T0247118

PENGUIN BOOl

WHY WOMEN DON'T TALK MONEY

Sharon Sim, a financial industry veteran with over twenty years of experience, stands out for her commitment to investing in profit with purpose. As the Founder and General Partner at Purpose Venture Capital, she actively pursues a mission to build and invest in technology ventures that contribute positively to society.

Her extensive career includes senior roles at renowned global banks such as Goldman Sachs and Deutsche Bank, where she provided investment advice to institutional fund managers, sovereign wealth funds, and ultra-high net worth investors. Sharon's expertise extends to wealth management and private banking, with major institutions like JPMorgan and UBS.

Sharon's multifaceted role extends beyond traditional finance. She serves as the CEO of a Singapore-based Single Family Office and co-founded Women in Family Offices, showcasing her dedication to diverse leadership. However, Sharon's true passion lies in giving back and empowering women in financial matters, and shaping their financial destinies. Her journey reflects a blend of financial acumen, leadership in the investment space, and a strong commitment to social impact and gender empowerment.

With over twenty-three years of experience in the financial sector, Serena Wong is a seasoned advisor on family wealth, investing, banking, business development for family offices, and champion for women in business. She thrives where connections matter, particularly across cultures, family generations, and gender.

As Head of Advisory at Kamet Capital, a Singapore-based multi-family office, she led a team that delivered investment management, wealth planning, administrative services, and philanthropy advice to Asia's most innovative entrepreneurs.

Serena held senior management roles including Head of Indonesia market for JPMorgan Private Bank and won the Business Partnership Award for large cross-business lines transactions. She honed her investment banking experience with Société Générale Corporate & Investment Bank where she worked in Paris and London covering Metals & Mining and

Project Financing. She started her career at GIC Private Limited, Singapore's sovereign wealth fund.

Serena holds a Master of Business Administration degree from Tuck School of Business at Dartmouth and a Bachelor of Social Science (with Honours) degree from National University of Singapore.

Serena is passionate about amplifying women's voices in business. She was a founding committee member of JPMorgan's Women Interactive Network in Asia. She advocates for women and wealth and closing the women wealth gap. She is Co-Founder of Women in Family Offices, a professional group that supports women decision-makers in Asia's family office sector. To give back to her alma mater, Serena is Council Member for the Asia Pacific region at the Tuck School of Business at Dartmouth.

ADVANCE PRAISE FOR *WHY WOMEN DON'T TALK MONEY*

'As an educator, I have had the privilege to witness the growth and journeys of many individuals. I'm thrilled to share my thoughts on *Why Women Don't Talk Money* by Sharon Sim & Serena Wong. This book is not merely a collection of stories; it's a profound exploration into the intricate relationship women have with money and wealth.

Through engaging conversations with twenty-four diverse women, Sharon and Serena beautifully illuminate the complexities surrounding financial matters in women's lives. Each narrative is a testament to the unique experiences and perspectives that shape our understanding of money. From entrepreneurs to artists, from executives to an Olympian, the voices represented in this book offer a mosaic of insights, challenges, and triumphs.

What sets this book apart is its emphasis on inclusivity and intersectionality. Sharon and Serena have ensured that the voices heard within its pages represent a spectrum of backgrounds, identities, and experiences. Regardless of one's socioeconomic status or cultural heritage, there's a story in *Why Women Don't Talk Money* that resonates deeply and sparks introspection.

All in all, *Why Women Don't Talk Money* is not just a book; it's a movement. It challenges the status quo, celebrates diversity, and empowers women to embrace their financial prowess unapologetically. Sharon Sim and Serena Wong have crafted a masterpiece that is both timely and timeless—a testament to the power of storytelling in effecting positive change. I wholeheartedly recommend this book to anyone seeking inspiration, enlightenment, and empowerment.'

—Carmee Lim
Former Principal of Raffles Girls' School (1988-1999),
Mentor Principal at Mindchamps Holdings Pte. Ltd,
Chairperson of I'm Soul Inc.

'This book is both thought-provoking and profound. Sharon and Serena have brilliantly captured twenty-four authentic and nuanced stories around money, coloured by family history, cultural upbringing, and personal experiences. Invaluable insights that will change the way we talk—and think—about money!'

—Jayesh Parekh
Co-Founder of Sony Entertainment Television,
Author of *What Shall We Do with All This Money:*
Inspiring Perspectives on Wealth

'This groundbreaking book amplifies women's voices and sparks empowering conversations about money. Through candid first-person narratives from women across diverse backgrounds, Sharon and Serena have curated a rich collection of experiences that bring this complex topic to light.'

—Tom James
CEO of TradeFlow Cap, Author of *Commodity Market Trading and Investment: A Practitioners Guide to the Markets*

'"When women take charge of their finances, everyone benefits."

This line from the Introduction of Sharon Sim and Serena Wong's new book, *Why Women Don't Talk Money*, says it all.

It's not just the story of Serena, Sharon or the twenty-two other women featured. It's testament to their strength and resilience, an acknowledgement of the sacrifices that they made in order to be financially independent, not just for themselves, but also to support their families.

These are, after all, important lessons for ALL women.'

—Georgette Tan
President of United Women Singapore (2019-2024)

'As a young woman, I worked for my money and gave little thought to how I could make my money work for me.

I knew I should save, so I kept my money in the same bank account that I'd had since I was three years old. I knew I should invest, so I bought a handful of the safest stocks I could find and hoped for the best. Beyond that, money, investing, and financial planning seemed too complex, too specialized, and decidedly too foreign for me. More than that, it just didn't feel right for me, a woman, to openly talk about money (and not least how to make more of it!).

This story isn't ideal, but it's all too common with women.

And now's the time to change that.

Women should be empowered to proactively handle and grow their finances. To seek out information and mentors who can help them take control. To break through the barriers that make us uncomfortable talking about money. And to set themselves up for the best possible financial future.

As this timely book demonstrates, as women, we can all play a part even in the simplest of ways, by supporting and mentoring each other, and sharing stories of our own experiences and relationships with money, including lessons learned.

I hope that—like me—you'll come away from this book feeling inspired, uplifted, and ready to make your money work for you.'

—Simran Toor
CEO of SG Her Empowerment (SHE)

'An insightful read on the different approaches that women have towards money, as well as their perspectives towards relationships, adversity, success and wealth. These women generously shared their diverse childhood experiences with money, so it will resonate regardless of your background.

If you've felt alone and unsure in your money journey, this is a warm companion that gives you a glimpse of how other women started and thrived in theirs.'

—Georgina Chang
Founder of Georgina Chang Communications,
ex-Head of Mediacorp's The Celebrity Agency

'In *Why Women Don't Talk Money*, Sharon Sim and Serena Wong particularly highlight the journey of women in Asia, navigating the complex terrain of financial literacy and independence. It resonated with me deeply, as it not only confronts the societal and cultural barriers specific to this region but also emphasizes the need for women to have clear investment goals, embrace simplicity in investment strategies, and recognize their unique financial needs and strengths. The book passionately argues for the importance of understanding one's values and taking concrete actions towards financial independence, such as investing in oneself and engaging in open discussions about money within families. It underscores the power of women investing with purpose, aligned with their values, which not only fulfills personal goals but also promises better risk-adjusted returns.'

—Uma Thana Balasingam
Social Leader, Co-Founder &
CEO of Lean In Singapore, Co-Founder of ELEVATE

'There are dozens, if not hundreds, of charlatans and soothsayers out there claiming to have that magical formula to make you rich beyond your wildest dreams. Naturally, only they get rich while the people who buy their books and courses are left clutching sand, slipping through their grip.

This is not one of those books. I've had the pleasure of reading it and went away at the end, buoyed and invigorated by the stories and anecdotes. It doesn't promise riches. Instead, it offers wisdom that only gets from experience and time-worn financial mantras that sometimes needs to be repeated in a sea of bad advice. While the title might suggest that it's only for women, I dare say that it applies to anyone who wants to learn more about the vagaries of money and how it can help or hurt us, depending on how we approach it.'

—Farhan Shah
Editor-in-Chief at *a+ Singapore*

'Insightful, bold, uplifting!

"The softness in relationships can be in harmony with the hardness of money"—a profound line from the book, encapsulates the complexities of the relationship between women and money, and the lingering stigma surrounding money talk.

The book comprises twenty-four interview-style raw stories from accomplished women, brilliantly weaving insight and inspiration with practicality. Simultaneously, the authors provide key questions that readers can apply to initiate money conversations.

Three powerful messages resonate strongly:

1. Curiosity and courage are key in confronting and understanding our own money narratives, enabling us to adopt empowering narratives that unlock our potential for a flourishing life.
2. Open and confident discussions about money among women empower and uplift, sparking a revolution and transforming our financial mindset and decision-making.
3. Embracing our worthiness as women and openly discussing our relationship with money can make us unstoppable.

The book's challenge is to take action by initiating money conversations and establishing a healthy new norm that benefits everyone. When women unite, share their experiences, and support one another, we amplify and lift each other.'

—Winifred Ling
Couples Therapist and Relationship Coach,
First Certified Gottman Educator in Singapore

'This book is a reflection of our times, and one that is crucial towards the change needed in this part of the world. It is seldom that you get a chance to unravel the perspectives and emotions of women in Asia when it comes to an otherwise hush-hush topic such as money. By gathering female trailblazers and collecting their stories, Sim and Wong give us a precious look into their minds and how they navigate money. A must-read for any woman wanting to take control of her own finances and future!'

—Dawn Cher
'SG Budget Babe', Top finance influencer in Singapore

Why Women Don't Talk Money

Sharon Sim, Serena Wong

PENGUIN BOOKS

An imprint of Penguin Random House

PENGUIN BOOKS

Penguin Books is an imprint of the Penguin Random House group of
companies whose addresses can be found at
global.penguinrandomhouse.com

Published by Penguin Random House SEA Pte Ltd
40 Penjuru Lane, #03-12, Block 2
Singapore 609216

First published in Penguin Books by Penguin Random House SEA 2024

ISBN 9789815233094

Typeset in Garamond by MAP Systems, Bengaluru, India

www.penguin.sg

For my mother, my husband, Damien and Amelia,
who inspire me to be the best version of myself.

—Sharon

For Mummy and Papa, with my deepest gratitude.
You make all things possible.

—Serena

Contents

Introduction

Let's talk about why women don't talk about money.

From childhood to our adult lives, money triggers discomfort and insecurity, even among the most accomplished women who find themselves as the primary financial contributors in their households.

But money isn't just about numbers. It's an emotional journey, a roller coaster of feelings that we've all experienced at some point. The book wants to change how we approach this subject, by encouraging conversations around money and wealth.

When women take charge of their finances, everyone benefits. We invest for the long term, with a clear sense of purpose. That's what our world needs now. This book is here to remind you it's okay to talk about your financial goals, to ask for what you're worth, and to dream about creating wealth. Most importantly, we want you to own your power to make money.

In the following pages, you'll hear from twenty-four incredible women from diverse backgrounds, each with their own unique take on money. They'll share their values, their struggles, and their triumphs, giving you a glimpse into the complex and fascinating world of women and money in 2023.

These stories are raw and real, and in sharing them, these women become beacons of inspiration for all of us who are ready to embrace our financial journeys. It's time to read, learn, and connect with the incredible women featured here.

Preface

'Doing well with money has a little to do with how smart you are and a lot to do with how you behave.'

—Morgan Housel, *The Psychology of Money*

'If you know the enemy and you know yourself, you need not fear the result of a hundred battles.'

—Sun Tzu, *The Art of War*

I

I have advised global financial institutions and some of Asia's wealthiest families for more than twenty years on investing and have come to realize that stories about money are like fingerprints—personal, unique, and shaped by our beliefs, thoughts, and emotions. These narratives steer our financial choices and behaviours.

A pivotal moment in my life left an indelible mark in shaping my perspective on money. I was in my final year at university in London. My world, however, took an unexpected turn when a call from my mother delivered devastating news. She had suffered significant losses in the stock market, which left us unable to meet the mortgage payments for our family home. To make matters worse, our family business was facing failure, adding to the financial turmoil.

I was suddenly thrust into a world of financial responsibility and uncertainty. The weight of my family's financial situation bore down on me, and I felt a deep sense of helplessness.

Cutting back on daily expenses, refraining from dining out, and withdrawing from social events—as I was too embarrassed to share with others the challenges my family was facing. Sleepless nights filled with worry marked those months.

Resolute in securing employment (and the highest-paying job I could find), I spent months crafting and mailing out close to a hundred resumes. I received calls for only five interviews, with just one leading to a job offer, which I accepted without hesitation. I remember it being a bitter-sweet moment as I had to give up on my initial dreams of pursuing a career in public service.

My family's financial setback during my university years instilled in me the significance of understanding your financial health and planning for unexpected setbacks. These lessons aren't just about numbers and budgets—they're about knowing what matters, learning about our own blind spots, and taking ownership of our financial destinies.

But this book isn't just about my story, it's about a collective journey. It's about women coming together to share their experiences, triumphs, and trials in the world of money. Why is this important, you ask?

Well, let's face it—conversations about money can be intimidating. They can stir feelings of discomfort and insecurity, even among the strongest and most successful women. That's precisely why we must have them.

When women open up about their financial experiences—the mistakes, the successes, the ambitions—they create a powerful network of support and learning. By sharing our stories, we learn from each other's triumphs and setbacks. We gain insight into navigating the financial landscape and forge our own paths to financial freedom.

This book is an invitation to join this conversation: to learn, inspire, and empower.

It's a call to action for women to engage with our finances openly and without fear and an invitation to share our money stories, learn from each other, and elevate our collective financial well-being. It's time to break the silence, shatter the taboos, and empower ourselves.

—Sharon Sim
Founder and General Partner at Purpose Venture Capital,
Co-Founder of Women in Family Offices

II

I have worked in Banking and Finance my entire career, so I thought I knew something about money. And an indisputable truth I know is that I'm a woman. So, if there ever was a topic I fathomed I could confidently write about, it's women and money.

I have always felt safest and most at ease with women, chatting and laughing, pouring our hearts out. I attended an all-girls' school, co-chaired Women in Business during my MBA years, served as founding committee member of Women Interactive Network at JPMorgan, and recently, co-founded Women in Family Offices. It's easy to feel inspired when your guard is down, and this is why I surround myself with the positive energy of my tribe. Speaking to, encouraging, lifting, and giving women a voice, is my purpose.

But women have not felt comfortable discussing money—whether we experience its abundance or dearth. Money complicates our relationships with others—our parents, spouses, partners, children, friends, and colleagues. I could not believe my ears when I heard some of my most successful female friends say they wished they didn't make so much money, or that they would prefer their husbands to earn more than them!

We need to untangle and find money clarity ourselves. I had my fair share of low moments with money—taking a job that paid below my value in my twenties, an empty bank account in my thirties, depleting my own resources to finance others in my forties. I felt vulnerable many times. In retrospect, I realized it was because I was trying to take care of others before myself.

But I never felt like a failure. My inner compass guided and urged me to keep moving one day at a time and told me that if I don't compare, and continue to dig deep for inner strength, I will have the confidence to show up, fully and authentically, for another day.

This book is dedicated to all women. All of us touch money in everyday life. So, it is imperative that we exercise our financial muscles, ensuring they are well toned and functional. As we get older, we need to keep building and maintaining these muscles. Before that though, we do ourselves a huge favour by acknowledging and embracing the fact that majority of our attitudes towards money started developing from an early age. We can choose to keep, or change, those narratives.

The group of women we interviewed were across a spectrum of backgrounds, careers, passions, and age ranges. We hope you find bits of their stories that resonate with you.

I know my own perspectives, ambitions, and priorities have undergone a permanent transformation by being part of this movement to give women a voice in shaping, and reshaping, our own narratives about money.

—Serena Wong
Managing Director at Julius Baer,
Co-Founder of Women in Family Offices

1

Anthonia Hui

The sound of the coins hitting each other
was like music to my ears.

Anthonia Hui is not a shrinking violet. She has incredible vitality and throws it in different pots: love for her husband, love for her friends, the energy she puts into her daily life and health, the vigour she puts into life's finer things like art, theatre, and poker. In this interview, the head of Singapore for a Nasdaq-listed global asset manager chronicles how her values of self-determination, hard work, and giving back to the community gave her power to rise from childhood poverty and eventually build a long and successful career in wealth management. Anthonia co-founded AL Wealth Partners that was acquired in 2023 by AlTi Tiedemann Global.

KEY INSIGHTS

Live well in the present and be true to yourself.

Find your own gravity. Secure yourself financially, mentally, and emotionally. There are so many shortcuts that you can take on the path to financial independence, but that could mean selling your soul. As Anthonia shares, it is never worth it.

You are never too young to start on the path of financial independence.

Some start at six and others at sixty. Take responsibility and take charge. Look for role models and people you can talk to and who can be of counsel to you.

When facing financial difficulty, don't give up. It can be darkest before dawn. You have the power to change your path and fortune.

Start investing, no matter how little you begin with.

The earlier you start, the sooner you can enjoy the effect of compounding. The key is to find an investment that resonates with you and your objectives. Anthonia does not believe in taking too much risk. Stay committed to your financial strategy, rather than getting caught up in the cycle of emotional buying and selling.

THE CONVERSATION

Serena:

Tell me about your childhood and your recollection of money.

Anthonia:

My father was a traditional Chinese man. As the eldest son, he had to take care of the family. He was a straight 'A' student, but due to the war with the Japanese, he discontinued his education. So, he shouldered the entire responsibility of raising nine siblings and his own four children.

When I was six years old, my father put my two brothers in school. I wanted to go too, so I asked him. He said we didn't have the money and only if I brought him money would he be able to send me to school. I woke up at four in the morning and walked two hours from my home to the industrial area of Hong Kong. I had no bus fare. Child labour was common in Hong Kong back then in the 1960s and elevated many lives. Mine was one of them.

I found a job as a packaging girl in a factory and would start at 6 a.m. and finish at 4 p.m. every day, then walk two hours home to cook, clean, and prepare dinner for my parents coming home. That was my life, and I never felt sorry for myself. It felt normal to me. I worked for a month and got my first pay cheque in a little brown envelope with my name on it. It was only one American dollar equivalent and paid in coins. I remember walking back and feeling like I was flying. The sound of the coins hitting each other was like music to my ears.

I felt in control of my destiny. Without knowing at that time, my own financial independence was in the making at six years old.

Serena:

That's amazing, Anthonia. What did your parents say to you about money?

Anthonia:

They never talked about it, but I could feel they constantly worried about and struggled with money. For example, they gave me HK$10 a day to fix three meals for a family of six. It taught me basic financial management. I remember going to the wet market thinking how could I feed a family of six with HK$10?

So, I would go to the vegetable seller and ask for the parts that people didn't like. He would give it to me for free. Similarly, at the butcher, I'd ask for the scraps, and at the fishmonger, I could not afford live fish so I would ask for the fish that just died. Now, food waste recycling is on-trend.

But that was how my family could have three meals a day.

Serena:

You were clearly ahead of your time. Was there a reason you were entrusted with this family task?

Anthonia:

It's a Confucian thing. My father believed the eldest daughter in the family must shoulder this responsibility. Even though I was the third child, I was the eldest daughter. So, I was tasked without even being asked.

Serena:

Did you end up going to school?

Anthonia:

Well, after working for six months, I took the money to my father, but he said it wasn't enough. So, I worked for a full year. By that time, the government announced free education for children from six to twelve years old. So, it was supposed to be a good thing for me!

My mother brought my sister, who is a year younger, and me to the government school. The principal apologized and said I was too old and past the age of entry into primary one. But my younger sister could join. It devastated me. I burst into tears, and I cried so hard. At that time, children were not interested in going to school, so the principal was shocked. He asked my mother what was wrong, and my mother told him I had worked one year to save for school.

Most people back then were refugees, so it wasn't entirely shocking to him I had worked for a year to afford school. He took pity on me and said he could do something. He could put a small table outside the door of the classroom. There were forty-five students in the class, and I could see the teacher and the blackboard.

That's how I started my education. Three months later, the teacher took out my exercise book in class and said, 'I have been teaching for fifteen years and have never seen a more fantastic homework assignment. And it's from an unofficial student.' She was talking about me. She finally brought me into the class. I knew that if I worked hard, I could prove to the teacher that I was worth it.

Serena:

Your resourcefulness and work ethic were clear even when you were a young child. When you started studying and working, did you think about the future and what you wanted to do next?

Anthonia:

Well, I was just happy to have food on the table and continue my education. I didn't think that far ahead. That's why I think it's important to live well in the present. Planning means nothing if you cannot afford to plan. The one thing I've learned is that you need to set your foundation well.

When I finished primary school, I headed to secondary school. I continued to go back to the factory and worked every Chinese New Year, Christmas, summer holiday, Easter holiday, and whatever holiday I could. The funny thing is this habit later had a profound impact on my career. I worked in the entire industrial revolution, from garments to electronics and toys, that mattered to the economic development of Hong Kong, and it helped me massively when I became a banker.

After I joined banking, I met my old bosses who I used to work for in the factories. I wanted to pitch the bank's services to them. I recognized their faces and remembered the factories they were from. Once, I met a former boss who was about to kick me out because he already had many banking relationships. 'What can you offer that I don't already have?' he asked.

I replied, 'Well, I used to work for you. I worked in your garment factory when I was nine years old.' Then, I mentioned the name of his team leader at that time and the address of the factory.

There was no Google back then, so he knew there was no way I could have found this information without knowing it first-hand. That's how I won his business. That's how I got many of my clients for the bank I was working for. The reason he became my client, he said, was because it said a lot about me as a person to get to where I am today. He also had values and a work-ethic that helped him become a wealthy individual.

A lot of hard work when you are young can pay you very well for the future. That's the message I'd like to share with young people today. I know many of them say that they worked very hard, but they have not seen hardship.

Serena:

When you think back to those days, what were your feelings associated with money?

Anthonia:

Besides growing in poverty, my family was also in debt. My parents passed on the responsibility to repay the family debt to me. So, they took away 99 per cent of my salary from me every month. I was left with only 1 per cent. When I was twenty-two, I worked as a secretary in a factory, and I only had HK$5 for the rest of the month. That covered bus fare and meals. I would buy a pineapple bun (*bolo bun*), eat one side for breakfast, one side for lunch, and the remaining side for dinner.

Serena:

Were you bitter?

Anthonia:

Never. I just took it as it was. I felt inferior and below many people in the community. It didn't make me angry though. I just wanted to understand how to improve my situation to make sure I didn't go hungry again.

I was sad, but the story was not about me having no food. My boss at the time recognized the situation and told me he could help me. Initially, I was happy knowing somebody could help. Then, when I heard his proposition, I was very sad. He said he would pay me HK$2,000 a month if I became his mistress.

From the woman's perspective, it seemed like a straightforward solution. But I was brought up with certain values and one of them was being able to look at myself in the mirror with some respect. I never told my parents what happened. Instead, I slept it over. I don't know how I closed my eyes. The next morning, I found my courage and quit. That's when I felt like I had reached the end of my rope. I didn't know what the future looked like. I just soldiered on and looked for another job. And then I found one that paid me double.

Serena:

For any twenty-two-year-old woman, many of us would not have the composure to fully comprehend what you struggled through. What about your personality helped you decide?

Anthonia:

I did waver for a second and considered the option because it was the easy way out. But one thing my parents taught me was that being poor doesn't mean you belittle yourself. Because of that statement, I realized the value of respecting yourself. Loving yourself is more important than filling an empty stomach.

When you think you have no choice, then you've already made that decision of not having any choice. I was pushed into a corner, and I had to make a choice. And I was true to myself. When I walked into his office, I looked into the eyes of my boss and said, 'If you genuinely wanted to help, you could have given me a loan. Instead, you prefer to take my body, which I cannot afford to give to you. Because of that, I cannot work with somebody who would make me feel this way every day.'

I never felt like he was attacking my femininity. He was taking advantage of someone who was weak, and it could be a man or woman.

Serena:

That's a precious lesson. The good thing is you walked away and found a new job that paid you double.

Anthonia:

Yes. And I was very shocked. Because of that, I learned the lesson that there is always light at the end of the tunnel and to never give up on yourself. It made me realize I can become a stronger person.

Serena:

Do you invest, and if yes, and at what age did you start?

Anthonia:

I never imagined I would have any spare money for investing. When I left Hong Kong and came to Singapore, I had just broken up with my ex-husband. I never like to owe anybody any favours, so I offered him the sale proceeds net of mortgage repayment from the sale of a house I had paid for, so that he could restart his life. I was on my own and had a job, and I wanted him to feel financially secure. So, I gave him all my savings and whatever money I raised from the sale of the house. I had zero savings.

Serena:

Why did you feel you had to give everything?

Anthonia:

Because I believe you cannot be married to somebody for fifteen years, call him your darling, and then become strangers when you go your separate ways. He wanted to raise a family and didn't have a job. But I did. I knew him for so many years, it's the least I could do. It was my choice, he didn't ask.

Funnily enough, he was supposed to marry another woman but then realized she wasn't interested in him, only his money. So, he realized that day that I differed from the other women he had encountered. We are still good friends today.

When I came to work in Singapore, I was fortunate that I had a good package, and I was doing well. I had a pleasant bonus. My current husband, Leonardo, told me it was time to invest my money. I never thought I would have money for investing. But it made me realize I can create wealth no matter how little I started with.

Serena:

That's a great message, get started with whatever you can and whatever you have. Just get started. How does your portfolio look now compared to when you started?

Anthonia:

Very different. We always worry that we don't have a lot when we start. But there are a lot of instruments available, like ETFs or Exchange Traded Funds. You don't have to put a lot of money in buying it, but you can get a diversified portfolio, and be exposed to multiple asset classes. So that's what I did. I divided my money into three major ETFs and kept adding to it whenever I had savings and bonuses.

When we are rising in our careers, we often start indulging in branded goods such as handbags, clothing, and jewellery. But you can still buy cheap stuff that looks good. It all depends on how you dress and carry yourself. Honestly, many times, I'm only wearing something that costs $100 or less, but it looks like it's worth thousands of dollars. I always encourage my younger colleagues to invest early because the earlier you start, the longer the compounding effect. Also, don't always listen to your friends who tell you to invest in things you don't understand, like crypto or digital currency. They might have made some money previously, but it's a roller coaster that will eventually return to equilibrium. Just remember that not everybody's investment is suitable for you. Find one you truly understand and believe in so that you can stick to it instead of flipping in and out.

I have been adding to my investments since the year 2000 and have taken nothing out. It's developed over time because I'm now managing our own funds and investing a lot of my money into my funds.

Serena:

That's another lovely message. Combining money and women, I know you have an extensive network of female friends. Do you talk to them about money and investments?

Anthonia:

Normally, I don't raise the subject, but my closest friends would talk about their relationship with their husbands, and it always concerns finance.

Often, they feel they shouldn't bother too much because their men are handling it. But I tell them, 'As long as your relationship works well, there's nothing for you to be concerned about. Men were not born ingenious investors!'

Most of my clients are male, and they are usually intelligent and capable business people and senior executives. But, in terms of investing, they are not as prudent as women. It's not about the gender divide. It's all about the ability to handle risk. A lot of men think that they can afford to make financial mistakes because they can always make more in the future. So, they let their ego get in the way. My role is to pull my clients back when they get too aggressive.

Sometimes my clients say to me, 'Anthonia, working with you is hard work,' because I challenge them. And they say, 'You even educated my wife. To tackle two women is difficult!' Because of this balance in our working relationships, I help the women feel more confident in managing their family wealth and educating their children about the value of money. The other thing I teach my friends is to save up their money for rainy days because you never know what will happen.

Serena:

How do you advise them?

Anthonia:

Well, first, I ask them to look at the way they apportion their budget. When you are given an amount, you put some aside as a safety net. Men tend not to ask you about financial decisions after you've empowered them to be fully responsible for it. Because of that, it's important for women to have a safety net. Also, invest so that the pot of money can compound.

And not only that, have your own will for your own money. You may have a joint account with your husband covered by a joint will, but what happens if one day you don't see eye to eye? You need to make sure that you can look after yourself.

Trust me, when you get to about forty-five, you worry about your financial security, no matter how much money you have in your bank account. When my father-in-law turned seventy-seven, even though he had a healthy amount in his bank account, he became incredibly concerned that he may lose all his money.

I think it's a psychological thing. When you age, you feel your health and mental capacity are failing, and you think money can fix all these problems. So, you grab very hard to hold on to the money, no matter how much you have. You don't realize how much that translates into problems that affect your relationships and mental health.

Serena:

Do you walk the talk? Do you have your own will? What are your wishes for your assets?

Anthonia:

Yes, I absolutely have all those in place. I have my advanced medical directive. So, if I become a vegetable, I tell the doctor, 'Don't resuscitate me and don't leave my family having to deal with the pain.' I have my will and trust, and the money in the trust will go to philanthropic causes that I support. I advocate the same thing for my husband.

Serena:

You mentioned money in the early days was for survival. Then you started working and accumulating wealth. Now, when you think about money, what emotions do you feel?

Anthonia:

I have learned that you treat money differently when you don't have enough and struggle every day to pay off debt and meet your needs versus when you have enough money to have financial security. Do you use money to control other people and situations, or do you use money to resolve problems? I must define my relationship with money. First, this money doesn't belong to me in this lifetime. I'm only a steward of the money that has been blessed to me, and I can benefit from it and enjoy it.

But beyond that, this money doesn't belong to me because I became who I am, not just because I'm smarter, or luckier, or worked harder. It's the community surrounding me who have given me opportunities and put me in an environment where I can thrive.

If I see another person in a similar situation to mine, it is my duty to give back and help them become 'another me', so to speak, so that society becomes more equal. 'I feel like I'm fulfilling my purpose, doing what I do.'

So, hopefully someone reads my journey in this book and gets inspired, and understands that they, too, can go through the hard journey. That it is not as hard as they think.

Also, many people overcompensate when they are poor by being too aggressive and too focused on becoming successful, no matter the cost. I never felt that pressure because I never felt worse off than other people.

Yes, I own up to the period when I felt inferior. I was trying to be someone else, thinking that it could make me a happier person. I realized I didn't need to be someone else to become happier. When I was twenty-three and working as a secretary, most of my peers came from wealthy families. They wore a different mink coat each day of the week. That was horrendous. I felt I had to be like them, so I did favours for them.

But they always laughed behind my back and said I could never be them because I was not born that way. I did not know that at that young age. How would I know? I worked in an environment where everyone was like that. So, I went home to cry again. I am very good at crying *[laughs]*.

One morning, I woke up and told myself, 'Hang on, I don't want to be that person. I'm not happy about it. So, to hell with it. I'm going to be myself.'

Serena:

So, do you now have enough?

Anthonia:

This is a complicated subject. What is enough or not differs from person to person. It's a mental thing. You must internalize the substance for that feeling. More handbags and more clothing does not make you feel full. It does not enrich you as a person. It's not about the money you spend; these things don't give you substance, that was how I felt. That's why I get upset sometimes when people call me a socialite because I want to lead a simple life and I try not to be involved in any such events, unless I absolutely must.

But some people see you based on the way you dress or what is on the outside, they don't attempt to understand you. When I mention material or monetary terms, I am cognizant of the other important parts of the world that are mental and spiritual. If you are mentally stable and have values and spirituality, you can reach the amount you deem 'enough'. Most people try to reach this amount by using money, but this is not the only way. So, money should be seen as a tool for you to impact the people around you, your family, and the community.

Serena:

You credit the community several times. How do you decide what to give back to the community?

Anthonia:

Some people like to put their name up on a building or create scholarships, but I prefer seeing real impact. I can make a difference in the lives of people that I want to support. I wouldn't use the word 'help' because we never asked these people. Most just want to find a way so they can survive. For example, when I was younger, I never wanted people to give me money. I wanted them to give me an education or an opportunity to do something more, like a career where I could do something meaningful and use my knowledge. Therefore, I have never asked for money.

This is why I think charity or philanthropy is misunderstood. It's not the money that's needed, but your knowledge and network. That's why I'm now putting myself out there to see what I can do to tackle human trafficking and modern slavery because when humans lose their right to make a choice and their lives are taken away from them, that's no way you can do anything. The financial support you give means nothing then.

For example, through my work with APC Malaysia Collective, I see that there are people lured and scammed into doing jobs they don't want to do. Many from Taiwan, Hong Kong, Malaysia, and even Singapore, are gainfully employed, but come to think that they have found a shortcut to make better and quicker money. Their friends lure them to Thailand where they are kidnapped and driven across the border to Cambodia. There, they go to a centre where they are trained to scam people, whether it's through sex, online gambling, or monetary investments. These people have to work sixteen to eighteen hours a day and are beaten and locked up. They have no freedom. Luckily, many of these rings can be shut down now, thanks to the use of technology. If someone in these centres can get a message out, the authorities respond and intervene.

But there's so many instances of similar crimes. For example, there are those who are smuggled into Malaysia to do illegal logging. Some Taiwanese young men are made to fish illegally.

Serena:

Thanks for shining light on a topic that's not much talked about. Coming back to our earlier discussion, you said that around forty-five years old, there is a vulnerable feeling around money. What are some of your experiences that you can share with women around this age?

Anthonia:

Let me share a story. One day, a client's wife called me to say that she wanted to have lunch with me. Alarm bells went off in my head, so I told my husband, who is also my business partner, not to come for this lunch.

So, I went and sat down and the first thing she said to me was, 'I think my husband is having an affair. I picked up a message from his mobile phone and this person was flirting with him.'

I asked her to calm down and probed more. They've been married for thirty-eight years and have two teenage children. The husband is sixty-two, and she's fifty-six.

I was straightforward and asked her about her menopause experience. Then, I asked her, 'Was it bad and had your husband been patient and standing by you?' She mentioned he had been. She was angry at him, of course, but still loved him. I told her it's important not to jump the gun.

When women go through menopause, we are often able to share our experiences and difficulties with friends who are going through something similar, and this helps us cope. For men, there is an andropause phase when they lose their so-called 'mojo', and they sometimes try to see whether they can attract other women, especially younger ones. Their success in doing so, makes them think that they still have this 'mojo', not knowing who they attract is after their financial power. These younger women massage the men's egos.

Many don't realize this. I think partners need to have empathy and respect for each other. When you're forty-five, you might start feeling insecure. Don't make it a big deal because if you believe in yourself, you can find your own sense of gravity. Secure yourself, first financially, then mentally.

Serena:

That's an important point and a potential blind spot for us women. Speaking of which, you now work together with your husband. Why did you decide to do that?

Anthonia:

It was a natural choice. I never actually thought about starting a business. I was always a career banker and believed in doing my best for clients, so I constantly fought with my bosses who would push me to sell more products. My philosophy is that if you take care of your clients, profit would naturally follow. So, it got to a point where I had enough. My husband, who was my colleague, said it was time for us to be independent. That's how I considered starting my business.

We talked about it and realized our skills complemented each other. We are a partnership, at work and, now, at home. Initially, we fought so much at work that sometimes our colleagues thought we hated each other, but when we got home, there was no more energy left to fight *[laughs]*. That's why the house is harmonious. I think the secret of our relationship is that we worked together for fifteen years before starting a business. We also share a common approach and developed hobbies together. I taught him how to play golf, and he taught me poker. These two hobbies take up most of our life outside of work.

We're partners in life, and I feel blessed. I found my best friend. To me, it is not about sexual attraction because that would die down once you're in a relationship for a long time. The most important thing is the friendship and the trust we have in each other. I can trust him with my life and vice versa. We never second guess each other.

Serena:

Is it an equal partnership?

Anthonia:

If you ask my husband, he will say no *[laughs]*. It's difficult because it was supposed to be fifty-fifty when we set up the business. But we needed to avoid a potential stalemate situation, so we had to decide who gets the final say. That's why I eventually got a 51 per cent share and he got 49. That's why he always says he's giving in to his wife to get more benefits.

But he is the one with vision and strategy, while I am better at executing, putting in the work, smoothening out the details, and making things happen.

Serena:

My last question, what is the kindest money-related thing anyone has done for you?

Anthonia:

Recently I attended the Asian Banking and Finance Forum conference in Kuala Lumpur. I didn't realize I had to change trains after the airport to get to the conference, and I didn't have the exact change. The machine kept returning the only RM10 note I had. I was panicking because I had to be at the conference for the opening. So, I asked the person behind me if he could buy a ticket for me, and I'd just give him RM10. But he refused the money and just bought the ticket for me.

It was such a blessing, and he expected nothing. He saw me stressing out and helped without asking for anything in return. It was very kind.

Serena:

Let's end on that optimistic note. You've given us much food for thought with your rich and colourful experiences. Thank you, and good luck with your philanthropic projects!

2

Quah Ting Wen

I feel bliss when I know I've gotten the
most out of myself at the moment.

Quah Ting Wen is a household name and national pride in Singapore. She is a three-time Olympian, and holder of eight national records for both team and individual events in swimming. Swimming is hard. Elite professional swimming is harder. But Ting Wen never complains because she loves it and does it with all her heart. In this conversation, she shares the importance of doing what she loves and is good at, and how she is building financial muscles using the skills she's learned in the pool to form a career outside of it.

KEY INSIGHTS

Money is its own thing.

It means independence, freedom, and choice. Wealth is more complex. It includes family, relationships, health, experiences, and quality of life. When you are full of vigour, excited for life, and surrounded by people you love, wow, you are truly wealthy. Money is a tool to make you independent. Use it to get experience and create memories for yourself and the people you love.

Social media is a tool.

Find your balance between knowing what you are getting out of being on social media and engaging with it, and of holding true to yourself and your values. Keep control and be responsible and accountable to the people who follow you. It allows you to build a brand that can help you, and helps you understand its vagaries.

17

Do what you are good at and what you love, and you will have no regrets.

Chase that sense of satisfaction and fulfilment you get from throwing yourself wholeheartedly into your goal. There is bliss and peace when you know you have gotten the most out of yourself in that one moment.

THE CONVERSATION

Serena:

A lot of how we feel about money begins from a young age. When you were growing up, did you speak about money amongst your family members? What did you talk about?

Ting Wen:

I was fortunate growing up. My parents raised my siblings and me in an environment where we never had to worry about money.

I rarely heard them speak about money in front of us or heard them argue about the topic. I think my parents really wanted to provide us with as free a childhood as possible, and I cannot thank them enough for that. It was a childhood full of play, fun, and exploration. My parents made us feel like they would always support us no matter what we wanted to try. I never thought of it in terms of money. In my mind, I always felt like my parents would always be there and have our backs. But, as I grow older now and think back on my childhood, I realize that there was a lot of support money-wise.

Serena:

What is your first recollection around the idea of money?

Ting Wen:

When I left for university at seventeen, I learned about the cost of flights to the US and the cost of being an international student. That was my first time thinking about money in a big way. When I was young, the only time I really had any interaction with money was when my mom would give me my allowance for primary school. She would give me a dollar coin and two ten-cent coins. The dollar was to allow me to buy anything I wanted, and the two ten-cent coins were for me to call home in case of emergency.

It was very specific. She also didn't give me $1.20 every day. If I did not use the money from the day before, then she wouldn't have to top up. But I never had an issue with not receiving more allowance.

Some of my primary school classmates talked about how they would get more money during special occasions like Chinese New Year or their birthdays. For me, the $1.20 was more than enough because I grew up in a household where I was not left wanting. If I wanted to buy a book or visit a place, like the zoo, my parents were happy to fulfil my wishes.

Once, I took the bus home from primary school and left my coin purse on the bus. At the end of the ride, the driver stood up holding my coin purse and asked, 'Who lost this?' I said it was mine. He opened it, looked at me and said, 'Prove it. How much is in it?'

I told him confidently that it was a dollar and twenty cents because that's the amount I received every day. There was no way I was going to get it wrong [laughs].

Serena:

Did your parents have different narratives around money? Or did they have one voice?

Ting Wen:

They were of one voice, which was great. And they worked well together. If there was a time when my mom wasn't so sure if I could get something, she would tell me to ask my dad. It wasn't meant to be a good cop, bad cop routine. She wanted me to get his opinion. There was synergy between the both of them and their expectations in raising us.

Serena:

What were your feelings towards money when you were growing up?

Ting Wen:

I knew money existed, and it was there for me to attain things. But it wasn't the most important thing to me. I just wanted to play and have fun, read my books, and when my siblings were born, play with them. My younger brother and sister are four and eight years younger than me respectively, so I was fortunate that I had a playmate when I turned four.

Serena:

Are you a spender or a saver?

Ting Wen:

I'm a saver. I take after my dad, who is a low-risk person. It might have something to do with birth order. I'm the oldest and most responsible child. I also think it has a lot to do with my personality, how I was raised, and how I watched my parents spend money.

In my sport, we must do a lot of repeated practise to get something as perfect as possible. We must be as prepared as possible and know as much as we can about the sport, our body, and our mind. That means getting rid of as many risks as possible. I think that plays a big part in my risk appetite, which is probably lower than my siblings.

Serena:

Now, what is your mindset around money?

Ting Wen:

It's not too far off from when I was five, but more complex. Now that I'm in a stage in my life where I'm about to finish my swimming career and move on to the next phase of my life, there are a lot of things that I think about, such as work, projects I want to start, things I want to do, giving back to the swimming community, and giving back to my parents for being there for me this whole time. Money isn't the entire world for me even now. It's still a tool for me to be independent. I use it to get experience and create memories for myself and the people I love.

Serena:

I want to get more personal. As an elite professional athlete, in a country like Singapore you are subject to high expectations and given a stipend. Peers your age might have a different earning capacity. How do you feel about that?

Ting Wen:

When I finished university in 2014, I had to decide between continuing to swim for the country or retire from the sport and start working like most of my other university teammates did.

I came back home to Singapore to swim for the team. But I felt lost. I had spent most of my youth as a student athlete—swim, school, then swim again. After university, it was swim, a big empty chunk of time, then swim again. And I was young at that time, so I still had a lot of energy. The sudden removal of school left this big void, leaving me with a lot of time to compare myself to my other teammates, many of whom were getting jobs, finding their direction in life, and climbing the ladder. I felt lost because I was doing the same thing that I had been doing since I was eight, which made me feel like I was being left behind.

So, I tried to work and swim at the same time. In 2015, I was an executive in the high-performance department in the Singapore Sports Institute. It was a great place to work because everything was located around the same place.

I would train, walk to the office, do my work, and then walk back to the pool for training in the afternoon. It took a toll on my body, but differently from school. Also, I was getting older, and it just took too much out of me mentally. I did that for a year and stopped because I was throwing myself into the pool, then going to work and being the best I could, then coming back to the pool in the afternoon. I was burning the candle at both ends.

The following year, 2016, was the Rio Olympic Games, and I came to a consensus with my parents that it would be my last Olympics. They told me I only have seven months to train for that and encouraged me to swim professionally for that period before going back to work. Well, it's 2023 and I'm still here.

Serena:

What keeps you going?

Ting Wen:

The love for the sport.

Serena:

What does that mean?

Ting Wen:

That sense of satisfaction and fulfilment I get from a day of good work at the pool. It's the feeling you get when you are racing, touch the wall, and reach whatever goal you set out for yourself, be it winning the medal, getting a certain time, or breaking the national record. It's chasing that momentary feeling of bliss. I feel peace and immense joy, and I'm on top of the world. I feel like I've gotten the most out of myself in that one moment.

And the sport is hard. We train all year for those twenty to sixty seconds in the pool. It can be punishing and painful. But I still really love it and I still do it.

Going back to your question about how it's difficult to be an athlete in Singapore, it's getting better. The government recognizes our efforts and gives out stipends. Just like normal jobs we have KPIs[1] to meet and the amount we get each month depends on whether we reach those KPIs and the level we're at.

Serena:

And given that you're at the pinnacle of your sport, do you have a comfortable, financially independent life?

Ting Wen:

I wouldn't say I'm at the pinnacle. It depends on the level and language that they use in the contract. Have you reached the world stage? Or are you at a continental level? Have you reached the Asian stage? If you bring it a level down, have you reached the Southeast Asian Games?

So, the stipend that I am on right now is close to what I think most young adults would start earning when they first step out of university. I used to be more uncomfortable sharing this, not because I felt a sense of shame, but because this monetary value reflects how your employer views you. You are this good, so you get this much. For a long time, it was difficult for me to feel okay with that because I feel like I've been giving all of myself in the pool, but it might not always translate in the competitions and the results. Still, that's how much we get.

It was also difficult because sometimes I would go out with my old friends from secondary school who have been working for a decade. Many of them are incredibly successful. They're very ambitious and I'm proud of them. I love meeting them, hearing their stories, and learning from them.

But it's hard. Sometimes I had to tell my friends that I can't have a $200 meal every week. My lifestyle was not aligned with that of people around me.

---

[1] Key Performance Indicator (KPI)

So, for a while, I felt lost and questioned whether swimming was the correct path for me because I felt like I was falling behind.

My mindset has changed in the last few years. I've become a lot more confident in myself outside of the pool. I've explored different parts of myself and realized that I am good at many other things outside of the pool because of the values that swimming has taught me over the last twenty years. And once I realized that a lot of these things that I've learned apply to other areas of my life, I let go of that fear that I will lose who I am the day I walk away from the pool.

I've spent the last few years figuring out other areas that I really enjoy, so that when I'm done with swimming, I can find other things that I'm passionate about and be good at those things too.

Serena:

Absolutely. Very heartening! And thank you so much for sharing such personal details.

Swimming has made you physically strong, and the expectation is that athletes are also mentally strong. How would you rate your financial muscle?

Ting Wen:

I got better at it around 2020. It's interesting because it depends on the people and content you surround yourself with. At the end of 2020, I started hearing a lot about investments and financial freedom. I did not grow up hearing these words and I don't hear them at the pool because I've been doing the same thing since I was eight.

A lot of my swimming peers around my age have retired. They've moved on. I'm swimming with kids in secondary school and junior college, and that's not their normal lingo. They're thinking about whether the boy from last night replied to them or the date they have next week.

But, when I reconnected with a lot of my secondary school classmates, they were in the next stage of their life, whether it was getting a house, preparing for children, or just trying to take the next step in their jobs. These terms made me curious, and I wanted to learn more. It was actually a blessing not hearing about money talk growing up, but on the flip side, when, where, and who do I learn from?

So, I wanted to get out there and learn as much as I could. Talk to people, hear their experiences with money and investing, and try to dip my toes in.

Serena:

The one message I took away from all the women we've spoken with is that there is no one formula. Investing in ourselves becomes the biggest long-term investment and the one with the highest return. So, it's never too late.

What is your perspective on wealth? Is wealth the same as money?

Ting Wen:

I don't think so. Money is its own thing. It is a means to an end. Money means independence, freedom, and choice. Wealth is more complex. It includes family, relationships, health, experiences, and quality of life.

You can have a ton of money and be the unhappiest or loneliest person in the room. When I see someone full of vigour and excited for life and is surrounded by people they love, I think to myself, 'Wow, that person is really wealthy.'

Serena:

What is the kindest money-related act or advice that anyone has ever given or done for you?

Ting Wen:

Tiny things, but still a tremendous show of kindness. It was something as small as a parking coupon. I had parked around near where my grandma stays. I can't remember the name of the road, but in my haste, I forgot to put a parking coupon. The car was there for a long time too, five or six hours.

I came back and there was a parking coupon on the windshield. There was no note, so I couldn't find out who it was and contact the person to thank them. These little acts of kindness and slight gestures don't cost a lot of money, but most things nowadays are a transaction. You get paid and then you do something in return. In this instance, this act could have been a transaction, and I think the person felt good after doing it. But I don't really see how that could have benefited the other person in monetary terms.

Serena:

Outside of swimming, on social media, I see that you have partnerships with certain sponsors and corporations. How did that come about? Is this something that complements what you're doing, or is it quite distracting but you feel like you have to build your brand?

Ting Wen:

I only became comfortable with it two or three years ago, really putting myself out more on social media and viewing it as a tool for work instead of just a distraction with pretty pictures on it. That change in mindset was also because I am at this stage of my life where I want to be more than just a daughter, a friend, and a swimmer. I also want to provide for the people around me.

That shift helped me zone in on different ways outside of the pool that I could make money on social media—in the least physically demanding way—since I'm so exhausted from my time in the pool. I was wondering how I could turn it into a tool to not only express myself, because I enjoy doing that online but also to share more about my experiences, and teach and guide people.

I'm great around kids and youth. I volunteered with the Special Olympics for a programme that taught children with disabilities on how to be safe in the water and swim.

From there, I realized I was not only good at it, but I actually enjoyed it. I also learned that I was good at working with competitive swimmers who needed stroke correction. I preferred teaching one-on-one instead of a big class. So, I turned it into a side hustle.

As for social media, brands would occasionally come forward and ask if I could promote a certain item. I had to find a balance between knowing what I was getting out of it, like making money, but also holding true to myself and my values. I learned that I'm the kind of person who would not promote something if I don't use it, or if it is not good for the sport of swimming.

There have been some clothing brands I know my build might not look good in. So even if I promoted those, they wouldn't do that well. I've also turned down supplements we don't use or are not helpful to our sport.

Serena:

Do you make those decisions personally?

Ting Wen:

I do. At the end of the day, I keep complete control over my social media and because of that, I want to be responsible and accountable to the people who follow it and are curious about the sport and what we do. I try to be as honest as possible and I only really promote things I've used before, enjoy, and that have the same philosophy as I do.

Serena:

Rarely do we get a family of three outstanding swimmers. You strike me as someone with a strong caregiver ethic. What money advice would you give your siblings and other younger swimmers?

Ting Wen:

I'd tell them to educate themselves. It doesn't have to be about money. With anything that you come across and want to be best prepared to tackle, you must go out there, educate yourself, and make sure you are equipped with the right information before making big decisions. That's something that I learned when I first started my foray into investing.

Serena:

What has been the best way to educate yourself?

Ting Wen:

It's a mix of everything. Talking to people who have worked in that space, and talking to people like me who are exploring the space with no background information.

It's also been hard trying to find correct information online. There's a lot out there, and not all of it is correct or good advice. So, I ask for the opinions of professionals who have gone to school or have the background knowledge.

Serena:

When this chapter is done, what is exciting to you that you want to explore?

Ting Wen:

I've been invited to give talks at companies and schools to share my experiences in the pool. Depending on the audience, I relate it to what they're going through. So, if it's school children, we talk about setting goals and balancing school and studies. For corporate people, we discuss communication skills, team bonding, being a team leader, and related topics. I really, really enjoy that.

It's come to a point where I realize that I'm good at talking to people. I'm a great listener and I've even explored going back to school for Counselling certification because at some point, people have come to me with more personal issues, and I realized I cannot just keep using my experience from swimming or my personal life to guide them. I also don't want to give people wrong information.

So, I thought about getting a Master's degree in counselling. While I may not become a full-time counsellor, I imagine that I will learn many useful theories from the programme that I can apply in my life. I love working with kids and coaching. While I might not want to coach full time, I definitely want to give back to the sport by doing stroke correction and helping set up clinics in different swim clubs or schools. As I move onto the next chapter of my life, I'm using social media, too, to discover who I am outside of the pool.

I also love writing. I admit I have not been great at keeping at it over the last few years because other things have been picking up. But I want to go back to it, whether as a passion project or a hobby. I would like to make writing a part of who I am after I'm done swimming.

Serena:

We've talked a lot about money. Let's talk about women. In swimming, is there any physical attribute that is different between women and men in the pool?

Ting Wen:

The biggest difference between men and women is that women get periods every month, and this is something a lot of girls and their parents go through when they put their kids in swimming. It could be similar for other sports or activities like ballet, where you have to wear a leotard. It's hard to hide the fact that you might be on your period. That's one of the major differences and actually might hinder a child's or even a parent's interest in the sport.

So, I think another thing that I've been quite open to talking about, right, is just being a woman in sport and being a woman in swimming. And I've kind of broached that topic before on my social media because so many parents online ask me, 'Hey, I'm sending my ten-year-old kid to the pool. But, if she has her period, does she not swim for an entire week?'

Serena:

So, what happens when you have your period, and you need to go for training?

Ting Wen:

It depends on the individual and the symptoms they have. I'll use myself as an example. When I was younger, maybe between the ages of thirteen to seventeen, my period lasted for about four or five days. The bleeding was normal, but the cramps were pretty bad for two or three days. But nothing so major that Panadol couldn't help.

People also fear bleeding on the pool deck. They don't want to feel embarrassed if blood trickles down. It's not even just about educating the girls, but the boys too. My brother is comfortable around women because there are three of us at home. We talk openly about our body and bodily fluids. I think that has allowed my brother to not only be educated but also be more comfortable and understanding, and sympathize with his female teammates.

Going off that, I feel like if more boys and girls were educated, and kids were less uncomfortable around one another, things would be fine. All you have to do is have a towel and head to the toilet if an accident happens. That way, the problem is solved and there are no kids pointing, laughing, or saying it's gross.

Serena:

Were you subjected to that teasing when you were a kid?

Ting Wen:

Fortunately, no. When parents are worried that the kid will start bleeding in the water, I let them know that blood doesn't come out in the water usually. They still worry because they're not there with their kid.

So, it's all about the preparation. A dark towel, ensuring you know where the bathroom is, and when you are done with swimming, just run to the toilet. It won't start gushing.

Serena:

So, it's as simple as that: calling it out and educating?

Ting Wen:

Yes, that's also something I've been passionate about.

Sometimes I bring it up to my mom and she says, 'Ting, you have so many things you want to do. You are all over the place sometimes.' I discovered this when I went to talk to students at school and corporate people in the offices. I realized I didn't just want to talk about swimming. There are so many things I learned as a swimmer in other areas of my life that can really help these people. For example, communication, leadership, and management. These are things I've learned along the way while swimming.

And on the topic of periods, it's something that I realized since I have a sister and girlfriends—that sex education is not as well done in Singapore as it is in some other countries. That's why I thought about going back to school to get an additional degree in Counselling. There are so many ideas in my head, and I want to package everything and make it mine.

Serena:

I am so full of anticipation for the next chapter in your life, Ting Wen. So much to be grateful for and so much to look forward to. Thank you for sharing!

3

Cecilia Tan

Money should be your servant.

Cecilia Tan is a force of unwavering determination and resilience. Her extraordinary journey, from helping her mother in a neighbourhood provision shop to climbing the corporate ladder in the competitive realm of real estate investment banking and fund management, paints a picture of grit and perseverance. In this interview, we explore the remarkable life of a woman who defied the odds and embraced a healthy and rewarding relationship with money.

KEY INSIGHTS

Money should be your servant.

One should never lose sight that money is to serve your larger purpose in life. Your capacity to make money is correlated to how much you invest in yourself. If you do that, you don't have to worry about failing.

Don't be afraid of losing money.

Investing is a process of trial and error. It is okay to make mistakes, but pain is an outstanding teacher. Losing money makes us understand taking risks has its price. Knowing your own risk tolerance is key to long-term investing.

Build that wealth reservoir.

Money is the most visible representation of wealth, but wealth goes beyond just material trappings. Wealth encompasses your experience and values.

Having this reservoir will give you a more sustainable way to invest and make money.

THE CONVERSATION

Sharon:

Tell us about yourself.

Cecilia:

I'm in my fifties, married with a teenage son, and a Singaporean. I studied in local schools and graduated from the National University of Singapore and have worked in Singapore all my life, barring some short-term overseas assignments. My family environment is quite interesting, and this is the first time I'm publicly sharing this. I grew up in a shop-house owned by my Mandarin-speaking parents. So, from a young age, I encountered money and dealt with it while helping my mother.

Since graduation, my entire career has been about money. I spent a third of my career in banking and a large portion of that was in investment banking, handling multimillion-dollar transactions. The remaining two-thirds was in real estate investment banking, investment, and fund management.

I have always dabbled in investing and dealing with money. So, money has really surrounded me.

Sharon:

You grew up helping your parents with the provision shop. What was that like?

Cecilia:

My father had a chronic illness and could not work, so my mum managed the shop most of the time. To keep costs down, she didn't hire any external help. I naturally became child labour *[laughs]*. I started working at the shop when I was ten. Besides going to school, I spent my life there. My mum was hardworking and would open the shop from 7 a.m. She only closed it at 10 p.m. I grew up in the shop until my university graduation.

I felt deprived as a child, but also understood how hard it was for my mum to handle the shop alone. I struggled a lot while growing up and hated that I had to help her with the provision shop to make a living. However, I knew it was essential because it was the basic element for living and for bringing money back. In a lot of families, the father is the main breadwinner. But my mother brought home the dough, so women making money is normal to me.

Working with my mother also had a profound impact on how I looked at money. I knew making it was difficult, particularly when you work in a provision shop. It is a tough business, and we had to stay open almost every day of the year. My mum only closed the shop once a week. She worked through public holidays. It is literally hand-to-mouth because you won't have any income for the day if you don't open it. Growing up, I knew I had to be responsible for my own livelihood.

And interestingly, when I was going through this phase, I felt bitter, but also thankful. I had customers from all walks of life—teachers, office workers, drug addicts, prostitutes. When I reflected deeper, I realized I shouldn't feel like I lacked something because at least I had the means to earn an honest living. That shaped how I looked at money.

Sharon:

How did this shape your value system around money? And your marriage? What do you tell your children?

Cecilia:

I always told my mum that I wish she still had the provision shop. Then, I could send my son to work there, and he would realize how hard it is to make money, and how easy it is to spend it. My mother was frugal and hardly spent on herself. She would splurge on my brother and me, but not lavishly. We had some indulgences. For example, going to KFC was something to look forward to. So, I grew up with the mindset that money needs to be handled carefully and not squandered.

That philosophy has carried with me through life. Even at home, from the first day of our marriage, my husband and I discussed how we would handle money together. We started a joint account and no matter how much the both of us earned, we always contributed to it.

To some extent, I think my husband trusted my judgement with household expenses. He never questioned me and knew I would be responsible.

In comparison, my son has a privileged life. For one, he didn't have to work in the provision shop. Hence, it was important that I impressed upon my son the value of money. I've never bought him expensive things. When he was younger and we went shopping, he would want to look at toys. I'd always say, 'You can look at them, but does it mean that Mummy is going to buy it for you? You have a lot of toys at home.'

With children, sometimes this works and sometimes this doesn't. But my son has embraced it. I noticed he is always careful with money. I even think he is extreme sometimes. He goes to Carousell and buys second-hand shoes because he thinks that is a good thing to do! *[laughs]* But I never stop him because I think that this is a good value to have.

Sharon:

How has your perception of money changed ever since you started your career? You're mindful of money because you know a lot of work has gone into earning that dollar. But you also worked in investment banking and worked on large real estate deals.

Cecilia:

My mother came from China. She was not educated, so the shop was the only way to make a living. But she always believed that girls should get the best education. She felt it was the only way to stop depending on the shop. I'd have more options and opportunities in life. Because I had so few hours to study every day, I really maximized my time in school and did fairly well, which gave me a good start in my career.

Working in the provision shop and then, seeing people making millions of dollars in my career made me realize how wide the spectrum was out there. But it also made me realize that the lack of something doesn't make one less privileged. I didn't see money defining my worth.

So, I'm sanguine about seeing sizeable sums of money. I'm not impressed by it because I have seen the worst of life and understand that money doesn't define a person. But I have looked at people and wondered how they made such an enormous sum. Do they have a particular trait or a special skill set? If so, how do I gain that skill to upgrade myself so that I could earn the next rank of wealth?

Many thought I was ambitious, but I just loved my work and took pride in it.

Sharon:

There's nothing wrong with being ambitious. As women, we tend to not say those things. But you work hard because you like your job, enjoy what you're doing, and want to be compensated. Something I've realized is that women equate money to so many things and this might be because it makes you feel like you are valued by your boss, or your husband, or perhaps even yourself.

Cecilia:

I've never allowed money to have a powerful hold over me. It's my philosophy. The moment it does, I become a slave. Money should be my servant. I always feel that your capacity to make money depends on how much you invest in yourself, how you broaden your experiences, and how you craft your expertise. If you do that, you don't have to worry about not making money. Of course, if you want to make more, you need to work harder. But I always try to strike a balance. If I find the environment no longer productive or conducive, or if I disagree with the corporate culture, I step away, even when they dangle a large retention sum. I've never regretted it. I've always felt that those were my defining moments because I stayed true to my belief.

Sharon:

How do you invest your money? How do you balance risk and reward?

Cecilia:

My mother is an enormous influence in my life. Even though she had little education, she learned about the stock market. At the time, we got our stock market information from Teletext. She could not read English, but she understood how the stock market works. In those days, there was a lot of speculative trading, buying, and selling stocks on the basis of rumours. My mother profited from the stock market. I was intrigued. So, I also started looking at Teletext. During those times, if you bought stocks, you had to transfer physical stock certificates. I remembered going to Lim & Tan Securities for those. It got me thinking. You work hard, but you could also be smart about growing your money, especially if you think you can manage the risk.

When I turned twenty-one, the first thing I did was open a CDP and brokerage account and start buying Singapore IPO shares. It was a lot of balloting and pure luck, and I had little capital, so it was pure trading. I made some money, which gave me confidence. I started becoming serious about investing and went with things I understood. Thanks to my banking job, I knew about real estate companies and some of the larger government-linked companies, so I invested in them. I also invested in real estate investment trusts in a big way. Beginning that journey early to build passive income gave me even more confidence.

It was not all rosy. I have also lost a lot of money. I blamed myself, but also consoled myself that at least I didn't lose someone else's money. Whenever I lose money, I would step back and ask myself, 'What's the lesson?' I might have been too impulsive or impatient. Or perhaps I didn't read the market well enough or didn't do enough research about the company.

I was a lot more gung-ho when I was younger. Once you get married and have a child, you are more measured and gravitate towards safer investments. I ventured into corporate bonds, building a diversified portfolio. I also began investing in private equity. It was my method of testing different instruments.

I have many female friends who are afraid of investing because they fear losing money. But you can't make money all the time and never lose. The stock market goes up and down. The investing journey is one of self-discovery and I've discovered a lot about myself—the good, the bad, and the ugly.

Sharon:

What have you discovered? What kind of investor are you?

Cecilia:

That I can be too risky, and my husband has to pull me back. At home, when we want to make large investments, we have discussions. I don't agree with him all the time, but I respect him. Sometimes, I shouldn't have listened to him. I should have invested!

But, in the spirit of family harmony, I take it in my stride. Opportunities to make money will always be there. Just don't be bitter about it and let it strain your relationship with your loved ones. For the women I know, I say: get started with small amounts and if you're not sure, bring people with you and build a community to help each other. For me, my husband is the community.

Among my friends, I think I talk about money the most. I know many women who feel that money has nothing to do with them. They feel that women are money-faced if they talk about money.

Sharon:

You must feel judged.

Cecilia:

Yes. The reality is that money is all around you. Not talking about it doesn't mean that it doesn't exist. So, confront your fears and deal with reality. It's fine if you don't want to invest because everyone has different approaches.

Sharon:

We want to invite more women to come to the table and discuss their fears about investing and money, and even ask questions they are ashamed of.

Cecilia:

Yes, we're on this journey together. We're now in an age where information is readily available. Can you imagine how it was twenty or thirty years ago before the Internet? Investing was so opaque. Now, investing is a lot more scientific. Sometimes, I think women are embarrassed to let people know they don't understand the stock market. There is nothing to be ashamed of. The key is: Are you willing to learn? When I was managing my money, I spent a lot of time educating myself. I read a lot of macro-economic and company-specific news and thought about the impact.

I sat in a community where people shared their views. If you feel frightened as a woman, bring one or two trusted female friends. You might always feel that the man is always right. But no, they can be wrong. Women can make money too. You need to be comfortable with who you surround yourself with and ensure that they don't judge you, whether you're making a lot of money or not at all.

Investing is a process, and it also helps you to grow. The way you handle that will distil down to your children. They will see how their parents not only spend money, but their reaction to it. When you make money, people are glad. When you lose it, however, everyone keeps quiet. It's embarrassing to lose it.

Recently, I lost a lot of money during the Covid-19 meltdown. I took a step back, studied my philosophy, and realized that part of the problem was because I had too much leverage. I was too adventurous and overconfident because I thought I could handle it. Unfortunately, I had to unwind the positions I was leveraged in and lost quite a fair bit.

My husband and I did a post-mortem. We are analytical people and don't get too emotional about it. In our lives, we see many transactions. Money comes and goes and there will be many opportunities to make it back.

What did I learn? I became a lot more conservative. I'm building again from the ground up.

Sharon:

Covid-19 was an excellent lesson for all of us. It helped you realize your portfolio might not be stress tested.

Cecilia:

Yes, it wasn't just one market. Every market was affected. Then, when the US dollar went up, that caused a lot of pain in my portfolio because my base currency is the Singapore dollar and it depreciated in US dollar terms. So, now, I also look at my exposure to multiple currencies.

Sharon:

For many people, wealth implies that they are rich to you. What is wealth to you and how is it different from money?

Cecilia:

Money is the most visible representation of wealth, but wealth goes beyond just monetary terms, right? If you think of wealth more philosophically, it encompasses a holistic approach, like your wealth of experience and expertise, your wealth of values.

If you have built a reservoir, it will give you a more sustainable way to invest and make money. Some people made a lot of money during the pandemic because of the high volatility. But those things don't happen every day. What do you do then? Do you wait another ten to twenty years?

That's why I place little emphasis on money. What I consciously do is to build that wealth reservoir as a person. If I joined a company or community, how can my wealth add to it?

Sharon:

We've been talking a lot about money, what it means to you, and how it has shaped your life. Is there a number that will make you say you have enough?

Cecilia:

When I was in my forties, one of my ex-bosses randomly asked me, 'Cecilia, how much money do you want to make in your lifetime?' I just said twenty million. I wasn't sure where that came from. But I suppose it was a subconscious aspiration. The thing about money is that it's subjective. How much is enough? Everybody will say the more the merrier. But nobody in their whole life can pursue money to the maximum. At some point, there'll be moments in a life where you need to smooth out any other things that take priority.

So, I feel that money must be the place that you feel content and that you feel at ease with whatever little or much you have. I've seen people who suddenly have a lot of money and can't handle it. They feel anxious and insecure because they fear losing their millions.

So how much is enough, seriously? I think that question is personal. I think everybody deep down will find the answer if you stay true to what you are searching for because everybody wants to make money. But money doesn't represent everything. There are bigger things that money cannot buy.

Sharon:

Let me flip the question. You have a scenario where you have so much money, okay, let's say a billion in your bank account. What are you going to do with it?

Cecilia:

I've thought about it, and I think the first thing is doing something about climate change. Governments are just not doing enough.

So, I hope all the billionaires can do something worthwhile with their money. How much money can you spend in a day? You don't need a lot of money.

But if you put those billions to help the earth and the underprivileged, to help the poor countries deal with climate issues, you can be a superhero to humankind. I think that's where the billions really matter.

Sharon:

That's true. I think that's where you can really get meaningful results. If I can ask you a fun question, what is the kindest advice you've received related to money?

Cecilia:

Many people can give you kind advice, but action speaks louder than words. So, the kindest action I've received in my life is from my auntie, my mother's sister. I think she knew how difficult it was for my mum to put me through university, so she always gave me a big *ang bao*[2] during Chinese New Year when I was young.

It was enough to pay for my university. It was in the thousands. So, if my aunt sees this, I want to tell her it helped me to go to school, and she gave it to me in such a dignified way. Her generosity touched my heart a lot.

Through her, I also try to help people around me through action, not just advice.

Sharon:

Thank you so much. I think that's one of the most touching answers we've heard so far.

---

[2] Ang bao refers to the red envelope containing money given by elders on Chinese New Year, birthdays, and other days of significance. It is a traditional form of blessing bestowed by those older to the younger members of a family.

4

Ong Bee Yan

Life is about understanding that it's okay
to make mistakes.

The transformation of Ong Bee Yan, from a self-described introvert with low self-esteem to a confident, elegant presence gracing covers of fashion magazines in her sixties, holds profound lessons about self-discovery and reinvention. Bee Yan's journey from self-doubt to social media influencer encourages older folks to step out of their comfort zones is a testament to the power of personal growth and self-belief. In this conversation, Bee Yan shares her pragmatic and uplifting insights regarding our capacity for change, no matter where we are in life.

KEY INSIGHTS

Investing in your greatest asset: YOU.

As we age, it's common to neglect self-care and self-development. Growing older doesn't mean fading into the background. Taking care of yourself, whether through grooming, staying healthy, or simply feeling good about your appearance, radiates positivity that others can feel. Imperfections are part of being human and embracing them is crucial.

The power of betting on yourself.

For Yan, betting on herself is linked to understanding that it's okay to make mistakes. While she has a prudent approach to money management and investing, she is a risk-taker in living her life. She has never shied away from pursuing her ideas with determination, from starting a cold-brew coffee business with her husband or pursuing a career in modelling. It's often in those leaps of faith that growth is achieved.

Down-to-earth money advice for the younger generation.

One, hard work pays off. If you're looking to increase your wealth, it's going to take effort and dedication. There's no such thing as a free lunch. Two, embrace contentment: Avoid the trap of constantly comparing yourself to others. Instead, focus on being content with what you have. Finally, pay yourself first: prioritize your future financial well-being by saving at least 15 per cent of your income.

THE CONVERSATION

Sharon:

You made an interesting transition in your sixties when you came out of retirement to start a business with your husband and then went into modelling. How did that happen?

Bee Yan:

It's never been in my wildest dreams to be a model. I'm not tall or gorgeous. I didn't meet the requirements to be a runway model. So, modelling has never crossed my mind. We would go to a lot of pop-up market events because of our cold-brew coffee business. At one of these events, a local fashion designer approached me. She was looking for ordinary people to be her models.

I think she liked my grey hair because she asked me if I'd like to be one of her models. And I thought to myself that at sixty-three, it's almost impossible to avoid wrinkles. But that she trusted me to be a model made me accept the offer.

It was also a chance for me to get out of my comfort zone and challenge myself because I've always been camera shy.

Sharon:

That's hard to believe because you post a lot of your modelling pictures on Instagram. How did you get over this fear?

Bee Yan:

I guess it's because I'm being made to dress up in an outfit that I don't normally wear, so that helps a lot. So, I'm assuming a different persona in front of the cameras. It's a bit like Beyoncé. When she performs, she becomes a different person.

Sharon:

So, this book is about women and their relationship with money. If I can ask you to think about your early years growing up, how was money discussed in your family, if at all?

Bee Yan:

I don't think my parents ever talked about money. I don't come from a well-to-do family. Both of my parents worked as hospital attendants. Whatever money they had, they spent on us and on keeping a roof over our heads.

While they never talked about money, I remember my mother being an incredibly generous person. She would help my uncle financially, who was a sailor and had five children. This is what I remember of her.

Sharon:

It's a little different for me because my parents worked in finance, so my siblings and I naturally talked about money. I think having that comfort level of knowing that your parents are taking care of you, so money is not a thing you think about.

Bee Yan:

I only know that if you wanted money, you had to work hard and save up for it. Money didn't grow on trees. No one is going to give or even lend you the money.

Sharon:

So, how did you help yourself when you were younger to look out for money?

Bee Yan:

I actually couldn't pursue university because my parents couldn't afford it. So, I decided why not come out to pick up some classes? I did a secretarial course and had to work hard to pay for it. For the things I wanted to pursue, I had made sure I saved enough for it. I was definitely self-reliant and resourceful.

Sharon:

You have kids of your own. How did you talk to them about money?

Bee Yan:

I was a bit like my mother when talking about topics like money. But when my children were younger and had uncles come over for their birthdays or Chinese New Year, I'd keep their ang baos in separate accounts. When they reached a certain age, I showed them they had this amount of money and told them they could have it now and do whatever they wanted with it. It's my way of telling them it's good to save money.

Sharon:

Yes, saving is definitely an important lesson to pass on to the next generation. Are you personally a saver or spender?

Bee Yan:

I don't think I'm a spender or saver. I'm just practical and only spend if I feel that there's a need—for example, investing in a personal trainer to train me. Actually, I spend more on things that motivate or discipline me. I donate to welfare organizations and rescues because I think that is worth spending on.

I don't spend on luxury items such as branded bags. I've told my husband many times that I feel like buying this or that, but the thought of paying thousands of dollars even for a second-hand one is hard for me to wrap my head around. Maybe one day when I get wacky, but not now.

Sharon:

So, you're pragmatic then. Do you think about your household finances the same way?

Bee Yan:

Well, ever since I started work, I put aside 10 to 15 per cent to pay myself first as savings. Then, the rest goes to expenses. I have money for rainy days. That's how I manage my finances.

Sharon:

That's an excellent lesson. It's a way of saving, for sure. But how do you invest in yourself? What do you think is worth spending or investing in?

Bee Yan:

Honestly, I don't know. I guess, as we age, we tend not to look after ourselves thinking that no one's going to notice us or that we're invisible. That notion actually changed as time went on. As you grow older, you have to be visible out there. It's still a life. People have to notice you and you have to empower yourself by doing that. If I groom myself, I look good and feel good and people can feel that positivity.

Nothing can remove those wrinkles and I'm fine with that. I think that's an important point. Investing in yourself is not just about upgrading your skills, but also self-care such as your health and your appearance.

Sharon:

I think you touched on a good point about being visible, and I think it's a significant point to look at your new career in front of the cameras as a model. How did you make that mental shift? And did it change the way you think about your financial freedom?

Bee Yan:

Modelling gave me the opportunity to do a few things. I actually donate half of my earnings to charity. I also use it as a platform to promote this idea I have called 'Grey Evolution'. So, I use my Instagram account to encourage other older folks like me to get out of their comfort zone and challenge themselves. It gives me a platform to run interview engagements where I can talk about empowering the silver generation. I also use it to organize charity events. If not for my modelling career, I wouldn't have been able to do all that.

It lets me think about my later years and still feel empowered and to have that financial flexibility to reach out to my peers and encourage and empower them to think about themselves differently.

Sharon:

Do you have any fears around money? Now that you're in your sixties and thinking about retirement, what are some of the financial worries you have?

Bee Yan:

I actually don't think about it because I guess one has to be content with what one has and be practical. For example, if you have it, don't overspend it. As long as you have that mentality, you should always be content.

Sharon:

I'd like to ask you something more philosophical. What do you think money means to you? Is there a particular value you put to it?

Bee Yan:

Money is essential because it puts food on the table, and gives you a roof over your head, and clothes to wear. It's also a way of helping others as well.

If I had more, I might also do something related to animal rescue. I might buy land and perhaps build a sanctuary. It'll be like a rescue centre and hospital, so all the street rescues can come for free medical treatments.

Sharon:

That's my dream too. I have a dog and I love animals, so it's always good to have such a dream, especially in a land-scarce space like Singapore. I'd like to ask you this question differently, but are there questions around money or finances that you're embarrassed or too afraid to ask?

Bee Yan:

That's a question that I'm not sure how to answer because I've never thought about it. I've never really been afraid to ask how someone grows their money.

Sharon:

That's good because I know a lot of ladies who are too embarrassed to ask questions like these even though they don't know enough, which is what this book is all about. It's definitely not a one-size-fits-all situation because of different risk appetites. In that vein, what is your risk appetite?

Bee Yan:

I'm a risk-averse person. But I have this mentality that if I put aside a certain sum of money, no matter how big or small, for investments, I am prepared to lose that. If it happens, I don't feel sad about it. I just move on and see it as a lesson learned. For many people who make the wrong investment, they feel very terrible about losing money and stop doing it after that.

Life is about understanding that it's okay to make mistakes along the way, especially in finance and investing because you cannot pick one stock and expect a massive return from it. So, when making your first investment, be prepared to lose money if it's the wrong decision. But you get some experience, learn from your mistakes, and make your next investment in the future.

Sharon:

To your point about you being risk averse, I don't think you are. The choices you have made in your career clearly show that you are a risk-taker because you've done so many things that none of us would have thought about.

Bee Yan:

In setting goals, I challenge myself especially ever since I came out of school. I give myself certain goals that I want to achieve at a certain age, such as retirement. And when you talk about risk, if I have an idea, I just go for it. For example, I had this Fashion for Cancer event, which was a fashion show and charity event. I just went out and knocked on doors. It's a risk, but if you don't try, you won't know. For projects or goals that I want to accomplish, I go all the way out.

Sharon:

You have no fear. Earlier, you mentioned retirement. How much money is enough for you? Is there a number you're looking at?

Bee Yan:

There is no number. As long as I'm comfortable, have enough money for rainy days and can be independent—not having to stretch out my hands and ask for money from my children—that's financial freedom to me. That's the end game. Having enough money is to have the freedom to do things you want. Lifestyle plays an important role too. So having enough savings makes a big difference.

Sharon:

And what about the rainy days? How do you plan for the next twenty years, especially to have that financial freedom for all expenses?

Bee Yan:

My husband pays, but we do plan for our future. He has decided that we shouldn't have any more new animals in the house. Because we are getting old, we'll wait for all of them to go before downgrading. Right now, I've got my retirement money from my previous career and the passive income from modelling. We'll probably downgrade once the animals are no longer around. We'll sell our house and downgrade to a two- or three-bedroom apartment.

We have joint and individual accounts, and we have looked into the future and discussed retirement.

Sharon:

What kind of legacy do you want to leave your grandchildren?

Bee Yan:

Besides us being financially independent, we would like to leave something behind for them that is a legacy. But I would really like them to know that if they want money and a comfortable life, they have to work hard for it. They can't expect anyone to help them.

Sharon:

And you're a good example for the next generation because you're still working and modelling and doing a lot of charitable work. As we talk about advice, I wanted to ask what was the best advice you've gotten in your life?

Bee Yan:

The best advice was the one by Robert Kiyosaki: Pay yourself first. That's the best monetary advice I've gotten. Unrelated to money, the best advice I got was to treat others the way you wanted to be treated.

Sharon:

What about the kindest money-related thing someone has done for you?

Bee Yan:

This has stayed with me for many, many years. I don't remember his name, but we were in our twenties, and he was my ex-colleague. I needed about $2,500, which was a lot of money, and I went up to him to ask if he could lend it to me. Without hesitation, he just lent me the money. I paid him back, but I will always remember this kindness. It remains with me.

Sharon:

Would you do the same, perhaps for your loved ones?

Bee Yan:

I would, but everyone is different because of their commitments. My husband and I believe in investing in properties, and we are teaching our children that as well. When they started work, we told them, 'Why don't you get a small one-bedroom apartment within your means, and we can cover the upfront payment while you cover the mortgage loan?'

But the condition was that if they rented it out, they had to pay 20 per cent of the rental to us. So, it was a win-win situation for the both of us.

Sharon:

That's great and smart too. I'd like to understand your perception around money versus wealth. Are they different for you?

Bee Yan:

Money and wealth are different. The former helps you put food on the table and gives you clothes, a roof over your head, and to have extra for rainy days and to give back to charity. Wealth is something more, it's when you can lead a luxurious lifestyle and you don't have to worry about rainy days at all.

Sharon:

Are you someone who splurges on luxury goods considering that you're always in magazine shoots?

Bee Yan:

No, not really. I have to think many times before I buy a luxury item. I like to go shopping with my son. In Japan, we went shopping at thrift stores and my son was so happy because he could buy so many items. It was fun. I'm proud of that because that's not common.

Sharon:

Are there habits among the younger generation that surprises you?

Bee Yan:

Sometimes I hear they will work, then take a sabbatical for a year or two to go travelling. That was unheard of during my time. We graduated from school, went to work, and then saved enough money to buy a house and get married. There was no discussion about stopping work and if you wanted to quit your company, you had to find another job.

The trend of taking a gap year is one of the newer money habits I suppose, because the concern about job security is not as worrying as it was during my time.

Sharon:

Great, thank you so much. This has been interesting, and I admire that you're doing so much for charity.

5

Veronica Phua

I am not running the same race as everyone else.
I'm running my own race.

Laughter and lightness come easy for food influencer Veronica Phua. There is a joie de vivre and appreciation for life that shines through. But her easy-going nature hides a fiercely independent mind. From climbing the ladder in the advertising world to running and owning her own agency, and eventually winding down the business, everything was on her own terms. In this conversation, Veronica shares how passion can drive you to chart your own life path, and the only hurdle that matters is investing in something that you are comfortable doing.

KEY INSIGHTS

Trust yourself, and don't compare.

Trust what you like and what you want, and don't compare. You only have your own life to live. If you are busy comparing and competing with others, you are doing it at the expense of your own happiness.

Managing money requires discipline and structure.

Being creative is usually instinctive and free flowing, while managing money requires you to put your head before your heart. Surround yourself with those who can influence you in the money direction you want to go. When you are younger, you may think that income can support your spending. But material things only give momentary happiness. Also understand that as you get older, you may not work at the intensity to grow your income at the same pace.

Treasure time with your loved ones.

Spend time with your parents and those who really matter to you. Quality time and quantity time are both important. See them as often as you can, especially as they get older. Be there if they are sick or need help. Be in a good mood for them so they can be in good spirits.

THE CONVERSATION

Serena:

Veronica, take us to your childhood. What did your parents tell you about money?

Veronica:

They didn't tell me what to do with money, but they were always cautious about their spending. We were not rich. My parents met when they were young and got married early in their careers. So, they were not making much. They also quickly had three young children.

While growing up, I remember having only twenty cents of pocket money when I started primary school. I'd saved three cents and would be proud of it, putting it in a little leather pouch with stitching. In those days my school sold noodles for ten cents, which I enjoyed very much. I'm sure it's impossible to find these days.

I always knew that money was difficult to earn, and you had to treasure it and be careful with how you spend it. We had little treats. I had always wanted a Barbie doll. I never had one, and it was something I always wished I had.

Serena:

What were your first memories of money?

Veronica:

Initially, money was a means to an end. Having money meant you could buy something you really wanted, like a bowl of noodles. It was just a transaction. But as I got older, I realized money was freedom. I started earning my keep, and I felt free. Money could open the door to whatever I wanted. I know everybody sees the best years of their life in school, but I preferred my working adult life. My best years were when I started earning my keep.

Serena:

That's a fabulous start. I know you discovered your creative side early on. Could you share a couple of anecdotes around that?

Veronica:

As far as I can remember, the moment I could hold a pencil, I was already drawing. My dad encouraged it. He always gave me sheets of paper. Until today, he's kept drawings from my childhood. I remember being observant when I was drawing humans, and I used to draw fat sausage fingers like in the movie *Everything Everywhere All at Once*.

I was frustrated with myself because I knew that wasn't how they looked. So, I started referencing my own fingers. I made changes based on my observations so I could learn and improve. As I got older, I realized I didn't enjoy academia. I skipped the lectures on subjects that I had no interest in and realized early on that I wanted to do something in the creative field. After my 'A' Levels, I tried my luck at joining the Nanyang Academy of Fine Arts (NAFA). At that time, there wasn't much support for the creative industry. It was something different, but I had to do something I liked. Otherwise, what was the point? I joined NAFA after taking a qualifying test and in my final year, I met a family friend whose son was a supplier for the advertising industry.

He used to buy the rights to fonts from around the world so that agencies would get him to typeset the printer for the ads. This was before computers when everyone had to do their own typesetting. I interned with him for a month and that was when I opened my eyes to the world of advertising because I followed him around for meetings.

I saw all these top executives in slippers, shorts, and T-shirts putting their feet up on the desk. They were having a great time as far as I could see, and I saw what they were doing. They had drawings and sketches and shared ideas with other people.

I wanted to do this. I wanted to be like them. After graduation and taking a brief detour to fly for six months to visit a few countries, I started my advertising career.

I knew what I wanted to do from an early age. At that time, the education system was very narrow. After you entered a secondary school, it determined what happened later in life, such as whether you would go to university, which was the thing to do. After that, you were set for life, supposedly. But I didn't feel that was the case.

Serena:

You said the independence and freedom you received from working was very liberating. If I recall, advertising was hard work and paid little. Did you think about money when starting your career?

Veronica:

You're right. When I started, I was earning incredibly little. But it was fine because I was doing something I loved. If I loved it and was growing, I was happy to accept the smaller salary at the start. But I also knew that if I worked hard, I could grow in every way, including income. I had the self-belief and confidence that it would come.

Serena:

I know at least two good things came out of advertising. One was when you met your husband, and the other was when the both of you formed your own agency. Tell us about that journey.

Veronica:

I've always shared this with people, but one of the most pivotal moments in my journey was being retrenched from my second agency. It was really the biggest blessing in disguise. It felt horrible though.

At the first agency, I was on the Singapore Airlines account as a junior art director. It was fun because I had a wonderful mentor who pushed us hard. With the right attitude and mentor, you will learn so much. I always tell my staff: be willing to learn and to teach.

The second agency was bigger, and my career experienced a lot of growth. I had lots of opportunities because there were management changes. From junior art director, I rose to senior art director. About eight years later, there was a change in management and the new regional director had other plans in mind. So, the teams were reshuffled and unfortunately, my copywriter and I were let go. It was horrible. Nothing prepares you for it, especially when you know you've done nothing wrong.

But you can either wallow or turn it into a good thing. When it happened, I was crying. I was emotional but still had a strong sense of responsibility. I told everyone that I would stay on to complete the project I oversaw. My husband was wondering why I would do such a thing since the company didn't want me any more. He had a point. So, on the last day, I took charge. I could tell people weren't sure how to react to me. They didn't make eye contact. I told myself that I would not go out like that. I wanted to go out on top. So, I put a smile on my face and went around taking photos. By taking charge of the situation, I turned it into something positive by celebrating the times I had with them and the work we had done together.

Now, I have this mentality that if you let go of an opportunity, your hands are empty to receive something else.

Still, it was hard the first few days because I was used to the routine of coming in and having fun when I work, and the culture of the agency. At that moment, my husband passed me this book *Rich Dad, Poor Dad* written by Robert Kiyosaki. Reading it made me realize that instead of waiting for the money to come in, like what salaried employees usually do, why not the other way around? I could take control of how I make the money. And since I wasn't afraid of hard work, my husband suggested we set out together.

He was already freelancing, which he enjoyed because it gave him freedom and independence and exposure to different clients. When you work at one agency, you get stuck with one client and it can be stagnant.

Serena:

I'm curious. What was the experience like to work with your spouse?

Veronica:

We met in my second agency. He came in as a freelance art director and was part of the team tasked to win pitches and gain new businesses. He worked with his copywriter while we had to do the bread and butter. I thought he had a more fun job, but that's where the sparks flew. We ended up being together.

We had to separate responsibilities. Even though he's a creative person, he took more of a management role so I could focus on the creative side because otherwise we would fight. We're both very passionate about our creative ideas, and rightly so, because you must believe in an idea to see it through. Sometimes, we would clash if we were both working on the same project. We have to be very clear on who's taking the lead, so that one person can support and the other can lead.

Serena:

Some say that creatives are not interested in money or don't know how to make it. Do you agree or disagree and why?

Veronica:

I think there's some truth in that statement because being creative is usually instinctive and free flowing. Managing money requires discipline and structure, and you must put your head before your heart. That's where my husband influenced me a lot, because honestly, I was a big spender and money gave me freedom and independence. I was thrilled to stimulate the economy *[laughs]*. So, I saved little in my twenties.

But as I got older and slowed my shopping, I realized material items might be nice, but it only gave me that momentary happiness. It didn't last. Also, when you're older, you get more easily tired and don't have the same energy to work at the same intensity as when you were in your twenties, so your priorities shift.

Serena:

So, do you invest?

Veronica:

I don't really make it a point to invest. I rarely look at stocks. When I was younger, I heard horror stories of people losing their fortunes and being made bankrupt. That has somehow been ingrained in me. I put some money with my goddaughter when she explored Bitcoin, just to encourage her. But it was a token amount.

I make a lot of investment decisions with my husband. After we started our agency, we became closely tied financially. We invested in property. It was a case of optimal timings. We had rented an office, which was incredibly cheap at $600 a month. It was a tiny hole-in-the-wall and was pathetic. It was where you would go to work and don't want anybody to visit. When you start your business, you suddenly realize you must be very mindful of how you spend every single cent.

Previously, you would get a salary that would come in every month and it's all good. Now, you must minimize spending. The good thing about me is that I'm adaptable. I had the resilience to achieve my goal. Later, we had to leave the premises because the landlord couldn't maintain his loan repayments and we were on the lookout for a new office space.

At the same time, when you're a small agency, you do everything on your own. So, I was delivering some hampers for my clients, which took us to Arab Street and then, we saw Haji Lane. We had never seen it before. It was literally a back alley and so underdeveloped.

People mainly used it as storage space for their Arab Street shop fronts. We drove in and thought it was a great place, and it was near to our client's place. We called the property agent's number and spoke to a man named Hashim. He's still a property agent to this day and our friend. Instead of renting, we bought because my husband thought we should invest in this. I remember thinking if he was kidding. Instead of paying rent, we got a mortgage with the eventuality of it being ours one day.

I'm not brave. I'm quite timid. But when you surround yourself with right-minded people, you can reframe your mind. It was a big step for me because my parents have always been conservative salaried employees, so we've never had that streak. It was only my husband's family. Being exposed to that made me more open. So, we took that plunge, and it was the best investment ever.

Serena:

From not knowing to going with the flow and being surrounded with good trusting relationships, especially your husband, helped you on your journey to take risks.

That's amazing. Now, you express yourself differently. And you prioritize freedom more than making extra money. But what is enough?

Veronica:

We're not the kind to buy a new sports car or buy a lot of things. Those were great at one stage in our lives, or at least for me since he's always been a sensible person. I've always liked beautiful things. But I think having sensible spending habits, and being rational when buying something helps. I always ask like, 'Do I really need it? Will I want it and still enjoy it in six months?'

It's easy to be tempted by something and having the immediate reaction of wanting it. And of course, you can get access to easy credit. At some point I realized I don't want to be living life with this 'flight or fight' stress mode. It's just not healthy. So, 'enough' is a choice. It's not a number. For some people, perhaps a million is enough. They can churn regular income and have enough to get by and pursue their interests.

Serena:

What do you prioritize now?

Veronica:

Right now, freedom. What I really treasure is the time with my parents. I see them very often. When my mother fell and broke her hip, that's when I realized, I didn't want to be a salaried employee any more. I told my father that. They refused to have a helper, so I could help with her recovery. I visited her every day, making sure that she was in a good mood because it's easy to feel down when you're bedridden.

These are the things that really matter ultimately. I'm very close to my parents, so I really wanted to maximize the time I have with them because they're not young. We go on holidays together, for example.

If I was still chasing money, would I be as happy? No.

Serena:

You have lots of rich and successful friends. Do you ever compare?

Veronica:

I've always been an independent thinker. I just trust what I like and what I want, and I don't compare. It's really a shift in mindset. After I got retrenched, I remember my dad sharing a good quote that I've always lived by. 'I am not running the same race as everyone else. I'm running my own race.' That insight really stuck in my mind. We only have our own lives to live. If you are busy trying to compare and compete with others, you are doing it at the expense of your own happiness.

It is easy to slip up and chase that certain lifestyle. For instance, we love wine, but we're not the kind that will invest in lots of bottles. We prefer to enjoy the moment because money spent in experiences is something we enjoy more than accumulating. That's priceless.

Also, as you get older, you see other less fortunate friends or those whose fortunes changed, or those who are wealthy and successful but then get struck down by illness and are gone just like that. You realize they used all the money they had to get better, but still lost the battle. These moments make you think.

Serena:

I've always wanted to ask you. You're known as one of Singapore's key opinion leaders in food. Was this by chance or did you pick this path?

Veronica:

This is quite funny because like I mentioned, I would spend my ten cents on that bowl of noodles, and I really enjoyed it. I've always loved food ever since I was a kid and I'm influenced by my mother who was the OG foodie. As a kid, we would take the car on weekends and drive to wherever it was that her friends said had good food and ate that dish. I knew that waiting also comes with good food. It was my solace, comfort, and genuine enjoyment. As I got older and had my money, food was the way I rewarded myself. Fortunately, I had a high metabolism back then.

And since I was running an agency, I would look at food reviews online or in newspapers and magazines to find places to go to. While doing my explorations online, I found this app called Burpple at that point. I thought it was interesting and downloaded the app. It became my food journal. I would take a photo of the dish and write about it. I enjoyed it because it was a creative outlet not dictated by a client. The photo and text were up to me. It was fun and I'm the sort of person who would give something my all when I decide to do it.

So, I wrote a lot of quality content and posted often. One day, I got an email from the community manager thanking me for my contributions and saying that I was going to be a tastemaker. I needed no more stress. I was just doing this for fun and the manager said, 'Just continue doing whatever you're doing. It's fine. It's just something we want to reward you with.' They had apparently started this tastemaker programme, and I got to meet other tastemakers who contributed, and a great food-loving community started from that. We shared and ate together, and it was a great time.

Then, the app changed to become more of a food discovery platform. During that time, I wanted to wrap up my agency business, but organically, because we had a lot of projects that would stretch over at least another six months.

At the same time, the CEO of the platform invited me to join them as a full-time consultant. After giving it some thought, I agreed because I really liked the team and there was no conflict of interest. They gave me this nice title: brand evangelist. I was already spreading the word about the app because I was genuinely enjoying it, anyway!

Then, the Instagram app came, and I thought it was quite fun that I could share with more people about my food explorations and help people make better decisions in food. Eventually, one day, restaurants started inviting me to come and eat for free. I became more careful about what I accept because I didn't want my health to suffer because of this.

Serena:

How do you frame this role? Is this a job?

Veronica:

I never, ever want it to be another job. I don't want to be beholden to it. It was still something I wanted to enjoy and could do freely and have full control over. That's important to me.

So, Instagram started developing. They started introducing IGTV and Stories, and I enjoyed doing that because in my previous job, I was doing a lot of video content for my clients and I had a lot of exposure to full production crews, so I picked up a lot of things along the way for creating content.

When people asked me how I did it, I didn't know how to teach them. It's something instinctual and built over decades of experience. Most importantly, I enjoy doing it. But I must remain true to myself. For example, if I went to a place and didn't enjoy it, I would explain to them why I didn't like the meal. I will not say good things just because they invited me.

If I was paid for it, like on certain projects with banks or credit cards, I'd state clearly that it was a paid partnership.

Serena:

The experience of going out for a good meal and having some drinks has become rather exorbitant in Singapore. Why is that?

Veronica:

It started because freight and ingredient costs became extremely expensive, and restaurants couldn't absorb all of that. So, it was passed to customers. The situation has changed, but the prices have remained sticky.

Singapore is also a global dining destination. We have Michelin-starred restaurants and even hawkers and have several World's 50 Best places. So, Singapore is a beacon of light for those who love good food. But I have heard a lot of feedback recently from several F&B people that business has been affected. People are cutting back, especially with interest rates the way they are and many having higher property loans. The first thing they would cut is usually dining out because if they had to allocate their spend, it would probably be for holidays since many are still travelling with a vengeance. Now, people are saving their restaurant splurges for special occasions.

Still, there are a few restaurants opening despite this downward turn in spending. But they are savvy. They have priced their menus cleverly. For example, they would do a pocket-friendly tasting menu below the $200 mark and offer add-ons. If you have a bigger appetite, you can add a wagyu. You can still have a splendid meal at a price that might not have been easy to find a year ago.

Singapore is fortunate that we have the best of both worlds. We have great hawker food and fine dining, and a lot that falls in between. I think that delicious food can be found at every price point, and I would not want to waste my calories on a mediocre meal.

Serena:

I always ask this question. What's the kindest money-related act anyone has ever done for you?

Veronica:

In the second year of design school, we had a photography course and all of us had to buy a manual camera to learn the fundamentals of photography. I had my eye on a Nikon F2. My father wanted me to understand the value of money and that I had to learn how to pay for something that I really wanted. So, he worked out a payment plan for me. He paid for the camera, but he wanted me to return the money when I started working. Knowing that I had to earn it back made me treasure the item more. It also made me think twice about taking it for granted. The value of something is a lot more if you worked or paid for it.

Some of my classmates couldn't afford it and had to share one amongst themselves. So, I was thankful that my father gave me that loan.

Later, when I bought my first property before the age of thirty, my father also lent me some money. I repaid him. It was one of those things you only realize later that there are people you meet in life who will teach you little invaluable lessons about money.

Serena:

I love that your personal stories have a strong undertone of forging your path and not letting other people, and also money, define you. Thank you for sharing, Veronica.

6

Choo Oi-Yee

How can I make money my friend?

Welcome to the world of Choo Oi-Yee, CEO of Singapore's leading private market exchange, ADDX. Oi-Yee is passionate about empowering women through financial literacy and has a unique perspective on the world of capital markets thanks to her experience spanning over two decades in global banks such as Morgan Stanley, Citigroup, and UBS. In this interview, she discusses the intersection of progressive technology, emerging asset classes like cryptocurrency, and the humanistic aspects of wealth management.

KEY INSIGHTS

Investing is a personal journey.

Your approach to investing is unique, shaped by your risk tolerance, financial goals, and life experiences. It is a path of self-discovery and continuous growth. The market will always be volatile, so you must confront your fears, make well-informed decisions, and remain flexible.

There is no such thing as a good or bad investment, only the right one for YOU.

Evaluating an investment's quality shouldn't rely on past performance or market sentiment. Instead, evaluate how well it fits your unique circumstances and objectives. In this perspective, an investment becomes right when it contributes to your financial well-being and aligns with your life goals.

How can I make money, my friend?

Building a relationship with money is like nurturing a friendship. Engage in conversations with it and learn from its presence or absence. Similar to how friends provide opportunities for growth, money can also offer the same. By fostering this friendship, you can attain well-being.

THE CONVERSATION

Sharon:

What was your first memory of money and how did you grow up around it?

Oi-Yee:

My father was a remisier in the capital markets. Work and money would be part of the daily conversation. My first exposure to finance was about the stock market. What's happening in the stock market? How does it affect his job? It became part of our family life and conversation. Looking back, it wasn't so much about money, but about how to make and lose money in the stock market. It became part of my DNA. I don't consciously think of money and capital markets as a separate topic.

Sharon:

The 70s, 80s, and even 90s were volatile times in the stock market for Asia. How were some of the money conversations with your parents about investing and risk?

Oi-Yee:

The stock markets were in the early stages of growth, and therefore, volatile. News flow affected share prices more quickly and investors were always reacting on a day-to-day basis. So, in those days, there were some financial crises. Singapore went through a stock market crash, and I could feel the impact on how we thought about and reacted to it as a family, what we worried about, and our long-term financial sustainability. All of those built in some concept of risk. Investing in the stock market had a large element of risk, and therefore growing up, I started understanding risk management.

Sharon:

Are these the same lessons you share with your two children?

Oi-Yee:

With the children, it's a less deliberate attempt. For example, if we're thinking about investing in a property for rent and we have to explain to the kids, what does that mean? We explain simple things like mortgages and share what it means to make returns. That's one part of the spectrum. The other end could be something topical like Bitcoin. Why is it important to think about these various asset classes in a simpler way? We also share how money doesn't come freely. So, do we use money as a tool in our family to empower ourselves?

Sharon:

I'm glad you brought up Bitcoin and cryptocurrency. What do you think of money? What is the value of money to you?

Oi-Yee:

So, I didn't really consciously think about money or investing until I got married and had children. Also, it happened at a time when I was climbing up the banking corporate ladder and had more savings. As we know, savings sitting in fixed deposits is not enough to manage your financial resources. I was in my thirties when I actively started thinking, 'Now that I have children, how do I prepare? What if they want to go to private universities outside of Singapore? How do I prepare for financial protection? When do we think about retirement? What if I don't like this job one day?'

With these thoughts, money becomes important because it helps you optimize for your needs and all the scenarios that might happen.

Sharon:

That's an interesting long-term approach to money. You've always been confident around investments. What are some of the best investments you've made and what's the best advice you have received on that front?

Oi-Yee:

Investments are a personal journey. Every family is unique because everyone has a different financial life cycle. Some have kids earlier, others have them later, some don't have them. Then you decide whether you have enough in your portfolio to invest. Work has allowed me to develop my investment thesis. I'm grateful to be in the finance industry because you hear, think, and absorb a lot.

For example, in the early days when REITs (Real Estate Investment Trusts) came about, we did a lot of homework to design and pitch to asset managers explaining why REITs were good for diversifying portfolios. The concept of diversification started here.

The other part of the job is to look at different companies and their strategies and management teams. If I were to invest in the stock, are these things relevant? In the early days, I was not an accredited investor, so I didn't have the access to the different asset classes I have today. Stocks were the easiest to enter. As a banker, however, you had restrictions on what you could buy, so I bought them when I was in between jobs or banks.

As a wealth management hub, Singapore has deep asset classes and products that support wealth management. So, over some time and after much exploration, I started thinking: Where do I go from here? What's my risk appetite? How much money can I lose without feeling the pain? Is there a safer portfolio or do I invest in the fringes of a riskier portfolio? I recently explored cryptocurrency. My thought process was simple: If I lost my capital, I treated it as tuition fees.

Sharon:

What advice would you give to younger women who are just starting out? How should they plan for diversification?

Oi-Yee:

Don't put all your eggs in one basket. Have different products with non-correlated returns so you can thrive in different financial cycles. It's important to understand that it's not just stocks or even within stocks. There are stocks that will survive during financial crises and those that will thrive when times are good. Investing in different products will help to do that and give a positive outcome in the long run.

It also helps to understand different asset classes and from there, discerning your risk tolerance. For example, one of the simplest things we can understand is the relationship between risk and return for something low risk. You get low returns for fixed deposits or bank deposits. They are one of the lowest risk financial products you can invest in. In today's terms, 4 per cent is something we can call almost risk-free.

For every extra dollar you might make, 8 per cent, 10 per cent, or even 15 per cent, risks become commensurately larger. Could you comfortably lose 15 per cent? Once you understand these two dynamics, then you can be comfortable doing the homework first. It doesn't have to be just stocks and bonds. It could be something fun for women, like gemstones or even luxury bags.

Sharon:

Test it out, make small investments, and try not to lose everything. It's also a process of discovery. I want to discover your relationship with money. How do you view it so objectively? Do you get different emotions when you think about money? Are you excited when you deploy it or are you afraid to lose it?

Oi-Yee:

To me, money is a safety net. On one level, it provides protection. On another level, it provides empowerment once we cover protection. How do we build that stack? Do we start with safer things like fixed deposits and insurance policies? Then, I think about optimizing it. For me, the end point is to cover my bases, which are mortgage, food, and travel needs.

I also think about retirement. How do you earn enough for it? My emotions towards money involve understanding how I can make money as a friend and work for me. We don't have to fear or be obsessed with it. It's about realizing how we can be objective and calm.

If I thought it was so important and took a risky position because I wanted to make a lot of money, I might wake up one day and find my wealth destroyed. How would I feel about that? I don't want to be in a position where I am obsessed about one wealth class. I prefer a more constructive and friendly relationship with money.

Sharon:

Money is also an enabler and a tool for us to achieve our end goals, be it retirement or even a second career. I love the way you think about it systematically, dividing them into pockets of savings and insurance, and layering more when you become more confident.

You can manage your money. It makes me wonder, what is money and wealth to you?

Oi-Yee:

We equate wealth with being rich. The idea that you cannot manage wealth because you have a lot of money is completely untrue. There are so many platforms out there now that you can use to optimize your personal wealth.

We need to rethink how we teach our young about wealth. When I think of wealth, I think of the financial resources that need to be optimized for different needs and scenarios. They will benefit from this thinking. Wealth is not just about savings but knowing how you optimize that resource. Of course, wealth means many other things. This is where your friendship with money comes in. Does money support you in your health, friendship, and mental journeys? For example, sometimes you want to splurge on something because it helps you destress, like going to the spa and having a nice relaxing day.

Sharon:

I love it. I love how you encourage people not to fear, but to learn as much about investing and to learn who you are and how much risk you're willing to take at any point in time. In this vein, assuming you have a billion dollars sitting in your bank account, what would you do with that money?

Oi-Yee:

Well, there are lots of things you can do with a billion dollars, except maybe buying my daughter's Taylor Swift concert ticket [for the Singapore show in 2024]. She said that she won't even sell her ticket for a billion dollars! *[laughs]*

But, seriously, there's so much good you can do. There are so many things that the world needs right now, whether for non-profits or organizations. I know Singapore has been thinking about working with wealth, or family offices, by giving them tax incentives to do blended finance and incorporate charity.

Singapore recognizes that will be the trend in the future. So how do governments and wealth work together to make an impact, whether it's for charitable causes or for growing different areas? One of the biggest is clearly climate change, where a lot of funding has been going.

But I also think it's the sector where we need a blend of governmental support with creative financial instruments. With a billion, you can do a lot in this area.

There was a point when I didn't have a job. It was quite scary because I'd had a salary for years. Then, I had to rely on my husband and that was frightening.

I tied a lot of my professional expertise to my identity. The ability to manage money and invest took a pause because I wanted to re-examine what I wanted to do. But that reflection also meant I had to ask someone, in this case, my husband or parents, which made me feel vulnerable.

So, money, especially a billion dollars, is empowering because it gives you the freedom to choose, to pause, or even take a break.

Once, I was working for a bank just before the financial crisis and I had a lot of options in a company that I exercised. During the crisis, the share price dropped like a stone. I thought it would be fine, but it went from something like $50 to $2. I still have some shares in that company today, although I'm not sure where I kept it. But it gave me the lesson of not being too wedded to an investment. The loss affected my emotions. No one likes to lose money. It made me question who I am because I'm so used to being in the finance industry every day.

Sharon:

On that note, what is some of the worst money advice you've received?

Oi-Yee:

Once, someone suggested that I should buy penny stocks because you can make a quick gain. Blue-chip stocks are, on the other hand, well-established companies with sound reputations, but there is barely any daily price movement. Instead of buying the penny stocks myself, I told the person, 'If you are so confident, why don't you take $10,000 of my money and deploy into the penny stock strategy?' It didn't work out.

But this is how we learn. If someone suggests something to you, even if you think it won't work, you should never assume you're 100 per cent correct. You can test the hypothesis by taking a small amount of money to learn. In this case, I stayed with my blue-chip stocks, safe in the knowledge that they won't implode overnight, and slept soundly at night.

Sharon:

On a broader note, what is your magic number? A figure that you're aiming for until you know you have enough to do whatever you want.

Oi-Yee:

The first thing I would do is to know where your data is. Here, it would be your financial inventory. I'm quite bad administratively, but I'll understand how many stocks and bonds I have, my remaining mortgage, etc., and then take stock.

What do I do with this information? Do I want to work for another decade and figure out my income from then? I'll also have to know how much it would cost for me to send my children to school. And if I were to pick my retirement age, what is the lifestyle that I want to achieve?

From there I work backwards and calculate what amount I would need to be happy enough that it could sustain us. Anything else on top is a bonus.

Sharon:

And what is the legacy you want to leave your children, whether monetary or something else?

Oi-Yee:

I think they would be happy if they had an apartment. But ultimately, I want them to not think so simplistically, and be responsible for their financial well-being. When they are thirty and have their own children and partners to worry about, the wealth management space might be different, but the fundamentals remain the same.

I want my daughter to think about what money means to her and then get out there to earn it. It doesn't have to be a glamorous job. She could be a server or part-time gymnastics coach to earn some money. From there, I want her to think about what to spend this money on. Does she go for driving classes in the future or go to Starbucks to spend $6 on a drink? I also encourage her to think about micro-investing ideas, perhaps in some of those super apps like Grab, playing around, and understanding what they give back to you. I think these basic skills are important and if they are conscious of it and use these skills, then I think we would have left them a lot.

Sharon:

Do you think women are more hesitant to experiment and take a risk, especially with investing?

Oi-Yee:

A lot of women I know leave the thinking to their husbands or other halves. Men are more confident about sharing ideas, and more often than not, share what they make. Even with myself, I share more with my male friends about investing.

We definitely need to rethink this. Women should step out and be more conscious. It's never been a topic of conversation and we need to make it more common, which is why I'm glad that you are doing this book. Whether you're a stay-at-home mother or professional, we need to kick-start that conversation, and I guarantee you that a lot of professional women don't talk about investing. Even at the baseline, thinking about the security and protection of the family is a good starting point.

Money isn't a common topic and I think a lot of us shy away from boasting about our profitable investments. We downplay it compared to men who are not shy to talk about their wins.

But sometimes, I also have female friends who see investment opportunities and ask me if I think this is a wonderful investment, being in finance.

My response is never yes or no. Instead, I ask, 'What does this investment do for you?' Every person has a different financial life and portfolio to start with. So, any random investment isn't necessarily good nor bad. Does it fit your risk profile, and does it fit your portfolio? Even if a person says you should do this, that doesn't mean that's the best investment. Women need to take a step back and understand that there is no such thing as a purely good or bad investment.

Sharon:

That's a good point. It's about understanding who you are and your financial position. You said your friends come to you for advice, but who do you go to for advice? Do you talk to your husband, for example?

Oi-Yee:

I think I see more products ahead of him. So, I usually start the conversation first. The question then becomes about the collective risk appetite. Those that I feel I can take; I do in small amounts. Those that are bigger and involve a deeper discussion, we'll go into it together. It's all about having that conversation with each other and coming to a consensus.

Sharon:

I'm glad we're having this conversation. Thank you for sharing your thoughts with us.

7

Joy Tan

Know your value and articulate your worth.

Joy Tan is deeply invested in the growth of people around her. With nearly four decades of legal practice under her belt and her role in WongPartnership's Executive Committee, Joy takes the responsibility of nurturing the firm's future leaders to heart. Beyond that, she generously dedicates her time to corporate and non-profit boards. Her role as the chair of the Singapore Repertory Theatre, a non-profit theatre company, highlights her commitment to diverse facets of her community. This section delves into Joy's journey, showcasing her dedication to mentoring the next generation while addressing pressing challenges in her field.

KEY INSIGHTS

With wealth, comes stewardship.

Wealth carries responsibilities—to ourselves, our families, and our communities. It's not just about what we have but what we do with it. While money is essential, the most valuable aspects of life are often intangible and cannot be bought. Wealth has the potential to yield dividends for the people we care about. The realization that we cannot carry our wealth into the next life drives us to use it to enrich our families, communities, and the world at large.

Assert your worth.

Understanding your own value and having the confidence to communicate it, especially in negotiations, can be transformative. Information and education are your most valuable allies, so be prepared to do your homework thoroughly. When making a request, it's not just about framing the ask, it's also about identifying the key decision-makers. By combining preparation with an understanding of your audience, you can pitch your case with confidence. Doubt is contagious, so believe in yourself.

Female role models shape the next generation.

It emphasizes the profound impact that visible female leaders have on the aspirations and achievements of the younger generation. The more women are out there, the more young women can see ladies in society doing good in positions of power.

THE CONVERSATION

Sharon:

Joy, if I can take you back to your childhood, how did your family discuss money?

Joy:

I grew up in a traditional Asian family. My father was the sole breadwinner, and my mother was a homemaker. We were a middle-class and fairly progressive family. My parents didn't hold my sister and me back. They encouraged us to further our education and focus on our careers. We didn't need to get married just for men to take care of us. We needed to study hard so that we could make our own money and take care of ourselves. While we talked little about money, we held progressive narratives.

I think my mother is proud of my sister, who is also a lawyer, and of me.

Sharon:

What's your first memory of money?

Joy:

Growing up, we discussed money, but usually with uncles and aunts at family gatherings during Chinese New Year. And of course, we got pocket money. I was a saver, so I'd set aside the pocket money I got together with the ang baos we would receive.

Sharon:

How do you talk to your kids about money?

Joy:

I'm open about money matters with our children. In our household, my husband and I have an egalitarian household. We share childcare duties and the mortgage and are very open with the children about everything.

I have an older daughter and a younger son. The former just joined the workforce. She is one of our overworked doctors and is finally earning her own keep. She is also a saver rather than a spender and took us out and treated us with her first pay cheque. When she had to open a bank account in her name so that the company could deposit her salary, we toured the various banks and compared the terms and conditions. She likes to do her homework. I also introduced her to my trusted insurance agent to protect her life and health.

My son is interested in finance and investments and is interning now in a Singapore fin-tech firm. We'll see where he goes with that. There's so much to learn these days.

Sharon:

How do you talk to your spouse about money?

Joy:

My husband and I discuss household finances openly. There is a joint account for family expenses, and we have our own personal accounts. That's the typical way couples arrange their finances. The both of us went away to study and then work, and we're familiar with making and managing our own money, so that shouldn't change even after you get married.

Sharon:

How do you think about managing your money?

Joy:

That's an interesting question. To go back a bit, I realized when I joined the workforce that few women had the same opportunities. I grew up in a progressive household, but I see women abandoned by their husbands and those in abusive family relationships. Many of them feel they can't leave because they didn't have the means to take care of their children or because their names weren't on the title deeds.

It isn't just in the matrimonial context. In families and family companies, you'd have the traditional Asian patriarch who passes everything on to the son. When there is a dispute about the estate or succession, it's usually gender-based because, invariably, the sons would get the lion's share.

Daughters and mothers are usually left out of succession planning and, hence, getting their inheritance. I often see how women are worse off in these cases when something goes wrong, and lawyers get involved.

Sharon:

What does money mean to you?

Joy:

It means freedom and choice. These things resonate with me. That's also my approach to investing and managing my savings. There's also an aspect of stewardship. We owe it to the next generation, to our community, and country. All of us have a responsibility to do more with what we have and not just focus on material items and ourselves.

Sharon:

Tell me more about your approach to saving and investing.

Joy:

There is always this sense that you need to store up for a rainy day. It's the traditional Asian approach to money, which makes many of us savers. I am risk-averse and old-fashioned, and don't believe that there's a thing such as free lunch. I believe in hard work as an occupational hazard. If something is too good to be true, it probably is. And so, because of that aversion to risk, I prefer safe assets. I take a similar approach in my personal life. My personal finances drive my investment philosophy.

Sharon:

What are some of the money lessons you have picked up?

Joy:

I joined the workforce during the Asian economic crisis in the late nineties. Since then, we've had the dotcom bust cycles, the great financial crisis, and now crypto winter. All these catastrophic market and economic crashes are largely driven by inadvisable risk-taking behaviour.

It is about fear and greed. You see that time and time again through the cycles. So, we never learn from our mistakes, unfortunately. It seems like human nature means we will repeat the same mistakes.

Obviously, in my personal life, I try not to do that. I hope to learn from my mistakes and similarly advise my clients the same way. My takeaway is to watch out for exuberance, especially when times are good. And as you've seen, the market goes through economic cycles, which also influences how I view my own personal finance. I am cautious about certain things, especially when it's looking too good to be true.

Sharon:

Do you think women receive enough opportunities to rise the ranks and get a seat on the negotiating table?

Joy:

I'd love to say yes. I feel that all the gaps have been closed and that there's no issue, but across the spectrum of society, there will be cracks, unfortunately.

The Singapore Association of Women Lawyers and the Financial Women's Association of Singapore have great programmes to encourage women, particularly from more disadvantaged families, to engage in estate planning and improve their financial literacy. Unfortunately, societal bias is another component.

Despite the strides women have made in the home, workplace, and communities, there is still that structural gender bias. In my firm, we do well in terms of gender on our executive committee. We have three women partners out of seven and several more bright, young, female lawyers in the potential partner pipeline. Unfortunately, we're an outlier compared to other professional services firms in Singapore. That has to do with societal bias.

I will say that women can be our worst enemy sometimes. We deliberately take ourselves out of the pipeline and hold ourselves back because we think the work or balance is too challenging. Women disproportionately shoulder the burden of childcare and care for elderly parents. We juggle more on average than the average man with family. The gap is there because of a variety of reasons.

But I think the gap is closing thanks to better education, more emphasis on this issue, and more women lending their voices. For example, in the board leadership space, we have the Council for Board Diversity. It's encouraging that 30 per cent of directors on listed companies should be women. The target is 30 per cent by 2030. I am involved in BoardAgender, a gender-blind business advocacy group under SCWO. That's a big push we're making.

Women are making strides. But while the trajectory is correct and bright, we shouldn't forget that there's still hard work to be done.

Sharon:

What's your advice for women who want a seat on the table?

Joy:

Know your own value and have the confidence to articulate your worth, especially on the negotiating table. Information and education is key. There is no substitute for that, so do your homework. That's step number one.

Second, work the ground. When you are making a request, you must do your homework and frame the ask. But you must also look at who the decision-makers are. If you frame the ask, work the ground, and know who you're talking to, you can pitch confidently. Crucially, if you have any doubts about the pitch, your audiences will have similar doubts too.

Sometimes we lack that self-confidence to push ahead. Even getting to the stage of doing your homework and preparing for it is a big step. Reach out to the community for advice. Mentorship is also gaining widespread acceptance. At BoardAgender, we have a mentorship programme for hopefully ready young women to come up into the pipeline of independent directors in Singapore.

The more women are out there, the more young women can see ladies in society doing good in positions of power. There are more role models, which helps. Individual mentoring is also useful.

When I was younger, I received this advice. A company has a board of directors that oversees the management of the company and provides strategic direction. It's useful for you to have your own personal board of directors to help you with your strategy. They can help to frame your goals and give advice. So, I took that to heart and assembled my board of directors.

They may not know that they are and it's an unpaid relationship *[laughs]*, but they are my trusted advisers. They're more senior than I am.

These days there is also this concept of reverse mentoring, which is having younger folks in your life who can help you look at things from a different perspective. I learn from my adult children all the time. We learn from the younger generation. Their perception of life, what's important to them, and even their financial goals are so different.

Sharon:

So, are there any particular takeaways you have from the younger mentees?

Joy:

I've had a traditional career trajectory. I was in the public service, then I left to join the firm and worked my way up through the ranks. Today's employees don't have these goals. They're more flexible. They have more choices, which is a good thing. And many of them have exercised this freedom in ways that are good for them and the community. Many of our young lawyers have stepped away from the profession to contribute to the community in other ways.

You hear a lot of your noise about this, but I don't actually see it as a bad thing. We talked about flexible work arrangements and while there's a push to get everyone back to work full time in the office, the pandemic taught us that remote work could be even more efficient than in-person work.

The lessons I've learned from reverse mentoring is really about flexibility of choice. I'm always energized by their opportunistic approach. That energy and hunger is great.

Time is valuable for everybody. Unlike money, you can't make more time. So, it's a different way of looking at financial security.

Sharon:

What does money and wealth mean to you?

Joy:

To me, money is more than just the materialistic aspects. We have a stewardship responsibility to ourselves, our families, and our communities to use it wisely. So, wealth encapsulates that concept of stewardship responsibility.

I strongly believe that the important things in life are those that money can't buy. For example, your personal relationships, your spiritual life, your health. While money helps with these things, they are just a means to an end. Money is not the end itself.

The accumulation of wealth has a lot of different aspects, but most tie back to friendship and family ties. Wealth is usually more forward thinking, and just like an asset, if we invest it correctly or think about it the right way, we can generate more for the surrounding people. You can't take your money with you to the next life, so you use that money to generate wealth that makes the family, community, and world a better place.

Sharon:

How much money is enough for you?

Joy:

I don't have a number in mind. I still enjoy my job and the practice. So, I'm not looking to retire soon. I'm still paying off my mortgage and I still have a child who's going away overseas to study. So, I have a long way to go. I'm assuming that the magic number varies from person to person and is a moving target for many. But providing for the family and sending my children to university tops the list of priorities.

I'd need a comfortable nest egg for retirement and philanthropy will feature in my retirement planning.

Sharon:

Yes, we need to plan for retirement. If I can ask you another way of looking at that, if you have a billion dropping into your bank account, how would you want to spend it?

Joy:

That is serious money. It's a world changing sum of money and I would feel the need to use it responsibly. I'd probably want to invest in projects that might move the needle, especially with all the major problems facing the world today like climate change and poverty.

I would obviously do research and homework, but I'd like to invest in the climate space. We've spoken about carbon capture technology that might reverse the terrible burden we've placed on our environment.

In terms of poverty in Asia, I sit on the board of an insurance company and have therefore been exposed to several interesting projects in Singapore and overseas. So again, I'd look to fund something that can get meaningful results for the needy in our society.

I'm passionate about the arts too. It holds a mirror up to ourselves, and is part of what makes us human. So, closer to home, I would want to invest in arts education and support some of the placemaking approaches that the National Arts Council have engaged in.

We must grow our audience. Bring arts to the heartlands and put on diverse, inclusive theatre productions. We have been supporting inclusivity in the arts. It's something I feel strongly about. And hopefully with my diminishing pot of money, I can move some into that space.

Sharon:

How do you view money and philanthropy? Do you need to have a lot of money before giving back?

Joy:

I always believe you need a bit of a critical mass before you think about philanthropy. Otherwise, it's better and more sustainable if you look at contributing annually.

Just like how companies have annual corporate social responsibility budgets, you can look at your own budgets and start early when you want to contribute instead of waiting for a big event.

Sharon:

What is the kindest money-related act or advice you have received?

Joy:

Well, I've had the privilege of a lot of kindness in my life and good grounded advice from my mentors.

When I had my second child, I continued working because lawyering is a twenty-four-seven job. The conventional wisdom was that if you took too long of a career break, you would not rejoin the workforce. If you take over eighteen months off, you never come back. Hopefully, the numbers are different these days because of the emphasis on flexible working. But, in those days, when I expressed a desire to work flexibly, the senior leadership of the firm had no problems.

I'm glad that they saw the value that I brought in the moment to the table. And they were incredibly supportive. They did everything they could to encourage my flexible working journey, and that's one of the main reasons I've stayed in practice and in my firm. I was very grateful for it. It was one of those pivotal moments in my career.

On the topic about women in the workforce, we have so many burdens on us, right? Having that openness and the help is something very kind even in today's world. I don't think it's something that we take for granted. It is something that we have done consistently in the firm. So, I've tried to encourage this in the firm. We have many instances of supporting our female partners to work from home and it has paid dividends in the long run. It's good for the individual, organization, and society.

Sharon:

I can completely understand because I came from banking, and I really struggled after having kids and going back to work full time. Moving on, can you tell us a bit more about how you think about investment, asset allocation, and risk?

Joy:

I'm very risk averse. My allocation into risky assets is tiny. I'm definitely much more of a fixed income unit trust person.

In Singapore, many people invest in real estate. I am not the exception. Singaporeans like real estate as an asset class because it's tangible. We spend so much of our time at home. Real estate is also a core part of many people's investment portfolios because we've gone through various cycles and Singapore properties have done extremely well through these cycles. So, it's a good store of value.

Sharon:

I appreciate that you shared your vulnerabilities with us. It's not easy to expose a core part of yourself to the world. Thank you for this conversation, Joy.

8

Petrina Kow

Wealth is the feeling of abundance.

The path to prosperity takes on many forms, and the story of Petrina Kow testifies to this truth. Based in Singapore, Petrina is a seasoned voice and public speaking coach. In this conversation, she showcases how her vocal mastery has opened doors to a plethora of opportunities. From her roles as a radio broadcaster to her accomplishments on the theatre stage and the world of voice acting, Petrina's story illustrates the avenues that wealth can manifest in our lives.

KEY INSIGHTS

Money is a means to an end. True wealth is investing in yourself and your relationships.

Money helps to secure our basic needs and is a tool that fuels the pursuit of our dreams. However, it's essential to remember that genuine wealth goes beyond the numbers in our bank accounts. It's interwoven with the richness of your relationships and growth. Embracing this perspective, you will realize what truly matters—the connections you build and the quest to become the best version of yourself.

It's okay to fear money.

Money can seem daunting and sensitive, and it's natural to feel apprehensive about managing it. This recognition is crucial because it empowers you to face your financial fears head-on. By acknowledging that these concerns are not unique, it creates a space for open and non-judgmental discussions about money. Seek advice, educate yourself, and make informed choices.

The best things in life are free.

In the frantic pursuit of financial freedom, you may lose sight of your health, family, and happiness. Especially after facing the journey of losing a loved one to cancer and battling the disease yourself, it powerfully underscores the notion that money cannot quantify life's treasures, like health, love, and happiness.

THE CONVERSATION

Petrina:

I'm excited and also slightly nervous, which is a huge admission for me because I can talk about a lot of things. I said yes to this because I am never asked to give money advice. That is not my area of expertise. But because I know nothing about money, I told myself this is a scary but great opportunity for me to learn.

Sharon:

You've spent your career in the creative field. What was your first memory of it?

Petrina:

I don't have an early memory of money. All I remember were the stories people told me. Once, my sister almost drowned me at Buona Vista Swimming Complex and I twisted my neck, so I had to be hospitalized for a night for observation. My sister felt guilty, so she brought all my little stuffed toys from home and left them with me. The next day, I was discharged. I don't remember this, but apparently, when my mother came to pick me up, I had distributed my toys to everyone else in the ward. She had to go to every child, apologize, and take them back. I guess I've always been a generous person and am happy to give whatever I have to anybody else and not worry too much about it. I'm not overprotective about the things I like. If I think about it, perhaps it also comes from a deep-seated need to be liked.

Sharon:

Was money a topic that you and your family talked about?

Petrina:

It came up once in a while. But upon reflection, my sister and I have different values around money. We grew up in a HUDC apartment, which is the executive version of the HDB[3] flat.

We were all right growing up. We had a country club membership. I did swimming, ballet, music, all of those things. We took family trips to Malaysia, which I remember with fondness. It was only when we visited friends in condominiums or bungalows that we knew we were different. However, we never thought we were poor. We didn't have a huge amount of money, but we lacked nothing. My parents were the pioneer generation of Singapore and came from poverty; they grew up in a kampong and had little schooling. So, improvement in the way we lived in one generation was great.

Sharon:

Coming from a middle-class family with a comfortable life. What was your relationship with money?

Petrina:

I saw having money as a buffer in the beginning of my career. And my income was measly back then. I think I was earning $1,800 or something like that as a radio broadcaster. I was staying with my parents, so I didn't have to pay rent and only had to pay for my personal expenses. Whenever I got down to less than $1,000 in my bank account, I started being more aware of my spending. It was my threshold.

I've never built spreadsheets or tracked my spending, and never thought about what I'm spending on or how much I should spend on it. It's a real luxury because I've never needed to scrimp and save. On the flip side, I also feel a great level of insecurity sometimes when I do not have enough money.

I've always felt I should get a handle on this. It's a sore point with myself. No one is putting any pressure on me, but I thought I should have some sense of managing my money since I'm so old. It has come with a fair level of shame, honestly.

---

[3] The Housing & Development Board (HDB) is a statutory board under the Ministry of National Development and is responsible for public housing in Singapore. Such flats are provided to those in need of financial aid.

I don't want my kids to have the same values as me. I want them to develop financial literacy a lot earlier in life, so I always use myself as a cautionary tale. The way things are, it looks like one child is listening to me while the other is like me!

Sharon:

How do you speak about money to your children?

Petrina:

The older one will be cognizant of the remaining amount in the bank and is quite vigilant about getting reimbursements on expenditure. She's very much a saver. The younger one is the opposite. He will be like, 'Yo! I have $200. Let's spend it!'

Still, I recognize that they're both from different generations. They're also more privileged than we were growing up. They've seen many things and don't want for anything. I don't think that this has had an enormous impact on them yet, and I hope that when they become adults, they will start growing an awareness of that.

Sharon:

Do you think you need to do more in managing your finances? Because you're a successful businesswoman and can run your own businesses.

Petrina:

I certainly don't feel like one! I would never label myself as a businesswoman.

But I've been thinking about this. I've been managing my career for the past thirty years. I've just never framed it that way. Maybe that was all I needed, to lean into this idea of a businesswoman. It's reframing your thoughts, right? As we grow and our life and career changes, we learn new things.

For example, I learned to balance my books because I had to report my returns. That was a hard lesson, and an interesting one. My work involves working with people and helping them get over their fear of public speaking or curating their voice. I'm always the most encouraging person in that space. But I am hard on myself when it comes to this subject. Sometimes I take a step back and indulge in self-love. I was dealing with a lot in the first two decades of my marriage, and not having it all together is okay.

Sharon:

So how did you overcome this fear around managing your money? Was there a pivotal moment in your life?

Petrina:

Yes, it was when I pushed myself to be a better public speaking voice trainer and taught in many fields—academic, artistic productions, business. When I looked at my competitors' training sessions and my own lessons, I thought I did it better. Then, I wondered: Why were my competitors charging more expensive rates when I was more effective? It made me realize that framing and narrative of the brand was important.

There was some hesitance and resistance on my part. To be honest, I wasn't sure why I felt this way too. But I got over it by saying, 'Look, if those people can earn all this money doing it, why are you short-changing yourself? Why do you make yourself less important when you know more?'

I had to understand my value and be bold. This comes up a lot in conversations concerning women and money, especially in the corporate workplace. We're so shy to ask for a raise. No one in my generation would have been brave enough to demand a salary increase. That was unheard of and because there weren't such examples, you think that as long as somebody gives you cake, you're happy. Your expectations are low because no one was breaking the mould and doing something baffling. Or even if they did, they never told you.

In today's social media age, with everyone sharing everything, it can empower you. It's not always a good thing. But there are benefits.

Being raised as an Asian female, we're always told to sit quietly. 'Oh, you're too loud now. You mustn't do this or that.' I was one of the loudest and most talkative in class, and fortunately, my teachers rarely shut me down. They encouraged my performing side, which was why I had the courage to go through with it.

The irony is that I work with a lot of female leaders who come to me with the same problem. They are being overlooked while the people around them are getting promoted because they cannot articulate what and how they are doing. It's important to be clear about your role and the value you add to the company. It's not about singing your own praises, but about understanding and recognizing what you do. Even then, it's hard.

Sharon:

What is the value of money to you?

Petrina:

In my line of work, there is little talk about money. It is a means to an end for me. I've always viewed money as a transactional item. If I want something, I need to have enough money to buy it. I feel stronger connections to people than to things and money. I want to spend more time developing relationships instead of trying to uncover the meaning and value of money. It might be an internal block for me perhaps, but I just don't think money is very important. It's just a tool to me. If I have enough of it, then that's good.

Sharon:

For you, wealth comes from investing in relationships, in the right people, and in yourself. How do you see money and wealth?

Petrina:

Money buys you freedom and choice. So, if you have more of it, the world opens up more for you. You have more choices. Vice versa, when you have less of it, your options shrink. Wealth, however, is an internal feeling. For me, it's about feeling if you have abundance in different areas. For example, do I have an abundance of things that make me happy, like friends or food, or significant moments?

It has little to do with actual money. I love watching my dog play with his toy, seeing my plants grow, or admiring flowers when I walk in the Botanic Gardens. It's these small moments now that bring me great joy. Then I feel happy without thinking at all about money. So, there is that difference.

Sharon:

Since you said wealth and money are different things, I'm curious to know. What level of wealth do you think is enough?

Petrina:

It could be monetary, like do I need $10 million in my bank account? Or it could be a safety net for myself and the family? It depends on what stage I'm in. I'm at a point in my life where both my children are going off into university. It's a transitional phase, an exit of two integral humans in our lives. It's funny because they're physically not here but are financial burdens *[laughs]*.

If we were to pay for their university, then when they finish and return, will they live with us? Should we provide a room? Are they even going to return? As Asian parents, I want them to come home. We will have a room for them. I've had a few conversations with my husband about either renovating or moving.

We've stayed put for now to focus on growing what we have. We don't want to spend too much until we are sure that they are really gone, becoming fully grown adults, and are not staying with us any more. Then we can decide what we want to do with our home. It's interesting because I read that no matter how old our children get, somehow, they will always find a way back to their family.

We've set aside enough money to clear the house and provide for their education. After that, they're on their own. I tell them to not ask for money unless they are really desperate. It might sound hard-hearted, but they must learn too. They need to struggle. But I also want to have regular conversations with them about where they are mentally. When I was their age, I wished someone had taken me aside and taught me how to manage my money. Even something simple as setting aside 30 per cent of your salary every month to save.

In the past, growing up, we talked little about these topics. Money, relationships, sex—these were all taboo. The important thing was—you shouldn't do it. Now, everything is wide open. Information is everywhere. It's more important to know how you can find and sift through what you need. Then, execute properly.

Sharon:

Yeah, there's a compounding effect of investing early. It's a mindset and if we have these mindsets earlier in life, we would be comfortable talking about money. I wanted to discuss more broadly about what you've achieved. You're quite successful in your own right and have been honest about your vulnerabilities. How full is your bucket right now?

Petrina:

It's pretty full. I consider myself extremely fortunate. I've had two gifts that changed my thinking early in life. The first was losing my mother when I was twenty-eight and just starting out to be a mother. It was a pivotal moment, and still is, to some extent. I'm still working through her death even though it's been almost twenty years. When it happened, I was raising my child, and it made things clear. Life is short and you cannot faff about with unimportant things. Focus on what really matters, which was this baby I had. So, I wanted to be the best person and mother I could be.

The second gift was getting cancer two years ago. I see it as a gift because it slapped me and reminded me again of what is important in life. How you choose to live every day, who you spend your time with, what you stress about, what you don't stress about. All the everyday small things matter because they can become big things. What you think affects what you say affects how you feel and eventually what you do.

Sharon:

Did your cancer battle affect how you view money? Did it make money less significant?

Petrina:

Yes, and no. My values remain similar, but I cut myself a lot more slack and not feel like I've wasted time, thinking I should have done something yesterday or three years ago. Now, I think about what I can do to simplify my life and live a better one.

And what is a better life? Is it waking up every morning, finding time to go exercise, and spending quality time with your loved ones? Or wake up, scroll through your phone, and stress about who's going to do what and who is thinking about me? Once you've had that perspective, deciding how you want to be every day and who you say yes to will give your mind space to move. It helps to take away all the distractions and focus on the important things in life.

People might think that what I went through was horrible. And it was. But I have the privilege of living through that and coming out the other side in better shape. I remember the first thing that went through my mind when I received the diagnosis was, 'Okay, can I look at the insurance?'

Thankfully, it covered everything. So, it became a physical task, right? I didn't have to worry about it financially. I didn't have to skip taking chemotherapy because I couldn't afford it. If I had to worry about the money, I would be in a different place. So, to have that worry thrown to the corner and concentrate day by day on eating and drinking enough helped. I told myself, 'If I can get through that, I can get through anything.'

When I look at other people and hear their stories, I feel lucky. Building that practice of gratitude is important. And when you get sick, you also see how the surrounding people respond to you and what they mean to you. I have been nothing but blessed to have the best family by my side helping me through everything, friends who supported me in so many ways. That I get to be here today and continue my work is a huge blessing.

Sharon:

What is the best money-related advice you've received?

Petrina:

My mother used to say that when you get married, your money is your money and your husband's money is also your money *[laughs]*. But, on a more serious note, when I was doing a marriage preparatory course, they mentioned that it's important to find out what the other person's attitude to money is like and see if that is a good match for you. It's less about money, and more about the values that we associate with it. If we can observe and talk about it and work through it, that would be helpful and helps with any relationship, not just marriage.

Sharon:

I don't want this conversation to end, and I'm so touched by the courage you've shown and the many refreshing stories you've shared. Thank you, Petrina.

9

Lily Choh

*Life is like gripping sand. Hold on too tight
and it slips away.*

You hear Lily Choh's infectious laughter before you see her. She is joyful and relatable and can establish rapport and engender trust quicker than most. It is fitting that she is CEO of Schroders Singapore, and Head of South Asia of Schroders APAC. She has committed her career to investment management and being a custodian of wealth. In this interview, she explores how her mindset towards money has shaped her life, and by having a healthy attitude towards money, she ended up being responsible for more.

KEY INSIGHTS

Women have money instincts.

Remember to trust your inner knowledge and intuition. Often, we have a deep sense of knowing when something doesn't sit right, even when we can't explain it logically. These instincts guide us in making financial decisions that may differ from what men traditionally do.

Have no fear of lack and less greed for more.

Embrace a mindset untainted by fear of scarcity or desire for excess. When we shift our focus from our own needs to the well-being of others, it provides us with a harmonious perspective. By letting go of the relentless pursuit of more, we can find balance in our financial lives.

Don't die wealthy. Live wealthy.

We can't take our wealth with us when we pass on. So, we should focus on living with abundance, whether it's for ourselves or for the benefit of others. There is a profound value in helping others when we can. It's not about the quantity of assistance but the significance of the gesture.

THE CONVERSATION

Serena:

Before we dive deep, I'm wondering if you would like to share a recent frivolous purchase?

Lily:

Well, the biggest purchase in the last two years was our house. I'm so glad we made that decision because prices just went through the roof. For frivolous purchases, I travelled with my daughter to London, and we just bought whatever we wanted that was reasonable. I guess it's not frivolous per se, but just us having a good time together.

Serena:

So, the theme of being a custodian of wealth has been a constant in your life and career. Could you tell us about your career journey?

Lily:

I started my career as a loans officer in a local bank. People would come to me for loans to buy houses, cars, and everything else. I had to make important assessments on peoples' credit worthiness. Then I moved to GIC, which is a significant custodian of wealth and assets for the country. There was a lot of responsibility, but what a great journey because I grew the most there. Then, I moved to investment management. Once again, it's a custodian role. Other people's money is our responsibility, so we have to think twice before we decide on assets entrusted to us.

Serena:

It's interesting you say that because I've always felt you're one of the most trustworthy people I know in the industry, and you have this amazing ability to make anyone feel comfortable around you. I'd love to understand how you grew up and how money played a part in your life.

Lily:

I grew up in Malaysia and it was such great joy because we lived in a big house and had twelve dogs running around the garden. One day, my father came back and said that his business was at risk. He was an established land developer and is usually optimistic, so we were worried when he came back and said that.

Money was always a serious topic at home. Fortunately, my mother is the exact opposite of my father. She's the typical conservative stay-at-home parent who always had a stash of money hidden somewhere, and that pot of gold helped us through the crisis. It was a long-drawn one, but thankfully, we all grew up well and began earning our own keep.

Serena:

Could you tell us how your mother and father dealt differently with money?

Lily:

My dad is the eternal optimist. He always says that if you work hard, you should play hard too. That mantra has always sat with me, and I share that with my company. My mother was different. She always said that we can play a little, but there's always a rainy day and when it rains, it pours. I'd like to think I got the best of both my parents. The storm happened when we were young and that pot of money she stashed away proved really helpful. That imprinted the DNA of my relationship with money.

Serena:

How did that situation make you feel? Do you remember the serious talks you had at the dining table about money and the emotions associated with that?

Lily:

We were young and didn't know what was going to happen next, so we were really worried. Our parents tried not to show too much emotion in front of us, but my older brothers knew what was going on, so they always told us we shouldn't be naughty because our mother and father are really stressed.

Serena:

Then, you grew up and came to Singapore for school. How did that influence your career choices?

Lily:

Well, I graduated in the late nineties. The economy wasn't doing well then, so I grabbed the first job offer that came. Then, my friends told me to apply for a role at GIC because it was looking for talent. I got a bunch of my older friends who are government civil servants to help me write my CV. They submitted it for me. That's how I got the interview and got in. From then onwards, the training, experience, and knowledge that was built up set the pace for what was to come. I'm really grateful for my earlier days.

Serena:

You are in a unique position to ask about investing, especially for women. What do you think is special about women when it comes to investing?

Lily:

I feel we can look at things in a balanced way. And there's instinct that tells us to do things differently from what the men are doing. That instinct helped me through my life journey. In the past three decades, I've snapped up some excellent property investments by instinct. My husband is objective and knows the value of items. But sometimes, timing is of the essence. I'm not saying women are better, but we can complement our partners with our instinct. For women, when our mind aligns with our heart, we make quick decisions. But I still fall back to my husband because he's the analytics guru in the family. Then, we make joint decisions. What I'm good at is acting fast and getting things done, so we complement each other really well. In the past thirty years, we've made significant investment decisions together.

Women are also great at building relationships and contacts. It's great for imperfect environments like real estate, where you need to hunt for something that you like at the right price. There might be locations that are off-market or that require special access.

Serena:

You mentioned time-sensitive decisions. But how should women think about investing for the long-term?

Lily:

My husband would disagree, but I think women can plan and multitask well. It's not a good or bad thing, but there are always opportunities in crises. People can get really stressed during a prolonged crisis. I work with fund managers who had never seen a crisis as bad as the pandemic and because the last financial crisis was such a long time ago. They are stressed and emotionally affected, and I think this is where women excel—our emotional strength.

Our clients trust us, so we just need to do our best. Bad decisions are inevitable, but we should be nimble and rectify them. This is what women are great at, coming in to manage and support during a crisis.

Serena:

How would you define your risk appetite? And in the same vein, what is the best advice that a friend or even a boss has given you?

Lily:

For our first marital home, we were trying to decide whether it should be public or private housing. My boss told me, 'You have a career path ahead of you. Borrow as much as you can. You've got a long-term horizon of twenty–thirty years. What is there to lose? What's the downside? Time is your friend. So, go for the best investment.'

I thought this was fantastic advice because I leaned towards my mother's philosophy of prudent risk management when growing up. So, I told my then boyfriend that my boss made sense and we went for the more expensive option. It shaped the way I manage risk. I would take the opportunity and risk if I feel the value of the investment is there. And don't hesitate too much, especially if you have a long-time horizon.

Serena:

What about poor advice? Have you received any you felt wasn't right for you?

Lily:

It's okay to take risks, but it has to be backed by thought. Don't invest on impulse. Let it sit a while. I've made many impulsive decisions that have gone south. When it's too good to be true, I think we really need to think twice.

We've all gone through quite a fair bit in the past several years. I have a driver in Malaysia for when I do business trips there. He's a freelance driver.

During Covid, when the country was in lockdown, he was down to his last $1,000 in the bank. A decade of savings got wiped out in three years of the pandemic. It was that bad, and it was so sad. This has really changed my perspective on life. If we can be kind to others, then we should be kinder.

Serena:

I'm curious, but has the meaning of money changed for you?

Lily:

I've reached a stage where I'm pretty content. I'm at a sweet spot in my life and I feel blessed in all ways, from family to friends and community to work.

That's why I feel my current relationship with money is balanced. There is no fear and I have less greed to want more. If we can focus less on ourselves and more on others, that gives us a balanced view.

When you focus on yourself, then you think about whether you should change your behaviour and how you should be living. As my father tells me, life is like gripping sand. When you open up your palms, you get more. The minute you tighten your grip, however, the sand slips away. Money is the same. Once you say you have enough, and let go, then you might actually get more.

Serena:

You said you are content and have enough so what is enough for you?

Lily:

Well, I still need to work *[laughs]*. But I'm not lacking anything. The bills are paid, and I don't have to worry about next month's bills and whether I can spend and pamper myself at the same time.

It makes me think about the question you asked me at the beginning: What have I done for myself? I haven't really done anything for myself. Everything has been for my family or the office.

This is where I am right now. Enough is no fear, no worries, and having confidence.

Serena:

In the spirit of not having fear, what happens if you wake up one day with a billion dollars in your bank account? What are you going to do? How does that change your perspective?

Lily:

A billion has never crossed my mind, but I would probably do something totally opposite of what I'm doing right now. It's not about taking the money and splurging on myself like a whirlwind holiday or private jets. It's about having no fear. The first thing that comes to mind is to go into art because I'm terrible at it *[laughs]*. I can't draw. Or go into music because I learnt piano a long time ago.

I'll also want to set something up that can affect individuals. I don't think I can change the world, but I can change the lives of many individuals with a billion. It's more practical, and smart, to change the world one person at a time.

Serena:

What are your teenage children's attitudes towards money? And what have you done to shape that?

Lily:

So, my children have very different personalities. Let's start with my twelve-year-old son, a cute and cheeky fella. I asked him what he got from mummy and daddy on investing, and he said, 'Take risks' *[laughs]*. That's his favourite line. He's sort of running his own business now.

There's a famous YouTuber that manufactured a series of energy drinks called Prime. It's not available in Singapore. You must get it from a US- or UK-based manufacturer.

Anyway, he bought the energy drink from his friend for $15 and I asked him, 'Why would you do that?' He said that he could sell it to another friend for $20, for a drink.

So, he's doing this on the side. He's a natural trader. I told him not to get into trouble because I don't want his principal to call me. But we love that he's so enterprising. He even recruited a few of his friends as business managers. He invested a bit of his profits in a Tesla stock, which he picked himself, with some top up from me. Now, he thinks he can beat 80 per cent of fund managers because it has been a great start and I'm worried that he gets too hot about it.

My daughter is different. She always says that I told her I could save and then spend on things that have value. I guess she's going to be a value investor *[laughs]*.

Serena:

It's interesting that they both have distinct personalities and I'm seeing this recurring trend of women being more conservative while men taking more risks. Is this what you see in the office too? Or is this too much of a generalization?

Lily:

Anecdotally, I'd say it's true. Our industry is still male-dominated, and the top fund managers are mostly male. They take risks when making investment decisions. Increasingly though, I think it's not so much about gender as it is about age. The younger generation in my office tends not to take too much risk. They're happy in their careers and don't want to do more to progress.

For them, work-life balance and mental wellness are more important. They feel they can earn money elsewhere and are usually risk managers instead of risk takers. It's interesting and sometimes, I have to push them a little more. The nature of risk-taking has changed.

When we were growing up, the career options were to be a doctor, lawyer, or accountant. Nobody wanted to be a banker. It's different these days and this might have shaped our thinking around risk taking.

Serena:

Returning to you, what has been the kindest thing someone has done for you? Something that's related to money.

Lily:

So, I shared earlier that my father's business ran into some problems. There was one stage where we struggled with the expenses for that month. An uncle and his wife came forward and gave us a few hundred to tide us over. It's not much now, but it was a lot of money for us back then. It didn't solve the problem, but that thoughtfulness and help were there when we really needed and it made the difference.

That's why we're still close to that uncle and aunt because of what they did for us. It's not the amount, but the gesture. It really ingrained in me that if we can help others, then we should. We can generate more kindness by helping.

Recently, I went to Malaysia to meet with a client who is the head of wealth in a Malaysian bank, and he told me something that gave me chills. He said, 'Don't die wealthy. Live wealthy.' It's so true. You can't bring money into your coffin, so you should live wealthy, whether for yourself or for others.

I thanked him profusely. My team was there, too, and heard this golden piece of advice.

Serena:

For our last question, what does wealth mean to you?

Lily:

The words that come to mind are comfort and stability. Wealth puts you in a position to do more and to do things differently. You can take some risk to make life a lot better. But wealth also comes with a lot of responsibility. Your community, friends, and everyone else is watching you, so you should be mindful of the responsibility that comes with wealth.

Serena:

That's so apt because it comes back to your custodian and fiduciary mindset!

Thank you for sharing so openly with us. Money can take us to the highest of places, but it can also bring out the worst in us. Your resilience and positive spirit really shine through.

10

Mint Lim

*Feeling sorry for myself was a luxury
I could not afford.*

When Mint Lim speaks, you listen. There is an assuredness and pace in how she connects and pours out her ideas, which is only possible when you've been tested by incredibly challenging experiences and met with folks from all walks of life. Mint is a serial turned social entrepreneur who distributed auto parts, ran a florist boutique, and started a tutoring business helping children in low-income neighbourhoods. She is the founder of School of Concepts and the first Singaporean to be awarded the Cartier Women's Initiative Fellowship. In this conversation, Mint shares how her struggles with money transformed how she views it and how she is using money as a force of motivation for her entrepreneurial journey.

KEY INSIGHTS

Honesty is the only way, with money and with people.

Have money discussions early in your relationship, particularly with your significant other. This helps to align your values and goals. When you meet financial difficulties, it is easier to hide it than to share it. But ultimately, you could be stressing yourself out and depleting your emotional and energy reserves. You may have the strength to power on, but finding a way to ease your burden can help in the longer run.

'Learning poverty' is a legitimate issue that needs to be solved.

Seventy-eight percent of children in South Asia today are suffering from learning poverty because of the pandemic. Learning poverty is when people are functionally illiterate. Being partially illiterate is as good as being illiterate. They can't move on from there. It's something people don't realize.

Money can be a tool for creating motivation or inciting fear, so choose wisely.

When you frame your mind to see money and its impact to drive you, you'll be surprised at what you can achieve. The lack of money can also be a driver, if you know what you are batting for. In Mint's case, she swung hard to alleviate financial problems for her family and to scale the School of Concepts.

THE CONVERSATION

Serena:

You're a woman of many hyphens, and one of them is being a social entrepreneur. What does being one mean to you?

Mint:

Being an entrepreneur is all about doing business and being resourceful. And being an impact-driven entrepreneur means doing business while doing good. When we do business, we always want to derive some level of satisfaction.

There is a product and an outcome we want to achieve and doing something good drives that kind of outcome. It's something intangible, but something incredibly important, akin to happiness.

Serena:

Let's talk about your childhood because it will help us understand where your drive comes from. Can you tell us how money played a part in your childhood?

Mint:

I was first introduced to the concept of money as a child when my grandfather played cards and mahjong with his friends. I saw how money was transacted across the table in honest, and not so honest, ways.

Later on, in school, I realized that all of us got pocket money. And I started asking myself how some of them could afford items that cost $1.20. That's when I realized that they might have gotten $2 as pocket money while others got $1.50. I got a dollar. And on top of this somewhat below market rate *[laughs]*, my mother had another request. She wanted me to save 50 per cent of it. That meant I could only spend $0.50 during recess.

So, I learned to pack my lunchbox, go to school, do a site recce, and look at the menu's prices. That's why I have this habit even till today of scanning through all the prices when I'm at a restaurant. Back in school, I'd find an item that fits my $0.50 budget. I always diligently saved. It stemmed from the home situation that I was in. I knew I couldn't ask them for more.

I began thinking, 'Surely this dollar can grow beyond asking my mother for an additional dollar?' I started observing trends in school and realized that there was this game called Five Stones that people were buying from the bookshop for a dollar. In my mind, I thought I could earn money by selling this game.

I would use scrap fabric that my grandmother didn't use, stuff them with random beads, and make them into a set. Mismatched Five Stones were a trend back then! So those were my sustainable Fives Stones.

Serena:

Interesting. So, you mentioned you had to be resourceful growing up because of your responsibilities. Were there certain circumstances at home that resulted in that or was it just good upbringing?

Mint:

I must credit my parents. They helped us understand the boundaries of many things and taught the concept of saving. But I must also say that my relationship with money was a roller coaster growing up. I had a lot of fear. What if I lose that dollar? What if I can't save that $0.50?

That's when I learned to be a bit more resourceful and tried to multiply my money. I felt a sense of motivation and that was very empowering. Things at home got a lot better. But then in my late teens, things happened within the family, and it became a lot tougher financially again. It was like day and night. You wake up one day nice and rosy, and the next day, everything crashes. So that was a lot to deal with.

Frankly, feeling sorry for myself was a luxury. It was just, 'Okay, now things are not moving well, but we have to move. I need to put food on the table and make sure that my three younger siblings are not affected.'

My nineteen-year-old self tried her best to do whatever within her means to put it together.

Serena:

What did you do?

Mint:

I tried many small businesses. I learnt how to spot trends. There was a tutoring boom at that time. There were also people exploring the idea of manufacturing with Alibaba. So, I opened a tuition centre, and the brand grew on its own. Then, I became the middle person and managed transactions between OEM[4] factories in China and some regions in the world.

It was very male dominated. I recall walking the streets in the Middle East and trying to make conversation for transactions. I'd walk into a shop to say hello and they would just look past me like I didn't exist, like I was part of the fixtures on the wall.

It made me realize this was what it felt like to be disregarded in a patriarchal society. I learned to work with what I had. Life was too short to feel sorry for myself or try something else. So, I hired a man to represent me, which worked really well because I could communicate certain decisions through him and push things across to find a solution. It also helped me to improve my communication skills. I looked at these as learning opportunities.

Serena:

That's incredible. It's hard to be alone in the Middle East and make transactions in a sector that most don't associate with women. I really applaud you for that. You mentioned you always take these challenges as learning opportunities, which brings me to your business School of Concepts. It was set up because of your own story. Could you share the childhood episodes you had to overcome?

Mint:

So, as a child, I struggled very much to identify the directions of certain words and letters and all that. I was too shy to tell anyone. So, it was incredibly challenging going through kindergarten and being around my grandparents who only spoke dialect. But I just tried my best until I sort of figured it out.

---

[4] An Original Equipment Manufacturer (OEM)

I was fortunate because the Sunday School teacher gifted some teaching material to my mother to help her help me. And along the way, after too many tears and trying to figure it out together, I figured out a way to gain literacy. That entire process was about embracing the journey. That was my first experience.

I learned different techniques along the way and during that process, I could pick up all those learning points and put them into today's school curriculum at the School of Concepts.

Serena:

What is the school's philosophy?

Mint:

The school was founded with the mission to leave No Child Behind. It uses a unique methodology and believes that every learner has an optimal learning style. In every learner, there's a superhero learner.

I still feel strongly that most parents should know about their children. Research and development took five years, and we spent this time formulating the methodology that we insert into our English literary curriculum to equip children with early literacy. It worked incredibly well.

So, we used that same methodology to create other curriculums: numeracy, financial literacy, even DIY toys. Now we've moved that pedagogy into edtech and created mobile learning games.

Serena:

It's amazing how you grew from a seed of a concept into a tangible product that's touching lives. You're Singapore's first Cartier Women's Initiative Fellow. Tell us about that recognition.

Mint:

I'm extremely grateful and humbled. The award acted as an affirmation for both me and the team for the work we've done. When you start a social enterprise or impact-driven business, it's not something that you just wake up and do every day. When we started, people didn't understand what an impact business was. Profit was still a dirty word. Double bottom-lines were unheard of.

I am thankful that in today's landscape, people understand a lot better and are building a more sustainable future.

The process was interesting and incredibly empowering. I had just given birth and was fresh out of confinement during a conference when a representative from Cartier spotted me. She messaged me over LinkedIn and said, 'Hey, I think there's something that you might be interested in participating in.' So, she told me about the fellowship and the application process. I was like, 'Oh man, I don't know if I have enough in my tank to do this,' because I had just delivered a baby and was out of confinement, so I was still adjusting.

I was adapting to a lot of things in my life while still managing School of Concepts. I thought many times about not applying. But the lady was so encouraging and empowering. She said we would do it together so that I wouldn't have to feel I'm doing it alone. That was fun. We sat down together, then she took out a notebook, and I told her about my journey.

So, I applied and was shortlisted. I didn't know what was going to happen after that, and they said I had to give a presentation. Being in hibernation after giving birth and just coming out of confinement made me feel like I didn't have enough in my tank to do it. But when I approached Cuili from Cartier Women's Initiative again, she said that if I got shortlisted, it likely means that I would be the first Singaporean to get the award. No pressure now, right? *[laughs]*

The more I thought about it though, the more I felt I should do it not just for my daughter or the women on my team, but for every Singaporean woman who was going through the same thing I was, being a founder, entrepreneur, mother, and wife.

So, I did it and became Singapore's first fellow! It was a truly humbling moment. I never once expected our little social enterprise in our little red dot to actually stand in Paris to receive the award from Cartier.

I think the maison saw how empowering the business was and how it would share that message with other women. They saw sustainability, not just to do good, but also in business. It was one of the most thorough due diligence I've ever gone through. The judges interviewed all the stakeholders, from my investors all the way to our beneficiaries. They left no one out. They scrutinized our numbers, projections, and everything else. It was an incredibly rigorous process.

Serena:

You mentioned double bottom-lines. Do you still encounter people who think that all social enterprises shouldn't be making a profit?

Mint:

From time to time, but not as much as before. I think the landscape has really grown and kudos to everyone who's contributed to this ecosystem. Today's consumers are clear now that businesses have double bottom-lines. They actually value the mission and vision behind these businesses. I remember that profit was such a dirty word when we first started the school.

We only had eight parents who truly believed in us. I always call them my most forward-thinking and loyal customers. Actually, they are not just customers. They are advocates who tell people how well their kids are doing. We value these things very much. This is what I call empowerment.

The ecosystem has definitely matured. Consumers today are very conscious about the value and the mission behind the business and this really affects their consumption decision. And I'm very heartened to know that. When we first started the School of Concepts, it was all about doing things right, doing things that would help, and enabling the team to say, 'Hey, I did something so good, I'm going to sleep tonight with a smile and wake up tomorrow feeling empowered to do more.'

Everyone had a mission to feel that way while still making a living for themselves and being able to put food on the table. I'm so happy to see consumers today exercise their choice when choosing what to spend on. It makes such a world of difference. In the past, people used to think, 'Am I getting the most value out of this dollar?' No one cared what happened beyond that dollar. Today, people are asking, 'What's going to happen to this dollar?' They are thinking forward. That's beautiful.

Serena:

I love that. I wanted to return to your points about choices and spending. Are you a spender or saver?

Mint:

Both. I'm a practical person and spend on necessities. I also spend on things that make my life more convenient. But I also enjoy saving as security. If something unforeseen happens, I know I have some savings to weather that.

Serena:

We spoke about profit and how that propels the School of Concepts. On the personal front, what is your mission for money? What do you want to do with it?

Mint:

Money is a great tool to make tomorrow a better place. It will make the world more liveable, enjoyable, and satisfying. So many can make this happen. That's the relationship that I think more people should have with money, where it's a win-win-win situation and not just the one person who benefits. The third factor is the environment.

Serena:

So, we're going from double to triple bottom-lines now! If you close your eyes and think about money and what it represents, what do you see and what are the emotions tied to it?

Mint:

A word came to mind when you were asking me that question: blessing. Money can bless many people with better livelihoods and better tomorrows. It can bless the environment and the economy.

Serena:

Do you invest? What investments do you make?

Mint:

Well, I'm an entrepreneur, so there's that daily investment I do with my business. That's my largest investment to date. For other forms of investment, I have a portfolio that contributes to my lifestyle, and the ratio depends on how much time I have to spend on each portion. I have long-term investments in some stocks and properties, but they're usually at arm's length and require a longer-term outlook. I don't micromanage these daily.

For the business, which is my largest investment, I put in more because that's where I spend most of my time trying to make it grow and become better.

Serena:

You see investing from a more holistic perspective. Let's dream bigger because I know you have the imagination and ability to do that. If you had a billion dollars, what would you invest in?

Mint:

I would try to rescue children from 'learning poverty', which is when people are functionally illiterate. Being partially illiterate is as good as being illiterate. They can't move on from there. It's a shocking number, but 78 per cent of children in South Asia today are suffering from 'learning poverty' because of the pandemic. It's something people don't realize. This actually translates into $21 trillion worth of opportunities for the global economy, which is crazy. In the long term, we will all suffer. So, I see this as an urgent need that needs to be rectified.

Globally, the trend is that the Asian youth is going to be the largest population and demographic in the world in twenty years' time. And this problem will not be eradicated within three generations because these children are the offspring of earlier generations and parents of the next generation. So, if they are not rescued from 'learning poverty', it's an enormous problem.

Serena:

That's a shocking statistic. Please let us know how we can be a part of this journey with you. Do you recall a time when you or your husband had your first conversation with money?

Mint:

It was direct and during a formal date. I brought a notebook and pencil. Very romantic right? *[laughs]* We were having fine Italian dining. Halfway through dinner, I said, 'Let's not waste each other's time. We are both mature adults. We have come to the stage where we want to get married because we want to have a family. So, let's be practical about it and talk about things that need to be talked about now.'

My then boyfriend was taken aback and probably thought I was weird and direct. But I was thinking about going big or going home. I asked him about the life that he envisioned for ourselves and our children. Does he want to leave a legacy? Does he want to work until he's sixty? What's his retirement plan? I shared with him mine, and he understood where this conversation was going.

I told him I didn't need to know how much money he had in his bank account because that's a different conversation. I just wanted to know where we were on our journey with money and how we were going to progress together.

It's like having a mission statement. You always need to remember it. That was my notebook and pencil moment, but it has worked very well. Every anniversary, I still take it out.

The notebook is affirmation and alignment that we are still in this journey together.

Serena:

What are the roles that the both of you play at home in money matters?

Mint:

We're both in charge of our own savings and spending. For the family pool, I'm in charge of spending and he handles the savings. But I'm in charge of investing the family pool.

Serena:

I know your daughter is still young, but have you already expected the money lessons that you'll be teaching her?

Mint:

She's sixteen months, so it's been very casual. She likes to count up and down and she loves it when we let her transact. When I want to pay for something, I get her to take the cash or card and pass it to the cashier. She recognizes that so much that she actually requests for my wallet most of the time when we go to the toy store.

Serena:

Was that also how you were brought up? Or was it a departure from your own childhood?

Mint:

That's something close to my heart because I think my mother was honest only up to a point about our financial situation. She felt like we wouldn't be able to understand, but looking back, I felt like it would have been easier if I had a better understanding and more clarity about what was going on.

And then later on, when things happened in the family, I did the same. I didn't tell my siblings how difficult the situation really was and was putting on a front for friends saying that I was fine. I was just trying to figure it out. No one really knew how difficult it was for me. In fact, my best friend only found out last month how tough it was.

I didn't tell anyone the full extent of it. My friend felt terrible because I used to buy lunch for the both of us thinking that I was earning more. But I had lots of responsibilities that I didn't think about telling anyone or being honest about because I felt like it was my problem.

Serena:

Did you feel shame or pity for yourself?

Mint:

I didn't want people to feel sorry for me and I didn't want my siblings to feel they were a burden to me. So, I was just masking it all. But today, I took a different approach to be very transparent about it in the organization. I realized the relationship with money needs to be a very honest one. If you have it, you have it. If you don't, you need to be rational about it. That's the lesson I learnt.

Serena:

Bringing it back to the School of Concepts, you said you are being more transparent with numbers, financials, and profitability with your team. How do you do it? And why?

Mint:

It's all a matter of saying things as is and being truthful because we are an impact-driven business. We wear our hearts on our sleeves, and we tell everyone that. I want the team to understand how they contribute to our sustainability because it is a sustainable business. And if they contributed to it, they should feel part of it.

I'm transparent about it because I felt that if they understand and they know how much their efforts have contributed to the sustainability of this business, they are empowered.

So, we have weekly meetings. There are two ways we run a meeting because there are double bottomlines. One talks about our achievements, how close we are to our targets, what we can do to achieve them, how it translates into our revenue, and how that drives sustainability.

The other side is what we call the Gratitude Circle. We get every single person in the room to give thanks. It's to help them draw that connection between gratitude, empowerment, and sustainability.

Serena:

What does sustainability mean to you in the business?

Mint:

Well, in a quantifiable way, to have enough money to pay off the rent, to pay our staff, expenses, and enough to share with our investors. That is sustainability.

Serena:

Coming to good advice, we're curious to know what kind of advice, good or bad, you've received around money?

Mint:

Back when I was working in China, someone said to me that money can solve a lot of problems. It sounded arrogant to me on the surface, but when I thought about it, if it's a problem caused by lack of money, it will surely be solved with money. And if these problems can be solved with money, then it's not really a big problem, right?

For example, if a relationship breaks down because of a lack of money, the solution will be to find more money. Then it doesn't become a problem because the relationship is fixed after that. But if a relationship is broken because of something else, then it's gone forever.

So, that was good money advice to me because it makes sense on a different level.

As for poor advice, I remember someone saying to me I should take a loan to do my business. Back then, I thought that would lighten my stress. But I thought, what's the skin in the game for me? When you have a sense of ownership, especially when your savings is in the business, then your decisions will change. If I'm offloading my sense of responsibility to someone else, that doesn't align with me.

As a serial entrepreneur, I started all my businesses with my savings and that gave me the motivation to push 200 per cent.

Serena:

Amazing. I wanted to ask you this. What is wealth to you?

Mint:

Wealth can be both tangible and intangible. Wealth can definitely mean having enough money. But then, what is enough? For me, depending on the season of your life, enough means making you happy, in that season.

Is it enough for people around you to be happy and comfortable? And if these boxes are checked, then a person is very wealthy. I felt happy in this season because I feel I have enough to provide for my child and for my family. I won't say we've got anything in excess, but we have enough.

Serena:

Do you have any fears around money?

Mint:

I won't call it fear, as it is motivation. As a business owner, money can be a motivating tool. It can also be a fear: not having enough to pay the bills, not having enough to expand, not having enough to scale. In the case for the School of Concepts, we needed more to scale the impact, beyond just business. It's beyond scaling in terms of size, it is also speed. The problem is real and also urgent because of all those children lost to learning poverty. It has been motivating to see the children coming out of our programme being equipped and ready for the future, and to seize opportunities.

Let me share with you a small story. Many, many years ago when I was just starting the School of Concepts, I taught a child who had no means to pay for his fees. His parents were not taking care of him. His primary caregiver was his aunt. It came to a point where she couldn't afford to pay me. But I didn't want to let the child go because I knew how important it was to him. So, I continued teaching him. He progressed and did well. If you look at the debt owed, it could have been used to expand the school or pay rent, but I put all of that aside.

One day I received a message and I still get goosebumps just thinking about it. This person texted me on Instagram and he said, 'You remember me?' I looked at the photo and replied, 'Of course I remember you.' I remember every single student I've taught. He thanked me for giving him education. He had recently completed his 'O' and 'A' Levels and was going to the next phase of his life, which was university. While waiting for his results, he was working at a salad bar and just got his first pay cheque. He said, 'You're the first person I thought of paying back. I can't pay you in full, but I want to pay you something.'

I was thinking to myself, 'This boy could have become a victim.' But he's reaping the benefits of those lost opportunities, and that, to me, is a positive outcome.

Serena:

Because of what you've done, this kindness is going to spread! On this topic, what was the kindest thing anyone has done for you?

Mint:

I count my blessings every day and give thanks for it, even to my head of school who buys me coffee every day. I've never gone in front of an audience to say that I'm raising funds, but I've wanted to open another school at many points in my journey. We needed to grow the education tech business, so I was having this conversation with a friend of a friend about this, and he said that he liked what I was doing for the children and was ready to write a cheque.

He was in business and knew how tough fundraising was, but he saw the same vision. The conversation helped us be aligned and see a vision that he had as well. We both wanted to work towards the same mission. And because of that, he felt like he could trust me to journey with him to achieve that mission.

That's why he wrote me the cheque. Similarly, the angel investor who gave us the amount to kick-start the education tech business saw the vision and wanted to journey together with us.

Serena:

You must have also spoken to their emotions or touched them in a certain way that made them believe in the School of Concepts. Thank you so much for your time, Mint.

11

Madeline Liu & Zheng Yizhou

For Gen Z, figuring out who we are is the bigger issue.

Madeline Liu and Zheng Yizhou are undergraduate students at the University of Hong Kong and University of Miami, respectively. We interviewed them when they were in Singapore for an internship with a financial institution. Madeline grew up in a large extended household in Hong Kong, while Yizhou spent her early and teenage years with her family in Beijing. They now live in Singapore. In this conversation, they share the voices of Gen Z, and how their peers view money and wealth.

KEY INSIGHTS

The most special thing about money is the smell.

Science has shown that scents form strong connections with certain emotions and feelings in your mind. For Madeline and Yizhou, money isn't just a currency to gain things but a tool that represents independence and freedom. Who doesn't love the smell of a crisp dollar bill from the bank?

Gen Z is more self-focused.

Some might consider it selfish, but the younger generation believes it's more responsible to figure out who you are before you even contemplate marriage and children. You have to love yourself first before you have the capacity to love others.

Wealth is an accumulation of wisdom.

Wealth is not limited to the money you own. Rather, the education and experience you've gathered, your thoughts, principles, and values that form the bedrock. The more experiences in life and reflections you gather, the wealthier you become.

THE CONVERSATION

Serena:

Thank you for lending your generation's voice to the narrative around money and women. Getting straight to the point, what does money mean to you?

Yi Zhou:

Money means freedom.

Madeline:

For me, the most special thing about money is the smell. Every time I open my wallet, I smell the bills, and I'm in heaven *[laughs]*. It represents independence and freedom. I get to choose how to spend the money in my wallet.

Serena:

Let's understand how money shaped your growing years. What were some narratives or lessons that you had?

Madeline:

My first memories of money would be when I was a young girl on the dinner table during Chinese New Year. It was one of my favourite and happiest moments of the year. Family members would give me red packets[5] and I'd put them in my pocket. My parents would keep them for me in a savings account. As I got older, I could keep them, and I felt accomplished and proud because it made me feel grown-up and in control. I could decide how I wanted to use the money.

---

[5] Ang bao

Yi Zhou:

The money talk in my household wasn't explicit. We don't directly talk about money, but always around it. I'd have different conversations with my mom and dad. With my mom, it's more like dating. She would give me advice on how I spend money when going out with someone. She would ask what certain people meant to me and how that made me feel about spending money. Was I comfortable and confident? She always told me to pay for my own bills, or even pay for the boys.

As for my dad, the conversation revolved more around having the correct financial mindset. He taught me to be brave and bold from a young age, and that I needed to learn the lessons of failure myself. He was teaching me to be my own money manager.

Serene:

Madeline, I knew you grew up in a large extended household. Did you see a difference between how your parents talked to you about money compared to your grandparents, aunts, or uncles?

Madeline:

We have a family groupchat and ever since I was young, I've been a part of it. We also discussed a lot of things related to money during dinner. I've been involved in the discussion, listening to the restaurants they go to, budgets, rents, and other money-related topics.

My household is more female dominated. When I say that, I mean the money makers are mainly the women. So, since a young age, they've encouraged me to be financially independent.

One lesson I remember from my mom is related to online shopping. For example, if I wanted to buy something but wasn't sure whether I really needed it, I would put it into the shopping cart first and then give myself a twenty-four-to forty-eight-hour deadline.

After two days, if I still remember, I would buy it. But if I hesitated or completely forgot about it, I wouldn't purchase it.

Serena:

Yi Zhou, what were the practical tips that you keep in mind?

Yi Zhou:

Spend on big things and not too much on small things. For example, the big things would be tuition and the house, and the small things would be clothes. Another way to put it is to spend on sustainable items. Everyone's different, of course, but this principle can apply to the new generation. It's not just money but many other things. We focus a lot more on sustainability compared to past generations.

Serena:

Let's talk about saving and spending. Madeline, would you consider yourself a saver or spender?

Madeline:

I consider myself more of a saver. I see the importance of money in the long term, and I think it's part of my personality, too, as I like to plan, and be organized and responsible. Then, I can guarantee a safe and comfortable life in the future.

I spend on daily necessities, and I occasionally travel. I also buy things that make me happy, but they have to be necessary and practical.

Yi Zhou:

I'm definitely a spender! *[laughs]* I spend most of the money on, like I said, the sustainable things, such as tuition or houses and relatively illiquid investments. I feel uncomfortable when I see the money just sitting there. So, I use it somewhere else.

Serena:

Let's touch on that because I know you actually bought your own place, right? How did that happen?

Yi Zhou:

I was in upstate New York finishing my high school, and applied for school in New York City, which is about a four-hour drive away. So, I decided that I'm going to get a place there just so I could feel homey and have a place to go to. I was looking around with my friend, and we found this really beautiful place in Chelsea. It was so perfect that I just rang up my dad and told that I found this perfect place. He said, 'Okay, sure.' So, I booked in and signed all the contracts. I didn't actually stay in that place for two years.

When I finally flew over, it was so great when I was there. There was a sense of belonging and it felt like a blank space that I could fill with my stories and memories.

I know it's a privilege and I never take it for granted. I really appreciate my parents for trusting me enough to allow me to find my place and being so generous to let me go for it. And, of course, responsibility always comes with situations like these. Having a house is a little different because you have to maintain it. I'm also in Singapore and Miami more often now; I don't live in New York City that often. So, I've rented it out and used the monthly rental to pay for my tuition. That creates a positive cycle and shows my responsibility.

Serena:

Thanks for sharing, Yi Zhou. Madeline, when you were growing up, do you recall any lessons or money mantras that people taught you?

Madeline:

One of the fundamental principles I learned is to spend when you need to and not spend on unnecessary things. So, since a young age, I've been careful about my spending. In particular, there is this one topic that I think makes for an interesting discussion. People like to buy these 'blind boxes' or 'mystery boxes' and a lot of friends around me really love this idea and the thrill of uncertainty. However, I don't buy it because I don't see the practicality behind it.

Serena:

Talking about friends, what's the common practice nowadays when you go out for a meal or a movie?

Madeline:

It really depends on individual groups. Even for me, with different friends, the spending habits differ. For example, with my closest group of friends, we split the bill equally among the number of people present. If it's with people whom I'm casually close to, then I will offer to pay for my share. For example, if I ordered a more expensive drink, I'll pay for it. And last, for dates in the future, I'd guess we would take turns. I would pay for one meal and the other person could pay for the next. I also think it's romantic because you could pay one time and there is an excuse for the other person to say the next date is on them.

Serena:

Let's speak about a different topic suited to your generation. When I was growing up, my parents taught me to study hard, get a job, get married, and then buy a house. That was perceived to be the formula for a good life. What do the both of you aspire to?

Yi Zhou:

The new generation focuses more on ourselves. Housing, marriage, and children are add-ons to who we are and want to be. Nowadays, I think figuring out who we are is a bigger issue. So, I think it's more responsible to solve this first before I even think about marriage and kids. If I don't know how to love myself, how can I truly love others? In a relationship, if we can love ourselves and each other, then we can talk about marriage and kids. But it is case by case. Everyone wants different things in life.

Madeline:

I agree with what you just said. And I guess what Yi Zhou said represents a proportion of the population because our family and cultural background shape our thoughts on financial independence and freedom. Coming from an Asian household, you would expect my parents to be stricter. But I was fortunate that my family shaped me to become independent and to think responsibly and out of the box. That's mainly because my family has the economic ability to support me. Others probably have it different because of their backgrounds.

I'm open to the idea of family and children, but I think I need to survive first before I can even consider that. I'm leaning towards no children. First, I see the amount of money my parents spend on me, and I think it's baffling. I even ask my parents, 'Why did you even decide to give birth to me when you could have used all that money, time, and energy on yourselves?' Of course, they keep telling me they don't regret it.

My mom works hard. She is successful in her career, and I always wonder why she would pause her career just to raise me before going back to work.

It's something that I don't know if I'll be able to do, to be as wise as her and make the sacrifices. They encourage me to think of myself before I think of marriage and a child.

Serena:

As you're about to graduate from university and enter the working world, what are your friends' attitudes towards money?

Madeline:

My friends come from backgrounds similar to mine. I live a comfortable life and don't need to worry about money at the moment because my parents cover my tuition. The only source of income I have are the few summer internships that I have done so far. It's not enough to make me fully independent, so I depend on my parents.

When we talk amongst friends about money, it's about budgets for our meals and, recently, our graduation trips. Because of Covid-19, we ended up going for a staycation in Hong Kong. We had to discuss the budget for the hotel, which led to interesting responses because everyone has different spending habits. Some people will spend a lot to get the best hotel while others will not.

Serena:

Do you talk about investments with your peers?

Yi Zhou:

Yes, we do. And it all came up because of the head of our high school. We were in a philosophy class one day and out of nowhere, he asked everyone if we had our retirement accounts set up. We were fifteen or sixteen and had never even thought about it. So, he was having troubles with his retirement account back then, and it made him realize that the younger generation should set up an account as early as possible and put in money regularly so that we would be more comfortable and confident when we are older.

From that point, my classmates got started. We went to the bank, set up our accounts together, and shared information and investment opportunities.

My risk appetite is low, and a low return is fine for me.

Madeline:

A lot of my friends are not in the financial industry or even interested in finance at the moment. They're a lot more social, I guess.

It's very mixed because there are friends who, like me, are working towards the finance industry. We regularly talk about the latest news and share some investments we want to make and our plans.

For those who are less involved in the finance industry, I talk less about money with them. They're not that willing or open to share, especially in front of people with finance degrees because they probably feel less confident.

Serena:

What are the differences or similarities between your male and female friends when you talk about money and investing?

Yi Zhou:

I'd say that the women in our generation actually pay more attention to the concept of money compared to men. I think it's because we realize there is a gender gap, and that money is a big driver if we want to close the gap. So, I would say that women, at least those around me, are more sensitive to money and eager to make it.

Madeline:

I agree with you. Based on my experience, I talk more about money with my female friends compared to my male friends. I also think it's inspired by my family because I mainly have this money talk with the female members of my family. So, likewise, I feel a sense of connection with my female friends.

Serena:

Interesting. This is going to be a slightly philosophical question, but when you think about money, how much is enough? Is it a number or a concept?

Madeline:

Enough is when I don't even have to think about not having enough money. I wouldn't even be concerned about not living a comfortable life. I have to go to school regularly, have a place to live, get to eat all the food I like, and be able to satisfy myself and not have to worry about spending a bit much on any day.

I guess that would be when money becomes enough for me. I'd say I have enough at the moment, but this is mainly because I'm reliant on my family and they have provided for me to feel enough.

Do I feel enough in terms of my money? That's definitely not the case.

Yi Zhou:

I'd say that money is never enough for me. When you look at the broader picture, money is never just money. It's associated with so many other things. So, I don't dare to say that it will be enough, and I think it will stay like this forever until the end of my life.

Serena:

What do you want to do as you gain more money and presumably have more access and control over money?

Madeline:

If money is just money, it's just paper bills. It is meaningful because we can use it to spend on things. We can get things we want from money, right? In terms of that, having more control over money means that I have more control over my life and my social network.

I'm more confident about who I am. My attitude towards money represents my comfort level in how I want to present myself to others. So, I would be thrilled to see how I manage money in the future.

Serena:

What about you, Yi Zhou? Do you identify with keeping money matters simple?

Yi Zhou:

A simple life can be happy, and often less is indeed more. But if it's art, then I think more is better than less.

In terms of attitudes towards life, relationships, and even investments, minimalism is a useful strategy because it eliminates lots of other factors so that you can focus on the most important few and navigate well.

Serena:

Talking about a conceptual question, if you had access to a billion dollars, what would you do? What do you stand for?

Yi Zhou:

I have been asked this question before, and my answer has always been the same. I really would not know unless I had the money in my hands. When this happens, I guess I'll see what to do. But, right now, I don't know.

Madeline:

If I actually had it in my hands, I would first want to pay back and reward my family. I want to make sure that everyone can have a comfortable house to live in. They can get anything they want and try to fulfil all their dreams, because I'm very close to my family. Even though a lot of us don't live in the same location, we have a tight bond. Then, of course, I would want to spend it on myself. Finally, I want to contribute back to the world. I like to volunteer and do community service during my free time, and I really see many people who need help. So, I'd like to use the remaining money to contribute to as many as possible.

Serena:

We talked a lot about money, but what is wealth to you?

Madeline:

Wealth is pretty much everything about me. It's not limited to the money that I own. It also includes all the education and experience I have, and even my own thoughts, principles, and values. The more valuable your wealth is, the more experiences you have in life and the more reflections you'll gather on what you are and what you want to be.

Yi Zhou:

I definitely agree with Madeline, and I think to add on, wealth is tied to richness, which is more than just money. Personally, for me, wealth is both ego to make it better, and responsibility to pass it on in the family. It's not just money, but a symbol of our family's contributions over generations.

So, I often think of wealth as something that's an accumulation of wisdom in a family.

It's something quite splendid and profound.

I always have this conversation with my dad. He grew up in a very poor countryside in China in the sixties and seventies, during a time of trauma. So, for him, he never had enough money growing up.

But he learned agricultural technologies from his elder relatives, his uncle, and his grandfather and that somehow stayed with him forever, even though he's not in the industry now. He always considers himself as a very lucky man because he knows that working hard doesn't mean you're going to be successful. You need a lot of luck too. So, he's very appreciative, which is why we volunteer a lot on different projects.

Serena:

Beyond money, one topic we want to talk about is kindness. It's an important element of life and how we live. What is the kindest money-related thing anyone has ever done for you?

Yi Zhou:

I truly appreciate my parents' unconditional love, trust, and support. When we talk about money and, like Madeline said, when you have kids, there are enormous sacrifices. I never take that for granted. I always look back, especially now in my twenties thinking about kids and marriage, and realize that if I were my parents, I don't think I would have been that generous.

Madeline:

I remember when I turned eighteen, in transition from teenager to adulthood, my mother and grandparents presented me with a lot of accounts. One had all the tuition money they had saved for me. Others were related to insurance and retirement. They had a lot of money for different purposes, prepared for me, and they passed over ownership to me. Right now, I can access these by myself, and I could even use them if I want to. I'm incredibly grateful that they organized this for me.

My family has really trusted me from a young age. I never received pocket money. I would ask for it when I needed it and that really is trust because they have to believe that I'm not wasting the money at all.

On deeper reflection, I feel I take money for granted. I know that money doesn't just come out of nowhere and I want to pay my family back in the future, hopefully.

Serena:

We have come to the end of our dialogue, and I feel so heartened that you both refer to your values and beliefs as a compass to guide you on your money journeys. Without you we would not have Gen Z perspectives!

12

Koh Huiting

I became a founder because I wanted to do something different. And I didn't want to wait.

Patience is not Koh Huiting's virtue. She moves with the tempo and energy of someone battling time, and she has much on her plate. In 2023, she launched Blueprint Ventures, an early-stage investment firm that seeks to uncover next generation businesses for the new Southeast Asia consumer. Before striking out on her own, she was the first female partner of Altara Ventures, double-hatting as Chief Marketing Officer. Her operator mindset was crystallized after years of brand management experience gained at Unilever and she laughs heartily recalling her times as an investment banking analyst in New York. Huiting is a Kauffman Fellow, a community that helps investors become more purposeful and deliver better returns. In this interview, Huiting retraces her financial and personal journey, and shares the vision of her entrepreneurial start-up.

> ### KEY INSIGHTS

Pay yourself first.

This is true for founders and start-up entrepreneurs. Pay yourself first because you have value. What you get paid can go to 30 per cent rent, 30 per cent savings, and 30 per cent discretionary spending.

Live within your means.

Just because you can buy something doesn't mean you should. You may get a momentary high, but that is about it. Money doesn't make you happier, though it sure makes life easier.

Create your own path.

Starting your own business is hard and requires a lot of financial responsibilities. However, founders often take the plunge because, strangely enough, not pursuing their passion is an even scarier prospect. Ask yourself: What problems need your solutions?

THE CONVERSATION

Serena:

Tell us about yourself Huiting.

Huiting:

I founded Blueprint Ventures in early 2023 after having spent five years at another fund. Blueprint supports Southeast Asia because we don't have many Southeast Asian brands. The thing I want to impart is that all businesses can differentiate on brand, you don't have to be a consumer product company only for that. The consumer consciously and unconsciously perceives the value of a brand. You usually choose something based on that perceived value and what it stands for. This brand image is even more important to the new generation of consumers.

Serena:

That's interesting. You have your pulse on the Southeast Asian consumer. What is unique about this region's consumer base?

Huiting:

Well, Southeast Asia currently lacks our own brands. If you look at other developed markets like China, Korea, Japan, or even India in the last couple of years, they've started welcoming the growth of their own national brands on the global stage. Why can't we have that for Southeast Asia? The time is now for the region.

The Southeast Asian growth story has really been about people growing into more discretionary income. So, the luxury for us is about being able to buy something other than the basics. But if you think about who is going to be driving the growth of the region, it will be the consumers—millennials, Gen Z, Gen Alpha—of today who will be the recipients of the largest inter-generational wealth transfer.

This is not just happening in Southeast Asia. It's a global trend. And this new generation is concerned with brand image. One interesting discovery happened in Seoul recently. I found out that 80 per cent of the under-thirty-year-olds used to own a Samsung phone.

Now, half of those have switched to an Apple iPhone. So even in Korea, Samsung has lost market share to Apple. The reason for switching? Brand image. That's baffling to me. I would have thought that Samsung would be the dominant brand for the Korean market.

Serena:

This is consistent with what we last discussed, you highlighted that the young Asian consumer is going to be the dominant force to watch out for. This is playing out.

Coming to women and money, what was your first recollection of money?

Huiting:

When I was growing up, the strongest narrative was—never spend beyond your means. Then I would go to school, and I'd be like, 'How come my friends have more allowance than me?' So, I told myself not to spend beyond my means. But then how do you contend with the fact that your peers seem to spend more than you? Growing up, my mindset was, 'I lack something.' For example, if my friends went out, I couldn't go out with them because I didn't have money. If I asked my parents for the money, they'd say not to be wasteful.

I felt like I hated money, but I wanted it a lot *[laughs]*. I wanted more, but I did not know how to get it as a child.

Serena:

You mentioned having to do chores around the house to get your weekly allowance. Tell us about that.

Huiting:

My parents wanted to instil the value of money in us. They didn't want us to take money for granted. My sister and I had to show our mother that we cleaned our bathroom. We also had to show her the T-balance we kept for the week. We had to draw the T, with credit and debit on either side. I was doing this till at least I was sixteen years old. When I eventually moved abroad and lived on my own, at least I knew how to clean my bathroom *[laughs]*.

Serena:

Did your parents view money differently or were they of one voice?

Huiting:

They were of one voice growing up. My mum is still saying 'don't waste money' and 'live within your means'. My dad now recognizes that you need some money to make money. So, if I or my siblings need help to start a business, we could go to him and try to convince him.

Serena:

When you moved away from home for school and started work, did your earlier mindset of scarcity change?

Huiting:

So, I went the opposite way. If you grew up constantly feeling like you don't have something, when you finally get it on your own, there are no guardrails.

I was a banker in New York and bought things for myself from Fifth Avenue *[laughs]*. But I quickly found out that you can't put everything on a credit card. During that time in banking, everyone knew you couldn't pay for your lifestyle just on your monthly compensation. You had to wait for your bonus. Everyone I knew in banking lived like that. We would put everything on a credit card and pay the minimum every month, then use your bonus at the end of the year to pay off the remaining owed.

Then, I quickly found out about APR or annual percentage rate. I did not know what that was. When the credit card company says this is your minimum payment due, I just paid that amount. So, the amount of debt I incurred grew exponentially larger since I only paid the minimum while the APR did its terrible magic on the rest. When my parents found out, they were so embarrassed.

For the first two years of my career, it was a constant balance between not wanting to feel like I lacked anything and figuring out how to get what I wanted.

Serena:

That's fascinating and such a valuable lesson. Then you transitioned to your passion, which is brands and brand management. Tell us about that.

Huiting:

This is why Fifth Avenue is my best friend *[laughs]*. I really hated my investment banking job because I felt so removed from real life. It felt like I was just manipulating numbers on a spreadsheet that had little real-world impact. I also felt like I could not find the purpose in my job.

For the first two years, I probably worked every single day. On the weekends, when going into the office, I would walk down Fifth Avenue slowly so that I could get to the office later. It doesn't change the workload but was a way for me to bring my sanity back. Because of that, I would walk past stores and ask myself, 'Why should I be interested in what you're selling?'

And there would be stores where the experience was great, and I always wanted to return. There were also shops with attractive price points, yet I didn't want to buy. It got me thinking about what actually motivates the consumer to buy it and it cannot be just about price point.

Even when I came from a mindset of lack, I wouldn't be spending it in a store where the price points could be attractive. That constant narrative and observation over two years got me interested in brand management and how brands influence a consumer's behaviour. I thought it was so interesting that it wasn't just about price point, but about experience, and what the consumer feels after they leave the store.

Serena:

You worked on household brands while in brand management. What was that experience like?

Huiting:

When I went into brand management, I worked on everyday household items like Paddle Pop and Breyers ice cream, and Suave hair products. These are value brands, but large, half-a-billion-dollar businesses for Unilever. When I came on board those brands, I thought they weren't sexy and were commodity brands, but that's when it became more challenging and interesting because these were cheap, value-oriented commodity products, the consumer could choose these or more premium options.

The challenge for me was understanding the consumer's psyche and still creating products and go-to-market strategies that would hook the customer to make the repeat purchase. Unilever was interested because these were their traffic driving brands. If you lose consumers at base level, then you are graduating a smaller cohort of consumers into Unilever's more premium brands.

Serena:

Transitioning from brand management to venture investing, do you have personal investments?

Huiting:

I have blue-chip stocks and a gold ETF[6]. I don't have much else going on because of childhood. When you come from a mentality of lack, when you have something, you don't want to lose it. Capital preservation has always been at the top of my mind. I feel most familiar with equity markets and so a lot of my portfolio is in stocks and ETFs. I only started investing in 2017 after I moved back to Singapore from the US.

If I were truly an active investor, I would trade public market equity stocks, I guess. But can you imagine the reporting you have to do every quarter?

I'm considered more advanced amongst my friends, who mostly keep cash in the bank. They do nothing more. They always ask me, 'What are you investing in?' or 'How do you start?', I just tell them to choose a company that they like—the one whose products they use every day and keep returning to. The inertia to start is definitely strong.

Serena:

So, are you a spender or saver?

Huiting:

I am both. I pay myself first when I get an income. There is a rule I follow: 30 per cent on rent, 30 per cent goes straight into savings, and another 30 per cent is on discretionary spending. I try as much as possible to not touch

---

[6] Exchange-Traded Funds (EFT)

savings because if I do that, there's always something to buy. I want to try every new thing to understand the consumer and where the trend is moving.

Serena:

You're fundraising for Blueprint Ventures. Has it given you any insights into people's psyche around money?

Huiting:

Nobody wants to lose money. As much as people say that they have an appetite for risk, that is caveated by the fear of losing money. Obviously, there is a spectrum, but you will never find somebody who says, 'Take all my money and invest in something that's 100 percent risky.'

Serena:

Warren Buffett says rule number one, 'don't lose money'. Rule number two, 'don't forget rule number one'.

I see similarities between your brand management days when you want consumers to spend their dollar and now you are getting investors to invest in your fund. How do you help investors cross that line?

Huiting:

Those who have crossed the line know me and understand my investing style and how I think. A lot of the people who have committed are within my close network. But it's harder, especially now the funding environment is unfriendly. A strong thesis and operational experience help investors to cross the line. That has been helpful.

Serena:

What does money represent for you?

Huiting:

Money is a means to an end. When I was younger, I thought I would be a lot happier with money. Now I realize that money doesn't make you happier, it makes life easier.

Serena:

What about wealth?

Huiting:

They're interlinked. You wouldn't call yourself wealthy if you didn't have a certain amount of money. But it's also feeling contented and at peace with whatever you have in your life. Money helps to facilitate that. You don't have to worry about paying your rent or putting food on the table, or wondering if you have enough resources to weather a medical crisis or a financial downturn. It eases a lot of stress.

I wouldn't consider myself wealthy. I definitely have more wealth today than twenty years ago when I started my career. And I think at the start, money is the primary indicator of the value you bring to the table. But, as you mature and progress in your career, different things take priority. And when you progress in your career, you make a certain amount of income that allows you to pay less attention to the absolute dollar and more on other things that make your life more well-rounded.

Serena:

Over time, circumstances change, and frankly, we can change too. Were there any 'aha' moments that made you think about life differently?

Huiting:

That has a lot more to do with personal growth than just my relationship with money. I don't know whether everybody goes through this, but I certainly went through it. I had a lot of things that I wanted to work through, so I went for a programme that helped shift my worldview. Growing up, my perspective of the world was negative, and I was quite negative as a person. It got to a point where I was just tired of feeling negative even though it was normal to me. That was the only state I knew.

But I looked around and saw how some people have it so easy and I wanted that too. So, I thought about going to therapy and then found a friend who had done the Landmark Forum.

She was a workaholic, and we had the same triggers at work. But one day she came back to the office and seemed so light. I asked her what happened, and she described the Landmark Forum. It sounded like a cult to me, but she told me it wasn't and asked me to come. The only reason I said yes was because she was so earnest.

The first time I went, I left at the end of the night, and went back to her the following day saying that this is definitely a cult. She told me she knew that was how I would think initially but encouraged me to continue. So, I said okay, probably wanting to prove my point.

But it changed everything and opened up certain perspectives that I hadn't thought of before. I did several other courses over time.

Serena:

What resonated with me was when you realized you were not in a good and happy state, and you did something different. The second thing was we should all have friends who give us that little push.

On this topic, have you received any particularly good or bad advice in your life?

Huiting:

'Live within your means.' *[laughs]* It's a reminder to yourself that just because you can buy something doesn't mean you should. When I was in my twenties, I would buy something just because I could. Now things have changed. It's good to have guideposts. I also realized that my level of happiness didn't improve even after I bought the item. It made me happy at that point in time, but it was fleeting. I needed to go through it to realize that material goods don't make me happier.

As for poor advice, it might probably be 'live within your means' too *[big laugh]*. I say that because there are certain things that you have to take leverage on, for example, buying a house or a car. You can't pay it all in cash. If we take it literally, it would mean you don't buy a car unless you can drop a hundred thousand dollars in cash. Right now, a HDB apartment is a million dollars on the resale market. Do you actually have a million dollars? And if you don't, then living within your means is not realistic advice. It really depends on the maturity of the person. Know when to flex financially.

Serena:

A fun question. If you woke up one morning and found out you have a billion dollars, how would that make you feel? What would you do?

Huiting:

Oh, I would buy a house. Give away to charity. Allocate 10 per cent to alternative investments. Then I can get someone to manage the rest of my portfolio? *[laughs]* I want to preserve capital so that my family and future generations can nicely live off the interest. Don't touch the principal amount.

Serena:

Thank you for being candid. Women sometimes feel shame because they don't know how to invest. Have you ever felt shame around money?

Huiting:

One question I always have is asking how I can make my money work harder for me. It's hard enough making money as it is. Some will say to put it into fixed income but that requires a certain number of dollars you will put aside and how many people can confidently say that they will not need that money. Many always say to make money work for you, but that requires money to begin with. If you're living from pay cheque to pay cheque, that accumulated amount is not enough to put this mantra into effect because you are at the mercy of the bank. I'm still figuring this out.

Serena:

Do you feel you are on par, ahead, or behind financially compared to your peers?

Huiting:

At this point, I feel definitely behind. Starting something requires a lot of financial responsibilities. So, it's tough when there's nothing coming in, yet you still have to pay utilities, rent, and all those bills. But I wanted to be a founder because I wanted to do something different and on my own. If there were other people in the industry with similar experience and vision, then I might not be doing this alone. But you have to start somewhere, and somebody has to do it first before other people follow. And I don't want to wait.

Serena:

Impatience can be your superpower, Huiting, as you scout and champion for Southeast Asian brands and companies. I am excited to see more of you in that space!

13

Felicia Heng

Don't be fooled by outward appearances.

Growing up in a conservative household gave Felicia Heng a strong work ethic. Following a successful corporate and banking career, her entrepreneurial spirit led her to start Wise Purpose, an Asian-focused consultancy specializing in family wealth advisory, leadership coaching, and next generation succession. Felicia works alongside business owners, family office principals, and board directors of charities and foundations. In this conversation, Felicia shares how the untangling of emotions from money can lead to clarity and freedom.

KEY INSIGHTS

Carve out different pools of resources for different purposes.

Creating different spending pools, such as one for lifestyle, another for emergencies, and a third for investments, gives you financial discipline and, subsequently, the freedom to make choices. You can rest easy knowing that you can tackle whatever emergency might come your way while still growing your wealth for the future.

The best time to plant a tree was yesterday. The second-best time is now.

Cliché as it may be, it's never too late to secure your financial future. You can begin with small, comfortable steps, such as a high-yield savings account or a regular savings plan into an ETF that tracks the best-performing companies. While low risk, the power of compounding interest will start flexing its muscle several years down the road.

If you can't spend it, it's not yours.

Credit cards have dragged down many who were seduced by the sudden ability to spend a lot more beyond their usual threshold. While useful for big-ticket items, most notably wedding expenses, that let you rack up significant credit card rewards, it's important that you take the appropriate level of risk and ensure you have money in the bank to pay the bill.

THE CONVERSATION

Serena:

I thought it'd be a good way to get started by asking about how you grew up and your earliest memories of money.

Felicia:

As a conservative Chinese Christian family, most of it was linearly associated with work ethic. It was all about working hard, saving enough, doing the right thing, and being responsible. If you did that, then you would have a comfortable sum of money and lead a happy life. That messaging has served me well and became a good fundamental basis that helped organize my life and finances. But I think over time, as many of us do, we discover that money has a lot of association with a hidden, perhaps emotional life.

My earliest memory was being in a car, looking across at the other car, and telling my dad that I wish we were in the other car because it was a more spacious and shinier car, and the people looked like they were having a lovelier time.

Suddenly I could feel the tension build in the air. The atmosphere didn't seem quite right, and it was quickly followed with, 'Oh, you should probably be quiet and be grateful for what you have. You don't know how lucky you are.'

And now, as I've grown up, I realized many people grew up with the same narrative of being grateful, which is interesting because when we look around us almost everywhere, even in corporate life, money is associated with rewards, doing the right thing, performance, and good behaviour.

And then when you look at how it stands in families, if you have two people from fiscally unequal families getting married, invariably, you will see a nuanced and subtle veering towards accommodating the slightly 'more equal' family. It also happens among business associates. So, you see money being used as an expression of goodwill.

Over time, I realized there was an emotional side with money. And that's also part of the reason I built my business because it represented a personal, deeply meaningful journey for me.

Serena:

If I could ask you a bit more on the emotions you experienced growing up in a conservative environment, how did money make you feel? Were your parents similar or different in their money attitudes?

Felicia:

I think money is very pervasive in our lives. You get an introduction to it very early on, regarding how it affects the lifestyle that you lead. As a child, it meant ang baos, and independence and access to prohibited items like sweets and trinkets. So, I quickly learnt that money could be quite helpful.

My parents had similar attitudes towards money. They were both educators, so the lessons around work ethic remained strong. It's remained a fundamental pillar for me and in my thinking. But you realize few things turn out the way we want them to do. We can do all the right things, but the outcome is not guaranteed.

So, over time, my investment philosophy also changed and developed more in line with skills that I gained throughout my career and my time in markets. I'd like to think that I have a healthy relationship with money, in terms of what it offers me, what access it gives me, and the opportunities and privilege to steward it.

Serena:

You mentioned your investment philosophy has changed. What is it now?

Felicia:

I believe that if you can take care of the downside first, then you can take care of the upside easily. Most people focus too much on returns and will risk 50 per cent loss for 60 per cent returns, but you're just making 10 per cent eventually and effectively at the same outcome as a more risk-averse person. So, my philosophy is to be conscious of the risk-return reward and think through risk appetite, factors, and time horizon.

Serena:

Sounds like you have a rather wide spectrum of holdings and asset classes within your portfolio. Could you share when you first started? It takes a lot of time and experience to build a portfolio.

Felicia:

You can start any time. I don't think there was a specific definitive date, but it's certainly from a time when there wasn't very much that I could put to work beyond just saving up. I've been fortunate in the last three years and saw how market cycles can be compressed, thus giving us bears and bulls and sped up my lessons by a fair bit.

I developed my skills and learned a lot through my clients. I was previously with an American bank and had the privilege to be brought into the private spaces of asset owners who are very risk aware. I learned a lot there.

It was small, comfortable steps, and not all at once. It's never too late. Start today and start as early as possible. There's that Chinese proverb that goes, 'The best time to plant a tree was yesterday. The second-best time is now.'

Serena:

You pursued a career in banking, which is a path I'm familiar with. Very often, I've seen advisers talk about asset allocation, portfolio construction, and long-term investing with clients and families. But it's hard to do so for ourselves. Does it matter when you have $100 million to invest versus building your own nest egg and bank account?

Felicia:

From what I've seen, the principles of long-term portfolio construction make a difference in how you think of risk and how you manage your own emotions. So, volatility doesn't really matter if you think intergenerationally and have a set of systematic principles you stick to because there is a lot of noise in the markets and the media plays up market movements. This is a personal view and I have nothing against the media. But if you sold 2,000 cups of coffee yesterday and sold 1,900 today, it's no big deal.

But a media headline might say that you've sunk 100 cups. So, stay focused on what you're after. That will make much more of a difference in your long-term returns.

Serena:

You mentioned you need to be aware of what you are after. So, what are you after financially?

Felicia:

That's a good question. There is so much entanglement between what money can do and solve. Those are money troubles. However, money cannot solve your emotional needs. Over time, I've learned to untangle them and have more clarity.

So, what is the difference between money and wealth? Money is my energy and time that I used to exchange for a currency that has stored value for transactions. Wealth is different. You can have a lot of money and not feel wealthy or have little of it and feel like a queen. There is a qualitative fulfilment aspect with wealth that money cannot provide.

Now, what am I using money for? I use it to fulfil all the important and functional basic needs important to daily life and be as worry free from money troubles as possible. Of course, I spend money on wants and discretionary items too.

At this stage of my life, I also understand what money cannot solve: the desire to be better than the next person and difficult emotional needs. The latter has become very important to me at this stage. There are a lot of things that more money can solve, but these are material problems. But if you read the biographies of taipans and tycoons, many of them are driven to succeed and make it big, but also get involved in economic rivalries and envy.

So, every time I get confused in my own tangled web of emotions or when I sink to the bottomless pits of envy, I go back to my basics—being in the car as a child and looking at the other car.

Serena:

That's lovely. You're self-reflecting to come to terms with our underlying emotions around money. What about your kids? How do you impart money lessons to them?

Felicia:

They're regular teenagers who look at their peers and make comparisons to benchmark their pocket money. And give me feedback *[laughs]*. I benchmark against other parents. It's been incredibly humbling and a real privilege to be their mother.

They used to be more simplistic, and I mean that in the best way possible. They make sure they spend their money wisely. We used to have simple mantras like 'be careful about borrowing from friends', 'don't buy for the sake of buying', and 'be responsible'.

As they grow up, their mindsets have changed, naturally. Our favourite mantra this season is: Don't be fooled by outward appearances because all that glitters is not gold. It's related to someone having bought something, or someone else with a certain lifestyle and has gone on an exotic holiday. The more important question is: Are they thrilled? Is there debt you don't see?

And this is where it's not about having more money than the next person. This is about being more emotionally independent, mature, and psychologically free to understand what your life is about. It's more important than trying to get into status rivalry or as I like to call it, status anxiety.

Serena:

Is there a difference when you look back at yourself? Do you feel you have a different mindset about money when you were eighteen compared to today?

Felicia:

When I was eighteen, it was about saving and spending well, and being wise about money and the fear associated with losing it. When you lose it, it's gone and you're never going to get it back. Looking back, however, made me realize it might not be the best advice because it's the opposite of a growth mindset, which is about learning from errors and not doing it again.

There's a quote from Alvin Toffler, 'The illiterate of the 21st century will not be those who cannot read and write, but those who cannot learn, unlearn, and relearn.'

If I lost money today, I would take a step back, think about the lessons, and try not to make that error twice. Women struggle with this fear of losing money and not making it back again. We are stereotypically nurturers and concerned about ensuring that the children have enough. That's why microfinance is more popular among women. Research points to the fact that women are more likely to repay that debt. It's almost instinctive, that concept of protecting, nurturing, and managing risk. So, that eighteen-year-old me was trying to ensure that all that hard work and sacrifice wasn't lost.

Serena:

On that topic, how is the responsibility shared or divided in your household?

Felicia:

We're a blend of tradition and modernity. He takes care of the children's and household needs, or anything that we consider as a need. I spend more on discretionary items. So, for investments, we consult each other occasionally and only if we feel that the other person has more updated information or has expertise in it. But we are mostly separate. I believe it's a good thing for couples to do that because you get diversification across styles and risk appetites.

Serena:

On that note, if you were to wake up one day and realize you have a billion in your bank account, no strings attached, what would you do?

Felicia:

Well, first, I hope it's in US currency *[laughs]*. On a more serious note, my answer would depend on how I got the money. If I had inherited it through massive inheritance, I would be immensely careful with it. I might be worried about losing it and concerned about what people thought of me or whether I was using it responsibly.

   If I made the money by myself, I would do something like good diversification with risk-reward considerations and a long-term portfolio construction. I'd probably do something longer term as well for those who could benefit from the money and spread it around the globe. I would take my early money lessons and past narrative into account. The idea is to work with an amount of risk that I'm comfortable with.

Serena:

How would you describe your satisfaction level regarding your current financial state?

Felicia:

It is about fulfilment, contentment, and having a plan and a vision of how to use it and how that is coupled with the other aspects of my life. So, money is just one dimension of life. While it might not be the topmost priority, it is just as important as the other dimensions. We always hear the adage, 'Time is money, health is wealth.' If we consider it, it goes back to what I said about money being energy. It's not a new view. If you have little spark left, you won't have enough energy to go out there. So, health is extremely important. Having time is very important. Great health means you get the time to enjoy your life. Having relationships to enjoy and share with you is just as important too. Taking all these into account, I'd say I'm satisfied with the healthy balance at this stage.

Serena:

I wanted to ask if you've heard or received any brilliant advice around money?

Felicia:

Honestly, what makes it good or bad advice really depends on how you started. My mentality around money is not something I'd consider expert advice. I was so risk averse with money and saved as much as possible. It probably skewed towards the opposite end of learning and growing, which is part of life.

One good piece of advice I received was that if you can't spend it, it's not yours.

Because of the way I started out in conservative circumstances, it gave me a ballast and that balance between holding, spending, giving, and taking the appropriate level of risk for myself. That balance has been helpful for credit cards. If you don't have it, don't spend it. However, what works for me may not work for someone who grew up on the opposite spectrum.

Serena:

Were there any moments in your life that you felt vulnerable with your money?

Felicia:

Many, many times. I think this is about untangling what is really a money issue versus the emotional or psychological issue. On bad days, money could trigger you because some people have superior achievements or spent on things that you can never afford. Who knows? And frankly it doesn't matter. The most important question is: How do you move forward constructively? You must be clear about whether having more money can help solve the problem. From what I've experienced and what I've observed with my clients, that clarity has given people a great deal of freedom. It's helped them to be better in the roles that they play in their business, in their lives as leaders and as investors. That's what we aspire to do, support them in that journey of clarity.

Serena:

I think that's meaningful work indeed. Coming back to yourself, what's the greatest money-related kindness someone has given you?

Felicia:

I've been quite blessed to meet kind people. I think it's also because I pay more attention to people who are kind to me than those who are not. The most significant things about money that people have done for me usually involve investing in my development or giving me the opportunities and skills to go further.

For example, my mother did a lot for me for my education, and my mentors have given me access to skills, expertise, and opportunities to widen my horizons. These are capabilities that have given me the confidence to move. So, even when times are bad, I remain as kind as possible, just like how those who have helped me before.

I've been blessed with generosity and skills that I continue to use throughout my life.

Serena:

That's a great attitude and aligned with how you use your experiences and empathy to help families in your consulting work. Thank you for taking the time to unpack these lessons for us.

14

Angela Loh

Dream big, work backward.

Meet Angela Loh, the woman reshaping Singapore's global presence in the jewellery industry. As the CEO and founder of Ultraluxe Global and Advocator & Co, she's redefining luxury. In an industry where established brands have long held sway, Angela is on a mission to build an inclusive and collaborative ecosystem that unites global international brands and independent talents. Ultraluxe is a festival encompassing all aspects of luxury, from jewellery and timepieces to fashion and home design. Discover Angela's transformative story in this section and how she turned her passion for beautiful things into a business.

KEY INSIGHTS

Always keep your eyes on the prize.

This mantra has guided Angela's remarkable journey. Her relationship with money traces back to her earliest memories of using it to buy small toys and stationery. But it was her passion for curating beautiful events, fashion, and jewellery that transformed into a multi-million-dollar business. Her approach is simple yet profound: Dream of the prize and work backward to figure out how to achieve it.

Wealth is a way to create opportunities and connect with people.

Money is a tool to create opportunities, forge connections with others, and fuel business endeavours. While understanding the fundamentals of saving, planning, and investing is crucial, it's also important not to fixate on the chase for money. True wealth is about investing in people and ideas that have the potential to grow. When you nurture this kind of wealth, money naturally follows, and it opens the door for others to contribute to this thriving ecosystem of talented individuals.

Do not give that power (to build wealth) away to anyone else, because only you can make changes.

Women often grapple with self-doubt, particularly when making financial decisions and pursuing our entrepreneurial aspirations. We may lack confidence to bring our business ideas and proposals to life, and instead, hand over these opportunities to others, assuming they are better equipped. Yet, the truth about wealth is that it begins with you. No one else can map out your financial journey. The ultimate responsibility rests squarely on your shoulders.

THE CONVERSATION

Sharon:

If I can start our discussion by bringing it back to your childhood, I wanted to ask what your earliest memory with money is?

Angela:

It wasn't so much about making money, as it was how I associated myself with it. I remember my uncle and mother mentioning that my nickname was 'Pay Pay Pay' when I was little. Since I was young, I always liked to shop. My grandma mentioned that I always bought something when I went out. I could never come home empty-handed. That was my reputation as a kid among my family members. It was just a desire for money to buy things.

My family never mentioned that I needed to make money, or that I spent too much. The funny thing is that when I spend money, I also make the money back. For example, when I was thirteen, I wanted to spend money on a gym membership. Who spends money on these things at that age and time, right?

So, I love going to the gym. One day, the gym staff asked me if I wanted to teach classes. That was when I made money by teaching aerobics. I thought it was cool that people paid me to exercise. I would wake up every day to teach five classes a week, which amounted to a substantial amount of money. I did the maths and realized that I could make the same amount as adults!

It felt empowering and kick-started the desire in me to do something I enjoyed and getting paid for it. Another time, I entered a fashion design competition, but I didn't have the money to produce the pieces I wanted. So, I approached a boutique, talked to the boss, and told him I wanted to create this collection for a competition. Then, I asked if he could help me produce them.

In return, he can sell the three pieces, and I would get a commission. Luckily, he said yes. Whenever I wanted to pursue something compelling, I looked for someone who can help me fulfil that.

Sharon:

How did those experiences and subsequent successes shape your life? You clearly see what you want to do and can enlist people to help you, especially with how you raise money.

Angela:

Yes, that's why I think my entire career journey has never been about doing a job. I'm fulfilling my vision of this individual I want to become. Working for PSA as my first role was a good prelude to the advertising world. There were a lot of administrative tasks that needed to be executed. Also, I received a fixed salary, which was lower than my earnings from my part-time role. But I continued to spend like I used to. Then I 'discovered' the concept of debt. I overspent and racked up massive bills on my credit card, which led to an enormous debt in my second year that I couldn't pay off with my income.

That was my first lesson about money: learn to control my spending. It's interesting to see what I spent, but I never thought about how much I earned. I forgot I was a 'President of Spending'. I needed to do what I needed to do to support myself. And this behaviour has translated into the way I run my businesses because my people only build according to what we are capable of and stop seeing what they can become. We should always look at the latter and then figure out how to raise the funds to reach that goal.

You always must work backwards and then figure out how you'll get there. It's almost like, 'I like this bag. How do I make the money to get it?' That was how I thought about life.

Sharon:

So, tell me about your career and how you settled your credit card bills.

Angela:

I paid it off with the help of my mother. Thanks, Mum! In my next job, I wanted to do something more, not just work. This was when I found something that could make money. My role at the time provided a great career path, but it was a defined route that gave little leeway to expand. You just get security.

So, I joined a start-up as an event organizer and looked through my contacts to see if I had any potential customers that needed to organize events. I told them I could help with that. I could call people, meet them, get rejected, feel deflated and depressed, and continue. That was my first sales lesson. You cannot have any feelings. You must just carry on because it's a numbers game.

Still, I felt depressed. It's hard to keep calling until you hit a yes. Then, I got one of my biggest projects for Hewlett Packard. It was 1993 and a $60,000 project, which was big at that time.

I gave them a dream. I realized I could score more clients by giving them the dream that both of us shared. Because of that, we are both invested in it. You always must make people's dreams come true. That's the biggest gift. It wasn't so much about the budget or the reward, but about helping them realize their vision to create greatness. That also gave me the realization that I had the knack for that.

Sharon:

If I can ask you, what does money mean to you?

Angela:

It is a way to create opportunities and connect with people. It helps to fund my projects and shopping *[laughs]*. I'm not attached to money in the traditional way. Yes, I know I need to save, plan, and invest. I'm not obsessed with or am dedicated to pursuing it. I just know that I must have certain things and go do them. For example, I was forty-eight and saw my friends having houses and paying for mortgages. I was just renting, and I thought I should get a house. I had savings, of course. I had insurance for endowment and medical coverage, and I had the basic funds in place for emergencies. But I didn't have enough for the down payment of a house. It was quite expensive, too, at about $2 million.

So, I knew I needed to make more money by doing more projects and getting more business. I worked harder and looked for more opportunities. The goal was to pay for that house. I finally got it after some time and now I'm staying in the space that I paid for.

I have a positive attitude towards money. I don't let it control me. If you put in the effort and use your creativity, you will get money. Some people tell me I'm an optimist or that I'm living in a bubble. I don't think so.

Sharon:

You took an enormous risk in 2020 to create UltraLuxe (a luxury festival celebrating designers and tastemakers). Could you share the thought process behind it?

Angela:

It was a dream. When Covid-19 happened in 2020, big events had to be postponed. I knew the pandemic was going to take a while. But I still wanted to make it happen. So, I split the festival in half and still achieved audience outreach. I was thinking of a systematic solution. When I have an idea, I will persist in doing it and find a solution. It may not be the same as an event in a big tent but spread out across twenty places. When I sold the idea to retailers, they liked it, and we pulled it off. Labour, however, was an issue.

The following year, I signed a lease for a retail space in Scott's Square for 365 days. It was the same idea but interpreted differently. We made a quarter more revenue than what we used to make. Unfortunately, most of this profit went to the rental.

I made a bet that the pandemic won't happen again, so I started talking to the Singapore Tourism Board and told the jewellers that they should come on board. Everybody signed on. I couldn't get insurance to cover it because the risk of Covid-19 was still around. Most wouldn't have taken the risk, but when I saw that Formula 1 was still happening, I knew the government was going to open, no matter what.

So, I took that gamble.

Sharon:

Yes, nobody could have predicted what happened in 2020 after how great 2019 was. But you took the risk and became creative in finding solutions. You also mentioned that you wanted to help your staff because you had many people under your employ. If I had known you in 2021, I would have advised you to hold your money and not take the retail space. But you took the calculated risk and gained more than just sales.

Angela:

Yeah, I went into that with my eyes wide open. I know it's a gamble, but it's a calculated risk that's also an amazing story because I don't think money and wealth is just related to dollars and cents, right? Sometimes, business is about pursuing your vision, as you said.

Sharon:

How do you see money and wealth? Are they different for you?

Angela:

Wealth is not just money. Wealth must continuously generate money for you and create a new generation of wealth-making possibilities. I believe in individuals and creativity that can grow. That's why everyone should invest. If you grow this wealth, the money will come, and everyone can take part and feed into this ecosystem of personalities and individuals with great potential. I don't have children, so my business and the people in it give that sense of community. I think of them as family, and I believe in them and want to support them. Fulfilling their dreams also fulfils mine and they become part of your wealth circle. It's a win-win situation. I teach them so that they don't make the same mistakes. It's a shortcut past my tribulations.

My job is to make them happy and help them grow, and I think that's richer than just giving them money.

Sharon:

That's very true. I wanted to ask you. How much money is enough to make you content? What is that magic number?

Angela:

I never look at numbers. If I need to raise funds, get investors in, or go public, I will start looking at that. That's a function that I need to do. But my mindset has always been about serving people and stakeholders.

I can live with what I have. I can eat simple foods. I also love watching YouTube and Netflix. These are the simple things in life that keep me happy. I've calculated how much I spend on food a day and it's about $10. It seems small, but I only eat two meals a day. Of course, there are days when I eat something between $20 and $30 but that's not every day.

Genuine happiness to me is doing nothing *[laughs]*.

But, to me, as I mentioned earlier, every hobby and activity can generate revenue.

Sharon:

You have a pulse on trends, and what people want. Are you creating a vision together with your client? Then wealth is about being knowledgeable and going with the flow.

Angela:

I feel I am blessed in my journey to learn capabilities and skill sets that I can automate into something beneficial for the community. And I feel that if anyone wants to create a productive, viable, and sustainable business, you must feed the community of many communities.

You put yourself in the customer's shoes, whether it's by supporting them in their business or their visions for their passion. It should be borne from their passion to help, which creates a happy relationship.

Sharon:

What would you do if you ended up with a lot of money in your bank account?

Angela:

I wanted to create a place that promotes sophisticated living. It's a restaurant for you to meet your friends, network, and enjoy good food. We can all come together to have fun, exchange ideas, and grow together. I want to create that.

Sharon:

I want to ask you something retrospective. If you had a time machine and could go back to a pivotal moment in your life, what financial advice would you give you to yourself?

Angela:

I would give that girl the template and the power to build wealth. I always used to have great ideas but never had the confidence to pull it off. So, I always gave these to someone else thinking that the other person is better equipped to do that.

It was only until I took it upon myself to stand up and take responsibility that actual change happened. So, I wish I'd done that earlier and not given that power to anyone else. I could have done this earlier by myself as an entrepreneur than to keep thinking that I can't do it. I need someone here. And I gave that person the power. Yeah, I think a lot of us are like this, or I think we doubt ourselves. Honestly, believe and invest in yourself. Do not give that power away to anyone else but yourself because only you can make changes.

Sharon:

That's a great moment to wrap up this conversation. You have a different and fresh perspective, Angela, and I think it is because you continue to grow and reinvent yourself. This has been a fun and inspirational chat.

15

Sunita Gill

Put it out there and the universe will listen.

Sunita Gill with her vivacious smile and warm voice, is a powerhouse in the world of international luxury property sales and investments. With nearly $2 billion in sales revenue under her belt and over fifteen years of experience in asset management, she's an industry leader. She's also deeply passionate about equipping women with financial knowledge and is a serial entrepreneur and investor. In this conversation, we'll delve into Sunita's insights about real estate, women, and money.

KEY INSIGHTS

Love-fear relationship with money.

Money is a complex puzzle for women, often sparking a love-fear relationship. On one hand, we cherish it for the financial freedom it offers. Yet, despite this affection for money, there's an undercurrent of fear. And it only takes a shift of mindset (a little courage) to strive for our financial goals, to chase after money with confidence, and to accept its power.

Believe in the universe and put your intentions out there.

Ask for what you want and believe that the universe listens. When you put your intentions out there, it sets a clear direction for your financial journey. It's about having the confidence to articulate your desires, whether it's a specific financial milestone or a broader vision for your life.

Support and lift other women.

Lifting each other up in our financial journeys is one of the most powerful things women can do for themselves. Sometimes, it is as simple as encouraging each other to take that new job, make that property investment, or get on that stage to speak. It's about creating a supportive network that empowers women to achieve their financial goals by being a mentor, being an advocate, and collaborating with women on business ventures.

THE CONVERSATION

Sharon:

Give us a quick introduction to yourself.

Sunita:

My name is Sunita. I have been in the real estate industry for about fifteen years now. My husband joined me from Canada about ten years ago. He was also in the real estate suite with a bank in Canada at that time. We have two young daughters, seven and nine years old. Real estate runs in our blood. We love it. I joined it when I was looking for a property and never looked back. I think that's a great story, too, to work with your husband and to be in the line that we are passionate about.

Sharon:

During your growing up days, did your family discuss real estate?

Sunita:

Coming from a typical Indian family, we talk about real estate all the time. Most Asian families have real estate as a safety component in their lives. However, renting and paying rent was taboo. You had to own a property, a roof over your head. My father was an avid investor, even though he couldn't afford much, but he pulled his family in to share property purchases and get rental yield. He had that foresight that Singapore real estate was the way to go.

At one point, everybody benefited from the sale. They had eight shops. Do you remember those old buildings similar to Queensway Shopping Centre that had small tailor shops? I used to go with him to collect rent.

I saw that real estate generated money and was fascinated with the collection of cash. It made me look at it from a different perspective. At that point, I didn't understand the mortgage that went with it, but my relationship with real estate and money was that real estate gives me money.

My dad didn't talk to us too much about money, but there was always that narrative that land is king. If you buy property, make sure you buy land. He was always against buying condominiums because of the management fees. He thinks that instead of paying somebody else, you should pay yourself.

So, when I grew up, I went into it because I was looking for a property and many of the male property brokers I met were unwilling to break down the numbers or explain the dynamics behind interest rates, SIBOR[7], and such. It can be quite confusing. When I asked them to tell me the difference between fixed and floating rates, they would reply that there weren't any differences and to just do what people recommended. That intrigued me. I wanted to learn more on my own.

Of course, people also said that real estate brokers made a lot of money, so I wanted to try for two years to see how I perform. Let me tell you, it's a lot of work. It's not as simple as opening and closing doors.

Sharon:

How old were you when you started looking to buy property?

Sunita:

I was twenty-six and had worked for two years, so I had some money in my CPF[8] account. I always asked, 'Why do I need to pay CPF?' And my father kept telling me I will thank him when I want to buy property and can use the money in my CPF account. So, I started looking at property when I was twenty-six since I had this amount of money I couldn't touch.

Sharon:

So that was where the journey started. What was the first property you bought?

---

[7] Singapore Interbank Offered Rate (SIBOR)
[8] Central Provident Fund (CPF)

Sunita:

It was a really old apartment in East Coast. It had two bedrooms and measured 700 square feet. I enjoyed going to the East Coast a lot back then, and I had followed a friend who wanted to buy it. The asking price was around $1.2 million, which was slightly higher than my budget. But if I pushed myself a bit, it was affordable.

That was when I became a landlord and had to handle tenants, which is another ballgame. At that young age, when you're talking to someone, they look down on you and wonder if you knew what you were talking about.

My father's health was not well, too, so I was thrown into the deep end to handle the family business. That was a steep learning curve. I remembered him buying an old beat-up second-hand car for me when I got my driving licence. He believed I should take care of the car on my own. He wanted me to learn how to handle the car when it breaks down, such as the air conditioning not working or the tires puncturing. Then, you'll learn to never be frazzled in any situation.

Sharon:

It's an excellent lesson to be thrown into the deep end then. How did you learn about the significance of money?

Sunita:

There wasn't social media those days, just newspapers. So, knowledge about money was hard to get. My biggest regret as an adult is that I wish I learned about money sooner. I wish I learned about savings, compound interest, and all of that. I always feel that the biggest thing I can teach my daughters now will be that concept.

I wished school taught money. It is such an important topic. My father used to guide me. He did well in the stock market. One advice he always told me was to understand the companies you're investing in. He would read every article in *The Business Times*, and I always asked if he really needed to do that. That was another lesson: dive deep.

I do the hard work now. It's not as simple as opening doors. There's a lot of research you have to do. Real estate has two components: emotional and financial. It's like managing money. I had a young client yesterday who walked into a place and fell in love with the view. She walked away and said to me, 'Hold me. I'm emotional and don't want to buy a property based on how I feel. Send me the numbers.' So, I did.

I'm in the game for the long term. I will not sell your property just to make the commissions today. The numbers made little sense for her, and I told her not to go ahead with the transaction. She appreciated that I told her not to shoot herself in the foot.

I always tell myself that if I could do it for someone, the universe gives back in different ways. Perhaps one day, someone will do that for my daughters or the people who matter to me.

Sharon:

How are you helping your clients to understand their investments for the long term?

Sunita:

One client asked me questions like, 'What can I sell it for in two years? In five years? In ten years?' And I did the projections for her. Your relationship with money should be an investment that you think about for some time. But I also understand that having that awareness around money comes with age. When I was younger, retirement seemed so far away, so it was okay to buy that handbag or more shoes and clothes.

Now, I just want to get rid of everything that makes little sense to me. In the long run, we need to look for assets that generate income, and real estate is always a good way to think about asset allocation.

Sharon:

I want to dive into what you shared that real estate is emotional on one end and financial on the other. How do you balance all those elements?

Sunita:

I have this theory. It's harsh. You either live in your property every day loving it, but don't make money, or you live, then love it. It's self-fulfilment, mental health, and happiness because sometimes you cannot get the best or you buy something and detach yourself completely from it. You only look at the end goal.

It's incredibly difficult to be honest. I've been in this industry for fifteen years and I rarely see absolute balance. There's always one side that's going to take more than the other. You will not love something that you're going to invest in, at least for real estate. Of course, there must be certain fundamentals that you are agreeable with. For example, real estate depends on location. So, are you okay with the location? Certain unfavourable districts in Singapore might generate a lot of yield and a lot of returns. But my clients sometimes tell me it feels strange to have that on their portfolio.

It is not always possible to separate your emotions from financial decisions, especially for property purchases. I remember being drawn to a place when I was picking out a property for myself. I simply loved it. The house was in a rough state, but I learned to remove my emotions from the equation.

I guide my clients in doing the same. It's a journey we take together, and I've advised them to step away from deals many times. This approach has led many clients to return. I recall one instance where a client's wife was deeply attached to a particular property, and she was upset with me because I wasn't letting her dream come true. I asked for a day or two to work things out. When I spoke to her, I emphasised that while she wanted a home she loved, her husband was the sole provider and investing a substantial amount to build assets for their family's future. We aimed for a balanced middle ground that worked for both of them.

So, we went out again, and we found another amazing property. It then appreciated $1.5 million in a year. She called me over for a housewarming and was so happy she bought the place.

Sharon:

I love your thought process and how you bring your clients through the journey of buying a property. Emotions are one thing, but there are certain things you can't run away from, right?

Sunita:

You can't escape fundamentals. For example, I'll tell you to stay far away from certain properties because I've seen the transaction history and know that you can never make money from it.

Sometimes, it can also be a discouraging year, so you have to take a step back and trust the selection process. Timing is important. I had a girlfriend who bought an 'emotional' property because of a divorce and when she tried to sell it, she couldn't do it for almost two years. It was all wrong. But she was in a certain mental state. She wanted to be near a beach front and didn't think of anything else. So, timing is important. You also need to have the right person next to you who can be honest and truthful. Unfortunately, she lost money on the property.

Sharon:

You mentioned quite a few times that timing and emotion makes a difference in the property experience. How different are men and women in this?

Sunita:

A lot more women try to make it work. That's interesting to men. I was with a husband and wife the other day and I noticed how different their decision-making process was. Even though he let her decide everything, she couldn't go beyond a certain amount. She got upset. Often for the men, it's about the numbers. Do they make sense? For the wife, it's more about whether they can do it together as a family. Men also make decisions quicker while women sway a lot more.

Sharon:

How do you relate to money? What does it mean for you?

Sunita:

I have a love-fear relationship with money. I love it because it gives me financial freedom. It's a tool for growth and freedom. It's also an instrument you need to pay for things. I think it's important for women to acknowledge the word money because women don't even want to talk about what they want to earn.

I have a co-worker who's worked with me now for the past two years. In all her jobs, she hasn't been able to go to her superiors or her bosses to say, 'I want to make those million dollars', because she's always told that we do not talk about it. We were having a discussion earlier about how women don't ask for higher salaries or promotions. Now, she feels so liberated when she calls me and says, 'Yes, I'm going to go for it. I'm going to make $500,000. I'm going to go to this client and I'm going to close them because I want this money and I want to use it to liberate myself to do certain things.'

I believe in the universe and that you have to put it out there. She's in a wonderful space now and she's one of the few girlfriends I can speak to about this. Sometimes, I feel defeated when my other girlfriends don't acknowledge this. Are they not willing to put a value on what they deserve? They feel like they are not worthy of that, and it irritates me.

Recently, I went on a girls' trip with three other girlfriends. One is a health coach, one is a fashion stylist, and the final one is an entrepreneur. Besides the latter, the rest of them don't think they can ask for much. They feel they need more experience. I asked them what's the worst that could happen. They replied, 'They say no.'

Sharon:

Exactly. A lot of us have imposter syndrome, especially when we run our own business or in a corporate environment where people expect women to sit back and appreciate the work that others are bringing to the table.

Sunita:

I've been an entrepreneur for a long time. Being honest, I had lots of self-doubt until I met my husband. We would meet clients and pitch for a property. They would pay us a percentage of the sale. For a long time, I was taking the minimum. I feel like I'm not delivering if I take so much from you. The fear is still around occasionally and when I bring it up with my husband, I still go lower. Then, I look at him and he'll do his thing and he always gets the higher amount he wants.

An important thing, too, is that women should speak to other women who can encourage them. I have a girlfriend who has been a sales professional for a long time. Even she is afraid to ask. Several times, I've pushed her to do it and she'll call me after the deed is done. So, it is important to find your tribe who can push you from the back. We just need someone who believes in us.

I remember my daughter going through something similar. Two years ago, there was a dance performance in school, and she really wanted to go for it, but her fear was holding her back. She sat on the steps for a long time, then she looked at me and I told to get up there. And she did it.

She comes back and tells me that if I hadn't told her to do it, she wouldn't have done it and would have been sad. So, it really comes back to someone giving you that push.

You know, I really struggled with finding female mentors for a long time. I was always pushed back every time I sought one. That was a titanic struggle for me in the past, which is why I strongly believe in giving back to women whichever areas I can. It may not always be the best advice, but I think it's still a form of support.

Sharon:

Yes, I remember you've mentioned mentorship is important to you. And financial literacy is another topic you're passionate about too. How do you reach out to more women?

Sunita:

It's more organic and usually through social events where I network. I also mentor at Halogen Foundation and other similar organizations when I can, and this isn't gender specific. I don't specifically look for women, but many have approached me. Recently, another lady in real estate reached out to me on LinkedIn and wanted to meet. It's just about letting yourself out there and sharing with the communities about what other women have gone through.

Sharon:

How do you talk to your children about money?

Sunita:

Children are a whole different topic. We do it differently since they're still young—seven and nine. When they get money, we put 30 to 50 per cent in the piggy bank. My husband read somewhere that it's good to get a clear transparent piggy bank because they can see the money. And it has worked! The girls always look to see how far more they need before it gets full. Another thing we do, which we picked up from Jim Rogers, is that we take about 30 per cent for investing and buy a stock for them.

It's funny because my daughter came up to me one day and said that she wants money to buy a toy. I asked her if she wanted to buy a toy or own the company. She paused and remembered that she owns Disney shares and bought more! I teach them to just invest the money in the stock and see what happens at the end of the year when you can make so much more and draw down on it to buy something they like. It helps to delay gratification, which

I failed as a woman growing up when I had good money. There were a lot of impulse purchases I feel are enormous wastes of money now.

Sharon:

And things like property and finances are all long-term journeys, right? It's also important for people to realize what they can do to crystallize the returns. Even now when I look at investing in a new company, one big question that keeps coming up is the exit, i.e. how you get your money back. But nobody speaks about exits for a lot of financial products like real estate or other investments. That's something that I think women need to understand.

Sunita:

Yeah, I think a lot of women whom I encountered were more impulsive in investing and more frivolous when they were younger.

Sharon:

How is it working with your husband?

Sunita:

Amazing. The good thing we did was to separate our daily tasks. We struggled initially because we overlapped a lot and weren't as productive. Then we took a step back. The good thing about both of us is that we will go through self-discovery. We are happy to be coached and to embrace our faults and strengths.

After speaking to our coaches, we separated our roles. I didn't feel that I was taking on too much, but the fact remains that I wasn't delegating, so the coaches helped us with that. He does more client servicing and I do more backend work because I get tired showing up all the time and I also have more things with the kids. He's a good hands-on father too. We alternate roles sometimes for things that we are good at, and we talk to each other all the time. Communication is important.

Sharon:

And how about finances? How do you talk about finance in the household?

Sunita:

That has been a journey for us as well. We came from different backgrounds. My husband's father was a chartered accountant. We grew up with different mindsets and it took us a while to have synergy in how we wanted to run the family and the investments we wanted to do. It's still developing, and we're still growing and learning. We're still going for finance courses because the landscape always changes, right? For example, the advent of blockchain, and how the property industry is growing with it.

We used to have a lot more clients in Singapore in the past two years. Now, with the world becoming smaller, clients are looking at places like Dubai and London, so we make it a habit to travel even for just a couple of days to connect with partners to learn about the market.

Sharon:

On that note, how much money is enough for you?

Sunita:

So, I tried to do that. I don't know if it's the right number, but this was in conversation with a few friends and people whose opinions I value. It seems like the magic number is $15 to $20 million until retirement based on our family's lifestyle and the children's education. For me, it's really important that I purchase a property for each of my children. They don't have to be fully paid up.

A mortgage runs for thirty years, and I want them to understand that I'm not paying for the property just to give it to them on a silver platter. They need to learn that. That was primarily my thought because I think women should have something to fall back on in life like real estate. I'm hoping and praying they have amazing relationships with their husbands. The property is a security blanket for a woman.

Sharon:

You're clearly comfortable with numbers and did a lot of planning. How do you aim to get to $15 or $20 million? How do you plan your investments?

Sunita:

Our investment portfolio is like many others. It's 50 per cent in real estate, 30 per cent in investments, and the rest is daily living. We constantly look out for high-performing markets. For example, we were told that Vietnam was doing well, so we took a trip to see for ourselves and study the numbers. The world is becoming smaller and one thing that my husband and I will never do is to go into an overseas investment without seeing, touching, and feeling the property or talking to the people of the land. $15 million is a big number, but we want to put it out there in the universe.

Sharon:

But I love that. I love the numerically driven approach to your business and your retirement planning. To you, what's the difference between money and wealth?

Sunita:

Wealth is preservation. It's about putting the jigsaw puzzle together to get to that magic number. It's beyond money, and it concerns generational legacy. I recently did a course on family offices, and it mentioned that wealth has degenerated over the years because of non-management. It's a whole new ballgame for me on how to manage money. I also recently learned about lasting power of attorney. It's so simple and cheap to do something and appoint somebody to administer your will for you. Wealth is really just so broad.

Sharon:

Wealth is really about putting together a plan for your assets for the next generation. About legacy, if you have a billion dollars, what would you do with all that money?

Sunita:

Pay off all my properties and probably buy more, specifically income-generating assets in prime locations. I'm close to my family, so I'll use the money to pay off the mortgages for myself, my children, and the people I love.

For the rest, I'd use it to create platforms that can help people in this space, like a boot camp about teaching financial literacy, perhaps for children in schools.

I'm also a big believer in giving back. I haven't given back to any specific charity because I wasn't pleased with the amounts that were going towards administrative costs. It's difficult to run a charity. But my husband and I would rather pay somebody who we know or help a beneficiary with more tangible payoffs, like the school education of our helpers' children.

Sharon:

What is the kindest act related to money that someone has done for you?

Sunita:

It was someone who paid for my father's funeral. Someone who was close enough and knew about the dire position that my family was in. This person stepped forward when my father passed away and asked us to allow her to do this because my father had helped her family.

It was karma perhaps? My father was in insurance at one point, during a time when many families couldn't afford it. But he would insist. Then this lady's husband passed away, and she received a good sum of money because he was the sole breadwinner. My dad passed away ten years later, and she stepped forward. That gesture was so touching for us.

Sharon:

We never know how our kind acts would be reciprocated in the future, but the act itself can make a real difference to someone else's life in that moment. I wish you all the best, Sunita!

16

Christine Amour-Levar

*I feel equally strong taking care of myself and letting
someone take care of me.*

Christine Amour-Levar founded two award-winning non-government
organizations, Women on a Mission and HER Planet Earth. With an
unwavering sense of adventure, she leads groups on expeditions around
the world to raise awareness and funds to support vulnerable women
globally. She is a climate investor, philanthropist, and author. Her energy
is infectious, and her work ethic is tireless, and when in her presence, you
feel that anything is possible. In this interview, she shares how her diverse
background helped her navigate money, and why she feels strong and
feminine charging through her career, saving her own money, and having
her husband provide for her and the family.

> ### KEY INSIGHTS

Discover your ikigai.

It's what wakes you up with excitement and fills you with joy. When you
channel your skills towards serving your purpose, you create something truly
remarkable. When your purpose and passion intersect, your vocation ceases
to be just a job, and you radiate with brilliance.

It's fine to let someone else take care of you.

You can make your own money, have your own career, and take care of
yourself. At the same time, be confident and accept it is absolutely fine if
others also want to care for you. It is not mutually exclusive. You are not alone.

Empower yourself by investing.

Get to know the companies you invest in, stay engaged, and provide support through introductions and more. Be an active part of their journey to success. By empowering founders and companies, you are empowering yourself.

THE CONVERSATION

Serena:

This is like asking to pick your favourite child, but of all the expeditions that you've been on, is there one that was particularly memorable or challenging?

Christine:

Gosh, this is a tough question. I've led over twenty-one expeditions and am privileged to take hundreds of women to some of the coldest places in the world like the Arctic and Antarctica and to some of the hottest deserts in Ethiopia, Jordan, and Iran. All of them have challenged us in different ways. We've had to climb up different peaks or tackle extreme heat.

If I had to pick one, I'd choose the time when we migrated with Nenet reindeer herders in Siberia. It was culturally unique. It wasn't the most physically challenging, although it got freezing, dropping to -36 degrees Celsius.

They were migrating, so we were riding with them. It wasn't so much trudging through snow, as it was living through their usual migration day− setting up camp, eating their meals, which mainly comprised frozen fish and raw meat and blood from the reindeers they herded. That was a cultural experience out of our comfort zone. We were in extreme conditions with beautiful, proud people who have been doing this for hundreds of years. They are one of the last remaining herders in the world. Travelling with 10,000 reindeer was a special experience for the team.

Serena:

Let's expand on the theme of culture. You grew up in different cultures and geographies. Tell us more.

Christine:

I was born and raised in the Philippines, so the country is still close to my heart. Some people don't know where I'm from when they look at me.

Deep inside, I'm Filipina first and foremost. I have a big family, especially my mother's side. My father was an expatriate there for many years. The Philippines is one of the poorest countries in Southeast Asia, but there is also a lot of wealth. I'd say something like 5 per cent of the population owns 99 per cent of wealth.

We have a growing middle class now, but growing up, I saw this inequality first-hand, especially during times of crises when the poorest are most affected. That touched me.

I knew I was fortunate to have a wonderful education, a roof over my head, and lots of opportunities. My parents weren't wealthy compared to the standards of developed countries, but we were in the wealthier class in the Philippines. I studied in an international school, so there were different cultures around me, and I spoke multiple languages.

I love travelling and had a head-start in life when I went to Japan. That curiosity has stayed with me. I've lived in Japan, the US, and Europe before finally coming to Singapore, so this desire to learn from other cultures and people with different upbringings has always been with me.

That's probably why I love picking exotic locations for our expeditions!

Serena:

Asian culture is close to your heart. What were the narratives around money that you were exposed to growing up in Asia?

Christine:

Growing up, talking about money was taboo in my family. I was the eldest child. My father, being a European, didn't like to talk about money. When we were children, it was brought up in the context of gratitude, such as how our holidays are nice, or I'm studying at the best school in Manila. We were lucky that my father was offering all these opportunities for us.

My mother came from a wealthy Filipino-Chinese family. Her father never worked. He had a hacienda plantation and was known as a sugar baron.

My father liked to say that he would give us everything for our education, but to not expect any inheritance. It was his way of emphasizing the need for education so that we could be independent in the world. I thought that was good.

My grandmother had a big house and many family businesses. Later in life, the family lost most of their money. Still, we knew we were from a privileged class, so it was at the back of our minds. My parents never made a big deal out of it. They would say that I needed to appreciate my privilege and give back. It was good that my mother brought us up with those values. I feel those stayed with me.

I always knew growing up in the Philippines that there were people who had money and those who didn't. I went to school with wealthy kids with drug problems and many psychological issues. It made me realize that having a lot of money can also result in more problems. I remember the random drug tests in high school because we had a massive drug problem with all these rich kids taking them.

My mother used to tell me that too much money can also bring problems, and that some parents would rather give money to their children instead of time. It's still something that resonates with me.

Serena:

Back then, how did money make you feel?

Christine:

I understood that money was important because it allowed us to have privileges. My dad worked hard. I remembered him coming home late almost every night. He worked almost every Saturday. Then, when I was seventeen, he had a heart attack. And I remember thinking, 'Wow, if something happened to him, what's going to happen to my mother?' She stopped working after I was born. As the eldest child, I felt this deep responsibility, and that motivated me to work harder.

I was eager to go to university and start my career so that I could earn money. It was important for security. Beyond that, I never aspired to be wealthy or to make a lot of money. I just wanted to make sure that I could be there for my mother and siblings if something happened to my father.

Serena:

After university, did you look for the best-paying job?

Christine:

Well, my parents never told me to marry a rich man *[laughs]*. When I graduated from university, I was living in Tokyo. It's an expensive city. I wanted to keep my visa, so I had to find a job right away. I went for interviews and got four job offers from Cartier, Kellogg, McCann Erickson, and Levi's, because I spoke Japanese relatively fluently by then.

I wanted to look for something in marketing. I didn't want to work in finance because I had done an internship with a French bank in Tokyo. Although they paid extremely well during the internship, I knew I didn't want to go back into that world. I wanted to do something creative.

In the end, I didn't pick the job that paid the most, but the one that seemed most fun and interesting. That was McCann Erickson. It had many blue-chip clients. Also, during my university days, I worked part-time as a French and English teacher and did some modelling, so I could save a bit of money. Even when I started working, I kept those part-time jobs because Tokyo was expensive, and I wanted to keep saving.

After my day job, I would leave the office around six or seven and teach French at a Japanese cosmetics company. I would come home late, but I didn't want to give up because it was a good income. It was a significant decision, as I saved up some money, which I was happy about. I was proud of myself. I wanted to make sure I had security.

I dated a wealthy American guy while I was in university. We're still friends now. Later, I met my first husband in Japan. He was a successful gentleman. It wasn't something I strategically thought about. I wasn't looking for someone rich, just someone who was a go-getter and had a work ethic. That was important to me. I had seen my father become a successful entrepreneur, so that vision of masculinity for me was still associated with someone who worked hard and succeeded.

Serena:

You're a strong, independent woman who knows how to make money. With that, would you consider yourself a spender or saver?

Christine:

Both. I'm balanced like that. So, as I mentioned, I started saving early on. Even when I moved to the US to work for Nike, I continued saving about 20 per cent of my income each month. I also bought real estate when I was twenty-five with my first husband. It was a beautiful apartment in Paris, and we sold it for a healthy profit. I've always been interested in real estate even today.

I like and spend on jewellery because I grew up with my mom, who also likes them. My daughters sometimes rummage around my jewellery box and ask to borrow some pieces. I always think it's nice for a lady to buy her own jewellery. Of course, it's also nice to get presents *[laughs]*. I'm fine with making my money and absolutely fine with a man offering to take care of me and giving me options.

I'm confident in saying that. It's funny because I was at a dinner party with some friends, and one of them told us she had just gotten a divorce. She has an illustrious career, and her ex-husband wasn't as successful as her, which caused some friction. Another lady at the table then said, 'If you date again, don't pick somebody who's going to pay for you and do everything.'

I don't agree with that at all. I think it's wonderful for women to have their own career, savings, and money, and I'm comfortable making my money and having my own savings. But I'm also okay to be with a successful man who likes to spoil me and takes care of the family.

I still feel as strong and as feminine that way.

Serena:

That's an interesting point. You bring lots of women together, but you don't come across as overtly feminist and aggressive. You are feminine and approachable. How do you toggle the spectrum?

Christine:

When I was starting out in my career, I was concerned about projecting the right image at work. I was at Nike for about eleven years, and I realized that as I got older, I was more comfortable being my authentic self. It also helps that the culture of corporations has changed with more people advocating for diversity in the workforce. Bringing your full self, they say.

Even though I loved sports and working at Nike, I suffered a little because I came from the Japanese corporate culture, which was more formal and conformist. Nike, on the other hand, is about bringing your authentic self to work.

But the wonderful thing about becoming more comfortable in your skin is that you are happy about being yourself. I'm open about my life on social media, I'm comfortable with my life as a mother, and I can be authentic, especially about the causes that I am passionate about.

I've created several movements through the non-profit organizations I founded that address the issues of violence against women and the impact of climate change on women. I've been working on and advocating for these issues for a long time now.

There was a moment in my life, however, when I remembered thinking, 'What's next?' I just had my fourth child, had a great job, and felt blessed in my life. Yet, I thought, 'Is this it?' It's only normal to ask these questions.

Then, I met a French mountaineer, Valerie Boffy. We had met a few times before and I always thought she was cool. I really like sporty women. She told me she was going to be away for seven weeks. I asked her whether she was going on holiday, and she told me she was going to climb Everest. That floored me.

I did a bit of mountaineering when I separated from my first husband and realized that I found strength in nature and the mountains. One of my favourite books is *Into Thin Air* by Jon Krakauer, which is about the disaster on the mountain in 1997. So, I knew how dangerous Everest could be. Valerie was a mother too.

I tracked her expedition and cheered when she succeeded on the first try of summiting. She had a banner that said, 'Bearing the flag for women everywhere.' She was climbing to support a charity called Women for Women International that supports women survivors of war, started by an Iraqi lady named Zainab Salbi. The latter is the daughter of the personal pilot of Saddam Hussein and wrote a book about her arranged marriage with an abuser and how she ran away from him. This was in the 90s. Then, she saw the television coverage of the rape camps in the Balkans and how the international community wasn't doing anything about it. So, she took it upon herself to do something. She found people in the US to write to these ladies in the Balkans, giving them $25 and a letter every month to give them strength and hope and to tell them they were not forgotten. Then, she started the charity, which has been going on strong for almost thirty years now and helped a million women around the world with various programmes.

When I heard about this charity, I knew I had to support it. So, together with Valerie, we organized a group of women to trek to Everest Base Camp and raise $150,000 at the same time. That was the start of Women on a Mission (WOAM) that I co-founded with Valerie.

I wrote a press release about how we were women on a mission to reach higher ground. Then I had women calling me to ask about the next one. That gave me so much purpose. It woke me up. I felt like I could use all the skills I had cultivated in my career to support women. We've added more charities now, and it's been the most beautiful thing I've done in my life. It's opened so many other doors for me.

Serena:

It's grand to have a mission and purpose. But at the end of the day, we can't run away from money.

Christine:

When I started WOAM, I chose a simple business model—we would donate all the funds we raised, and we were all volunteers. I decided this very early on with my co-founders. My husband told me it wasn't sustainable because I spent all my time organizing events.

However, literally after we returned from our first trip, one lady who was supposed to join us but injured herself while training reached out to me. She was the CEO of Temasek Trust. She asked me to come to her office and said that there were three jobs she would love for me to look at.

I was initially hesitant because I loved the flexibility I had and didn't want to work full time. But she insisted. I ended up picking a communications and marketing role, and eventually worked with her for five years and led the communications team. It was a wonderful experience that paid well.

The timing was right because I was advocating for women, and the corporate world was shifting. Many started advocating for corporate social responsibility and my work got attention. It showed me that if I follow something with passion, it doesn't become work any more and it helps me to shine. It opened other well-paid opportunities, and I realized I could find a balance between getting a good salary and the flexibility to continue with my NGO work. I was lucky, but also realized that I made my luck because I was active around it.

For my NGO, I could have allocated some of the money I had from fundraising for a salary and hired people. But I chose this business model because you must take risks in life to win big, right? Trying new things is scary, especially when you must let go of the safe cushion of corporate jobs. Of course, it's easier said than done, but I think my actions have shown that it's possible because I received multiple lucrative opportunities.

Serena:

Moving to a topic closer to home, between you and your husband, do you talk about money?

Christine:

We do. We talk about money a lot and it is a constructive conversation. I enjoy talking about it and I'm glad he's open about it. We talk about our children's education, what we want to offer them, what we hope for them, and also discuss real estate and where we want to base ourselves in. We also have our moon-shot goals.

Sometimes I plan longer, for twenty years, and other times, I just think five years ahead because you never know what's going to happen. No one knew the pandemic was going to happen. So, we talk about what we know at the moment.

I'm looking at a place to buy now and we talk about renovations and similar topics. We plan the finances together and discuss how much we are going to save and invest. We talk to our children about this too.

They're all different ages. My eldest daughter has already started working with *Financial Times* in the UK. I'm helping her with rent now because London is expensive and she's just started working, but she's been great at saving. I've told her I can't pay her rent forever and she's made plans to either get a roommate or a promotion. She's focused, which is great, and I'm happy to see that she's being responsible.

My other boy who is at university recently got a job to help with students coming in for orientation. It pays well, which will help with his pocket money.

I still give them some pocket money and used to give them money when their grades were good. That's how my parents motivated me and I'm okay with doing the same. Of course, I expected good grades, but if they're excellent, I give them a bonus. I remember trying harder when I knew I would get a financial bonus too.

When they were younger, I didn't talk too much to them about the cost of things because they won't be able to comprehend it. But now, I tell them how much we pay for schools and holidays because I want them to understand and appreciate the cost of things.

I think it's healthy to talk about money and we talk more about it at home compared to when I was growing up.

Serena:

Asian parents like to give their children a head-start financially, if possible. Is this something on your mind?

Christine:

Yes, it's interesting because my parents never did a mortgage deposit for me. I know I have a Singaporean friend who's done that for her three kids, which I think is amazing. Two of her girls are currently in California. They're Singaporean, and she put the deposit down on their flats, but she said, 'You pay the mortgage.'

I have another Filipina friend whose father paid the deposit for her and her husband as a wedding present. Both are working and paying the mortgage. I'd love to do the same for my four children, which is going to be a lot of money [laughs].

But if I can, I would like to do that for them because it's a delightful gift. I'll put down the deposit and they take care of the mortgage. I want my children to be around when they get older, and I'd love to host them as much as I can. Maybe we can rent a holiday villa and they can come during holidays. That's my dream.

I have high hopes for them. I'm not a Tiger Mum, but if I'm paying that kind of money for their education, then I expect them to get good grades and good jobs. They don't have to be rich. I just want them to be comfortable and successful and maybe have enough for a pleasant holiday. The world is becoming more expensive. Still, I expect them to be independent. We talk about these things and the children know that I have expectations.

Serena:

Let's pivot and talk about something that intimidates women. Do you invest?

Christine:

I invest, and it started a few years ago. I've invested in real estate the last twenty years because I believe in and enjoy it. We've also invested in our family business. My husband has a business in Singapore, and we've reinvested a lot of the profits that make sure that the company is going the right way.

I've also recently invested in climate tech, which is new to me. I started working in sustainability as a consultant with a few clients, so I've had the opportunity to come in at the right amount. It's something I enjoy diving into because I can follow the journey of the companies. I also believe in investing in game-changing technologies. Now I'm on the board of a venture capital firm, Investible, as well. As a board member, I get to meet founders and talk to them. The first two funds are sector agnostic. There is also a climate tech fund that's done well in Australia.

We're launching two funds in Singapore, with one focused on climate. I'm on the board for the Singapore fund, so I have opportunities to invest in projects personally.

Serena:

Is there something about investing that excites you?

Christine:

It's empowering. You are always educating yourself about the companies that you invest in. I like to stay close and support them with introductions. I want them to do well. A few of my girlfriends also invest. Some of them invest in the start-ups that I advise for with no encouragement from me. They like the concept, and they find that these start-ups are doing great work, usually around sustainability where my interest is. They're also usually led by women. A lot of the women who take part in my expeditions are also active investors in their own right!

Serena:

Absolutely. Now, let's talk about wealth. What is the definition of wealth for you?

Christine:

I suppose it's different for different people, right? When I think of wealth, I think of the assets I have that will grow. It needs to be protected and it could be generational or self-made wealth. But it's personal. Wealth could also be your personal connections.

Serena:

Some say everyone has a number. What is your number?

Christine:

For me, enough means being comfortable enough to not have to work, but I love working, so I guess having enough means being able to take the holidays that I want with my children and having the ability to help them live comfortably and enjoy life without too much pressure.

My husband and I have a number. We would like to live in different countries. I think the more realistic way is to look at your current earning capacity and then, how you would like to live for the next five to ten years. From there, we can extrapolate how much you need to save and study your investments. We have a financial adviser who is a family friend.

It's step by step. I'm a planner and I like to plan where I'm trying to go, but I must be flexible because life doesn't always pan out the way you want it to. I know what I want next.

It's an interesting topic, and I talk about it with my husband a lot.

Serena:

Do you still have vulnerability or fear around money?

Christine:

I'm a lot more comfortable now. Being a fundraiser for so long helps. I'm always very goal-oriented in getting a group of people together to hit a target, whether it's raising funds for a company or charity. It's about rallying people and telling them why they should support a cause or invest in a technology or firm.

It's been a big part of my life, especially in the last eleven years. It's almost easier to raise money for companies compared to philanthropy because you get measurable returns. I've asked people to part with their money for philanthropy grants and donations, so when I started working with investors, I had confidence even though I never worked in finance. It's the same principle: to convince people to put money where you believe it should be.

I'm still learning every day because of course we're dealing with more complexities, like carried interest and management fees. But once you pick up the lingo and you talk shop, you learn it.

Serena:

My last question, what is the kindest money-related act anyone has ever done for you?

Christine:

My father never went to university and sending me to Japan for school was expensive. He had savings that could support me, so that was very kind. My first bosses also pushed for my salary increases and bonuses and that meant a lot to me too.

The moments that really touched me were when people believed in me and supported me because I showed potential. It shapes your career and makes you want to do more and work harder.

Serena:

You have an amazing power to make others believe in you, Christine. It is coming full circle as you give back on many meaningful causes, harnessing many friendships built over the years. That's how I believe the world makes progress. It has been a privilege to speak with you.

17

Harmin Kaur

A pair of high heels and a good suit makes me
feel like I'm ready for anything!

Harmin Kaur's grace and poise are external foils to her fierce independence and inner fire. She started working when she was sixteen, driven by the desire to be financially free. Once she found her purpose—to empower women and close the gender gap in entrepreneurship—she has not looked back. Integrating the yin and yang of not-for-profit work with her own enterprise, she is equally at ease with the grime of entrepreneurship and the fineness of arts and culture. In this interview, she shares her developing approach to building her empire.

KEY INSIGHTS

Discipline and the right values are essential for your wealth.

You can have all the money in the world, but without discipline or the right values, all your hard work and sacrifices can be wiped out in a few years.

Your best investment is your family and the right partner.

The right partner is someone whom you can trust, who supports your dreams, and who will put aside his so that you can pursue yours. The wrong one can be mentally and financially draining, and will also affect your potential down the road.

You don't have to be rich to be generous.

Life really boils down to a few defining moments, when a simple kind act can change lives. Even a simple loan can change someone's life dramatically in the future.

THE CONVERSATION

Serena:

Harmin, tell us about yourself.

Harmin:

I started at a non-profit and had my business for many years before going into banking. I was in the sector for fifteen years before going down the entrepreneurial route and started Women Venture Asia with my board members in October 2022. It's a non-profit that works with women entrepreneurs to create a more inclusive ecosystem. Several months later, in March 2023, I launched Stellaire, a commercial entity for art lovers who are culturally curious.

Serena:

Did you grow up in a culture where your family could talk about money?

Harmin:

I've realized that the more comfortable you are with money, the less you talk about it. That was my experience. We didn't talk about it in the earlier years when my family was comfortable. Then, in the late 80s during the Pan-Electric crisis, my dad lost his job and business. Our investments with it. We went from being comfortable to struggling to pay the bills. My father and mother had to keep working even in their old ages.

We struggled for several years. I saw my mother stepping up and finally becoming financially independent. Now, she's in her seventies and has passive income. She's retired and doesn't need anyone to support her.

She had discipline. That's the other thing I learned about wealth and money. You can have $100 million, but if you don't have discipline or the right values, it can be wiped out in a few years.

Serena:

How did that discipline translate into her money journey? Was it savings?

Harmin:

Yes, it was. She had little to save, but whatever money she had, she put it into the house. She didn't have an intricate investment portfolio, but her discipline inspired me. I speak about this to my clients. It's not about how much you have. It's about your discipline, how you manage it, and how you put it to work.

Discipline is also about staying invested when the times are rough. I've worked with women from lower-income backgrounds to ultra-high net worth families and the common theme to their successful investment portfolios is discipline.

Serena:

Through your family's highs and lows, how did money make you feel?

Harmin:

It's developed over time. When I was younger, I felt money was essential and was a core part of me. The desire to be financially independent drove me. I saw how my mom had done it and experienced the benefits firsthand.

I started working at sixteen and couldn't wait to graduate. School was a means to an end. It gave me the opportunity to earn more and have the things I always wanted. If I wanted anything, I had to work for it. No one told me this. I learned it through my parents.

Serena:

What does financial independence mean for you now?

Harmin:

It hasn't changed. It just means that I don't have to ask anyone. I discuss it with my husband out of respect, but since I was sixteen, I've never had to ask anyone what I wanted to do with my money or how to spend it. It means having the power to make my decisions. It's empowering not to be beholden to anyone.

For example, when I wanted to leave banking, it was an independent decision. I talked to my husband because I needed his emotional support, but I had arrived at a point in my life where I knew I didn't need the financial support of someone else.

Serena:

What does being a social entrepreneur mean to you?

Harmin:

I've never thought of it as social entrepreneurship.

I want to build something and start a platform that lets me make an impact. That was important. Sometimes, we wait around or offer to volunteer, but you're never called upon or your expertise is never leveraged fully. I was tired of being passive and contributing while being confined. So, I went out and did it my way. It's important to carve out my own space and create impact my way.

Serena:

Why not create a for-profit start-up instead? Why did you venture into non-profit and create Women Venture Asia?

Harmin:

Fabulous questions. And right now, I have both. I still don't want to be in a place where I depend on anyone, which is why I still have my for-profit business. I'm still commercially minded at heart.

I think it goes back to the meaning of money for me and how it grew. When I was sixteen, money was essential, and it remained so until my thirties. Now, it's the diminishing marginal utility of income. It's a familiar term among bankers.

I'm not saying I've earned billions, but up to a point, the utility of money and satisfaction diminishes. You need a certain amount to survive, and then another amount for happiness. After that, it plateaus. That's where I am right now. What gave me more satisfaction was putting it to work for a purpose. I took a chunk of my savings to start this non-profit.

But every dollar that I spent gave me much more satisfaction than if I were to buy something with it. My perspective and outlook have changed.

Serena:

I feel that many women have that revelation that life is more than money, but few have the courage to take action. Tell us how you took that leap.

Harmin:

There was a lot of fear. And what works in a corporate setting doesn't quite work outside. Corporate settings are safe environments. It's tough and you don't take a lot of unnecessary risk, especially in banking.

There's also a lot of speculation and whatever has gotten you this far will not get you to where you need to be in entrepreneurship. Since a young age, I always needed that security, that assurance that there was always going to be a safety net for me, which meant working for someone else. The iron rice bowl served me well.

But that same fear of not having security stopped me from taking the leap. That was the most challenging part, and I had to overcome that. But the sense of purpose I felt was so strong that there was no way I could not do it.

I told myself to look at the women around me and all the things they've launched. I spoke to several people and rationalized the process. I also went through several sessions with a few coaches and realized that I needed to make the leap. It was a process.

Serena:

Why did you decide women's empowerment was your purpose?

Harmin:

I served a lot in different women's organizations. I volunteered and even worked at AWARE before. I'm on the board of United Women Singapore. In my banking role, I headed diversity for Goldman Sachs. I've been doing this for over a decade, so it felt natural to me.

But if I were to trace back the root of this passion, it probably started when I was sixteen and saw how empowered my mother was. She didn't have education or job experience. Yet, she became financially independent. Seeing it play out in my home made me realize that it's important to push that dream for the community.

Serena:

I love how personal your story is. Coming back to money, are you a spender or saver?

Harmin:

I go through different phases. Early in my career, I saved a lot, and it was amazing. I worked for a non-profit, then started a small business. The pay at a non-profit was modest, but I was amazed by how much I could save. I could even get a car.

Then, when you enter banking, your lifestyle changes. I didn't save the same percentage. Looking back, I would have done this differently. I went through this phase of being like a bird out of a cage and banking gave the opportunity to embark on a different lifestyle. I returned to the disciplined phase when I got married and started a family. By that time, you're no longer saving and investing for yourself, but for your family and your children's future. That forces me to be disciplined.

Serena:

What are some non-negotiables that you spend on?

Harmin:

Clothes *[laughs]*. I'm being very honest and unapologetic about it. Putting on a high pair of heels and a good suit makes me feel like I'm ready for the day.

Serena:

What about investing? How did you get started?

Harmin:

I wish I had started earlier. I only saved because that's what my parents' generation did. Obviously, inflation was not an issue then. So, they would save and buy a residential property. That was the formula back then, and they weren't wrong because the returns were amazing. Now, it's levelled off.

So, when I started my career, I thought I would save to buy a house, and that would be it. But the banking industry exposed me to a lot more ideas. You hear what people are doing and start educating yourself. Then you become more efficient with investing. This develops over the years.

My best investment has been the stock market. But I also think about the value I've derived from investing in venture capital. For me, it's not so much whether it's the best investment as it is the impact that investment makes. If something can give me similar returns and make an impact, I am incredibly passionate about it. These are the investments that I'm more focused on right now. I'd also say that these are my best investments.

I'm also invested in my business. It meant rejigging my portfolio and liquidating some assets to fund the business. It might have been painful, but it is worth it.

Now that I'm an entrepreneur, I prefer passive investments, too, since I can't spend as much time watching it. I take a safer route and look even longer term. I'd say 10 to 20 per cent of my portfolio is in longer-term funds, and it's a higher percentage than before. I still am invested in the stock market and believe in a buy-and-hold strategy, and I have money market funds, but my portfolio is no longer as highly diversified as before.

Serena:

Let's switch gears and talk about your new business.

Harmin:

It's called Stellaire, and it is focused on being at the vanguard of arts and cultural experiences. We are bringing bespoke, one-of-a-kind encounters and access around the art of living. It could be culinary art, art of winemaking, performance visual art, or even couture. Wherever there is an artisanal journey, we want to get intimate access to that. It's not just about the product, but making our members understand there is a heritage, a long legacy, and an artisanal journey behind this item.

For example, our community would get access to some of the most established winemaking families. If a guest chef comes in, we want to merge his or her culinary art with visual arts so that it's a differentiated experience. Our community is looking for something different they cannot find anywhere else. It's a one-of-a-kind experience.

For example, we soft launched in March at the Van Gogh exhibition in Singapore. Our guests had a VIP preview, and we hosted a dinner in the exhibition hall. It didn't even have a kitchen facility. We had to work with the venue partners to make it happen and flew in a Michelin-starred Dutch chef from Holland who created a Van Gogh–inspired menu. There was food, champagne, and the Van Gogh immersive experience rotated around the room. It was a spectacular night and the one-of-a-kind experience that we challenged ourselves to create.

Serena:

Are you trying to create an experience that money cannot buy?

Harmin:

Perhaps. It goes back to the diminishing marginal utility of money. Some experiences are just not about throwing money at them. It's about creating something, about access, and about the personal relationships and artisanal journey behind them.

It's not so much about going to a Michelin-starred restaurant and spending $1,000. But what we wanted to do is give you intimate access to these artists.

Serena:

Besides being an entrepreneur, you're also a wife and mother. In your home, what are some money mantras you tell?

Harmin:

So, every time the kids get their red packet money from their relatives, I've been telling them not just to save, but to put the money to work. For example, if they got $500, they had to remain disciplined. How much can they set aside to spend? How much should they keep? I've also been explaining to them about inflation and the dollar value of money and children these days are ready to consume information like this. They understand it.

So, my eight-year-old is very much like me. He's money-driven, but not so much about the pursuit of money as it is about success. To him, money means he's fulfilled a goal. It's like my entrepreneurial journey. It's not that I want to earn money, but money is an important indicator of how commercially successful and viable your business is.

Serena:

At home, do you and your husband split roles in money-related issues?

Harmin:

I'm blessed. The best investment I made is in the family and being able to find the right partner. You can have all the money in the world but if you have a wrong partner, all of that could be at risk. For me the right partner is someone whom I can trust, who supports my dreams, and who will put aside his dreams so that I can pursue mine.

When you have two people with intense careers who have kids, the reality is that something must give. Both of you can't have intense careers at the same time. Someone will have to take a step back so the other person can step forward and take the risk.

My husband is a surgeon. I'm sure that there are things he wants to do, such as taking a risk to start a business. But both of us can't be doing that at the same time. He loves what he does, but he wants to do other things as well. I'm glad that he's providing that stability so that one of us can take more risks and pursue our dreams.

He's also been very open to advice. As a surgeon, he has very little capacity to think or talk about money. The good thing is that he's a lot more disciplined than I am. For financial decisions, however, while we discuss it together, he leaves it to me.

Serena:

Do you talk about money with your female friends?

Harmin:

I don't. It could be an Asian mentality. When people talk about salaries or investments, they just say that they've bought a house. But that's the extent of what they will share. Some might say that they've been up late trading some stocks, but never tell you the full story. So, we don't share about our portfolio or even investment advice.

Serena:

I'm going to put you on the spot. What is the best advice around money you can share?

Harmin:

To be in control, do your research, and be empowered with the right information. Both men and women, particularly the latter, are always told how to invest and what we should do. And we're passive about it.

I know a lot of women around me who are educated and incredibly smart, but they leave the decision-making to someone else. But it's not rocket science, right? So, empowering yourself with information is great. Also ask questions and learn because there are so many resources out there. You just need to be more involved in managing your finances.

It also depends on what phase of life you're in. I'm very blessed to be at a stage where I've worked hard and can now invest in Women Venture

Asia. I wouldn't be able to do this twenty years ago. So, let your personal circumstances guide your investment goals and decisions.

Serena:

Did you ever feel vulnerable or ashamed when it comes to money?

Harmin:

There will always be those occasions, right? Especially when you're a banker because people expect you to know. But you must get over that. Even now, since I don't follow the markets as much as I used to, I have more questions and am getting comfortable that I'm no longer in the thick of it.

It's important not to assume that bankers have all the information because nobody knows how the market is going to behave tomorrow or even today. Don't let anybody tell you they know.

Serena:

The meaning of money has changed over time for you. But what about wealth? What does it mean?

Harmin:

Wealth is more than just tangible assets. When I think about wealth, I think about happiness. It's still important to have money because that secures your children's future, and we're investing right now for them. But it's also important to be content, happy, and healthy. If your money and investments can help you achieve that, then that's great.

The rest is mindset. I think of wealth as a mindset.

Serena:

A fun one. What would you do if someone gave you a billion dollars?

Harmin:

I would give it back because I feel that more money means more problems, sometimes. Don't get me wrong. I'm not saying that I don't want more money, but I have this traditional mentality that if it comes so easily, it will go away easily as well. I want to have worked for it.

If someone gave me a billion dollars, the reality is there are strings attached. At that level of wealth and money, there are a lot of challenges associated with it. I've seen that play out several times before and you question the people who want to be around you.

The example that always comes to mind is something my husband shared with me. He's a doctor, so he's seen people in their last days and some of them are incredibly wealthy people. He shared an example of this wealthy person who constantly had people coming to him with papers to sign. But when he was gone, no one was there with him.

Serena:

Our last question. What was the kindest money-related act anyone has ever done for you?

Harmin:

As I mentioned earlier, money was difficult to come by when we were growing up. My mother covered my university fees, and my father covered my sister's fees. Then, there was a time when the school fees came for the year and my mother didn't have enough. I had to sit for my exams. She borrowed the money from a good friend, who wasn't rich herself. Yet, she trusted my mother and knew how important my education was. She lent it knowing that it was possible my mother wouldn't pay back the money. Of course, my mother did. They're still good friends now. But that's the one thing that I remember because it enabled me to get an education and it was the kindest deed anyone had done for us.

You don't have to be rich to be generous.

Serena:

Indeed. Generosity is not correlated with how much money you have in the bank. The quality of a person's character has little to do with how rich you are. What a wonderful way to end this conversation. Thank you, Harmin.

18

Ning Chong

Investing in yourself is priceless.

Ning Chong is a connector of people to art and wants to make art accessible to all. She studied Economics and Economic History at the London School of Economics, and earned a Master's in Modern and Contemporary Art from Christie's Education in London. Ning is Founder of Family Office for Art, a premier advisory firm for fine art acquisition, and Founder of The Culture Story, a private space connecting people, building community, and promoting art. In this conversation, she ponders how different messages from her childhood shaped her views on money and how we can build wealth through art.

KEY INSIGHTS

When you collect with passion, knowledge, and commitment, you create wealth.

Build wealth through passionate, knowledgeable collecting. Whether it's art or any other valuable item, true wealth comes from collecting with intent and unwavering commitment. It's not about buying and selling for short-term gains; it's about the deep connection and understanding you develop through your collection.

Investing in yourself is priceless.

If you're presented with opportunities to enhance your skills and knowledge, seize them without hesitation. Your personal growth is an investment that pays lifelong dividends. It is important to spend money on yourself.

Own things with people who matter to you.

Share your passions and investments with those you care about. It's also a wonderful way to bond and share passions with those close to us and makes investing a lot more fun.

THE CONVERSATION

Serena:

A good place to start is to talk about what happens at home. If you could think back to when you were younger, was there any talk about money with your family?

Ning:

I lived in a household where my parents had two different ideas about money. My mom was frugal. She had a modest lifestyle and used to work part-time jobs to pay her way through tertiary education in the UK. She never went home, and practically stayed in the UK for five years studying and working at the same time because she was adamant in paying her own way.

My dad had it slightly easier. He was a Colombo Plan scholar with the government and belonged to the baby boomer generation. So, when he came back, he got a good job with the Economic Development Board of Singapore. He also did well as a stockbroker and gained a taste for the finer things in life. That's how art came into our life.

Since a young age, I've been surrounded by fine art objects and collectibles, and I never understood that these things cost a lot of money. I thought they were just beautiful things, and this was a normal life. But as I got older and went to the UK for school, which my parents paid for, I realized that this wasn't normal.

One of the deeper memories was when the pound was very expensive compared to the Singapore dollar. I would go on Skype with my parents every week and they would tell me to spend wisely. I'll run out of money and ask them to send over more, and they will tell me the exchange rate is now 'SD$3 to £1!'

It's interesting because this conveyed two messages to me. One was my mother telling me she worked hard so that I wouldn't have to suffer as much as she did. Then, my father would go to art galleries every other weekend. At that time, art wasn't seen as an alternative investment. It wasn't common; he was just buying things that appealed to his aesthetic and taste.

Serena:

How did that make you feel having two sets of messages?

Ning:

It was conflicting, and it still is because the imprint they had on me is permanent. I realized that as I got older, and now that I'm running my business with a young family at home, it's important to find your own voice. You need to make decisions you are comfortable with and not always have this guilt about spending money on certain things.

It's important to have some degree of financial literacy. That gave me the confidence to take care of my family and the household and run the business.

Serena:

Before we go into your current situation, could you share what it was like when you were younger? Did having conflicting messages from your parents shape your behaviour, especially since you're now working with your father?

Ning:

Even as a young girl, my father and I enjoyed shopping together. He would always give in and buy me nice things. My mother was more practical. When I started working and made certain purchases, I would stash away what I bought because I didn't want my mother to see it. I'd try to hide in my closet or under the bed before she came out of the bath, and deal with the discovery later. Even now I catch myself doing that!

It's an interesting process to go through. My priorities have shifted now, of course. I'm more discerning with these discretionary purchases. But I can imagine many young girls wanting to go after labels because it gives them confidence and a sense of identity. It helps you find your place in the world.

Serena:

Now, you run a business with your father. Was that a decision that came naturally?

Ning:

I didn't plan on becoming an entrepreneur. It happened gradually. Looking back, however, my dad has always been entrepreneurial. Since his retirement, he has been investing actively in start-ups. So, he's familiar with being an angel investor and gravitates towards art and lifestyle start-ups.

I didn't think I would be one of those start-ups though. My father continues to invest in me and our company. I also want to credit my husband. He might be a traditional fund manager, but he is really involved with entrepreneurs and start-ups too. So, somehow, I ended up with two important people in my life who are supportive of my entrepreneurial endeavours. They understand the challenges, pain, and relationships involved with investing. It's not a foreign concept to them, so it's been helpful because I think if I didn't have them, it would have been difficult to manage on my own.

Serena:

I'm glad you brought up your husband. Being married to a fund manager, how did that determine the money roles at home? Did the both of you have a discussion about this?

Ning:

Money isn't really something that you would talk about from day one. Currently, we have our separate accounts. But increasingly, we have to talk about finances because we have three young children under five, and we run our own businesses. So, one thing that my husband and I recently started is quarterly check-ins. We put these in our calendar and check in with each other, not just emotionally and spiritually, but also to talk about these hard topics. If we don't have this discipline, then nothing gets done because we have to deal with so many things—other people, things, and projects.

Serena:

What are some of these hard topics or questions?

Ning:

I apply the same approach I use in business and at home, which is deciding what our short- and long-term goals are. There are daily expenses to cover the household and the children. I take care of that. I'm the Chief Financial Officer, Chief Risk Officer, chauffeur, human resources, and everything else *[laughs]*. Then, the long-term goal is our nest egg. What is our approach and risk appetite? The both of us are not daily traders. We just invest and sit on it, while checking in every six months or a year. On this point, my husband and I are aligned.

One thing that I learned from my mother, which I've adopted, is the practice of giving our children a big ang bao during Chinese New Year. I remember going to the bank with her when I was in university and was shocked to see a decent sum of money in my account. When I asked her where this money was from, she said, 'It's from me! I've been quietly, diligently, giving you and your brothers a nice ang bao every year. It's mummy's money, not daddy's money.'

I've done that for our children. I explained this alien concept to my husband and told him I really would like to do it because we're already quite hands off, so this is one way to help them build something. So, when they turn eighteen or twenty-one, and want to take a gap year, they have something and can make their own choices.

Serena:

That's lovely because you're giving them options. You mentioned you read economics in university and now you're married to a fund manager. For money, was there any particularly good advice you received?

Ning:

There's no price to investing in yourself. You should also feel that you deserve it. Recently, during my maternity leave, I was hesitating about taking an online course even though I felt it applied to my business. I looked at the price and baulked because it was several thousand dollars for a four-week course. My father and husband told me I should do it because who else am I going to invest in? It's money well spent, and I shouldn't feel guilty. If anything, I should make the most out of it, get those contacts, do my notes, and complete the homework because that will set me apart.

So, I've realized that it's important to spend money on yourself.

Serena:

And it's important to continue learning as an entrepreneur while also remaining cost conscious. The best investment in the business is yourself. On this topic, what does money and wealth mean to you?

Ning:

I see money as fuel to drive our engines, whether family, leisure, work, business, or investments. I see two tracks, short- and long-term. In my line of business, where we advise people regarding their strategy for art acquisitions, there is a quote: 'If you buy and sell art, and know how to time the market, yes, you could make some money. But if you collect art or anything else of worth with passion, knowledge, and commitment, you create wealth.'

When you buy important historical or iconic works of art and have holding power instead of flipping for short-term gain, you create wealth in depth and significance of your collection. Everyone has a unique point of view in collecting. And at that point, you become a connoisseur because you are collecting with passion, knowledge, and a point of view.

I'm trying to weave this into the other aspects of my life. It applies equally to business and to life.

Wealth isn't just about the numbers. It's also enriching and food for your soul. It gives you the freedom to express yourself. A lot of collectors say that their collections reflect their personality, character, and points of view. It's an expression of themselves.

Serena:

Speaking about voice and point of view, what was the first item you collected?

Ning:

I've never looked at starting my collection until recently. For the past decade, I've been looking after my dad's physical and digital collection and properly inventoried it. He has over 300 pieces.

Then, a year ago, I read a book that inspired me and decided I wanted to start my collection because I now have a point of view that differs from my father's preference, aesthetic, and taste.

So, a confession. I was heavily pregnant with my third child and had this insane desire to buy something! I concentrated on female artists. It's nothing new, but I wanted to give my collection more focus and be really intentional.

One of the first works I bought was by a self-taught Indonesian artist called Murni. Her works are colourful and graphic, almost indigenous. I also recently co-bought another work with my youngest brother who is becoming interested in collecting art. He usually invests in whisky and sake, but he said he wanted to learn properly about my world.

I told him that there's no shortcut, and he has to do his homework. He has to go out there to the galleries and the museums. I didn't expect this, to be honest, and I tried to keep these conversations off the dinner table because otherwise, my father and I would monopolize the conversation and only talk about art. My brother and I went to an auction preview together, and I shortlisted several pieces and explained the track records. The next day, before the auction, my brother texted me to say he also liked a piece and asked if we could co-purchase it. During the auction, I wasn't sure if we could get it because the auction was very active, but combining forces meant we could go further. We had to get the condition report, decide who was to be on the phone, or to be present, for the bid. That was quite fun!

Now, we have to decide who's going to hang the work, at his place or my place, or that it would be rotational *[laughs]*.

Serena:

You also co-own some pieces with your husband. Tell us about that.

Ning:

Since we have been together, inevitably some of my art tendencies have rubbed off him. I did a big show for an American street artist, Futura, and it was beautiful. He's a graffiti street artist, but his repertoire is so much more. He's well known in North America and Paris. The latter is because of Agnes B. They used to do a lot of exchanges in the eighties and nineties. My show was his debut exhibition in Singapore and featured thirty recent works.

My husband came to the show and was looking at the pieces. At the end of the exhibition, he told me he really liked a piece and bought it. I didn't pressure him at all. Lo and behold, five years later, there was a request for a loan, which I facilitated. So, the piece is currently exhibited at the ArtScience Museum in Singapore, and the exhibition is called 'Sneakertopia: Step into Street Culture'.

Serena:

Can you also share with us how art and culture is part of our daily life here in Singapore?

Ning:

Lots of valuable pieces surround us, and all of us have encountered art. We just don't realize it. The Art in Transit programme is Singapore's largest public art showcase. Local artists are commissioned to create original artworks and there are over 400 pieces in our MRT stations. The artwork represents that precinct, and the station is built around art.

Serena:

Coming back to women and money, you mention you've been blessed by so many people around you. What is the kindest money-related thing anyone has done for you?

Ning:

When I started working, my mother told me she expected me to contribute to the household. She asked me to set aside 15 or 20 per cent, and I did it, albeit begrudgingly. Then, she told me that after I had done that, I should set aside another 15 or 20 per cent for savings.

I got older and started my own businesses, and my mother was unfortunately diagnosed with lung cancer and passed away about two years ago. Before she passed, she told me she had saved all that money I had given her. She never used it for household expenses. I was surprised because I thought the money was gone. But she knew me so well. She wanted me to save more for myself and it was such a blessing because I used the money to help the businesses and ease some of the financial burden.

It was the kindest thing anyone has ever done for me.

Serena:

What is the one thing that you wish for yourself from a financial perspective?

Ning:

Be easy on myself. Life is a marathon and having my account sorted today doesn't mean that I can close my eyes for the next two years. There'll be difficulties and I cannot always make the right call. I am okay with that now.

Serena:

That's a great approach to adopt and you always come across as calm and poised. The topic of women and money is such an important one and as you rightly recommended, we can go so much deeper in a safe environment free from judgement. I feel we achieved that. This has been such a pleasure, Ning.

19

Joanne Ho

Money is like a small seed you plant.

Joanne Ho is a seasoned professional in the communications industry and one of the pioneers. The founder at Brand Cellar, a PR and marketing communications firm based in Singapore, has built an impressive 500-strong client roster that includes prestigious names like the Michelin Guide, the Japanese government, and renowned wine critic Robert Parker. Beneath all her achievements, Joanne cares deeply about lifting and helping the people around her and is fully committed to building businesses with the right people. In this section, we delve into Joanne's insights on entrepreneurship, people, and money.

KEY INSIGHTS

Money is like a small seed you plant.

Money goes beyond just owning and accumulating it; it's about sharing and creating something greater. Think of money as tiny seeds that you sow. The more seeds you plant, the more your garden flourishes. If your intentions are noble and you genuinely aim to assist others, financial rewards will naturally follow.

Being rich is feeling content with what you have.

Money isn't just about numbers, it's also deeply tied to your sense of contentment. In today's world, where social media often leads to comparisons, it's easy to feel inadequate. But instead of measuring your worth by possessions, focus on your daily happiness. Love and appreciate yourself because life is too short to be constantly chasing more.

Wealth is about investing in the right people and businesses.

Success often hinges on doing the right business with the right people. It's about having your mindset in the right place and ensuring that your team is fully aligned with your vision. It's 1 per cent vision and 99 per cent alignment. When you and your team are on the same page, incredible things can happen.

THE CONVERSATION

Sharon:

Could you introduce yourself to us?

Joanne:

I've been running my own PR agency for the last twenty-five years, so we have many, many amazing clients, such as the Michelin Guide since they landed in Singapore and Robert Parker in blogging. We have about 500 F&B clients through the years, and we've served Japanese governments and the prefectures too. I'm so honoured to work with them. It's been a fun journey, and I feel blessed to have a job I love.

Sharon:

How was money or business discussed in your household when you were a child?

Joanne:

Both my parents are entrepreneurs. My father is a journalist, and my mother owned her own advertising agency. She always encouraged me to have an entrepreneurial spirit. We talk about money openly, but we don't obsess about it. When I was in primary school, my mother didn't want to give pocket money to me during the school holidays. She asked me to earn it. So, I sold Christmas cards. And I was empowered with three unique selling points I still remember vividly.

Sharon:

What are the three selling points?

Joanne:

First, you get free hot stamping for your first Christmas card. Second, they are beautiful and have selected designs. Finally, we can do it incredibly quickly for you. I carried a toolbox and walked up and down International Plaza knocking on doors. That was my first sales job. I was only ten.

Sharon:

Were you all alone in that job?

Joanne:

I was alone, and the first three doors were scary. When you knock on the door and they open, you must say hello and get their interest within the first three to five seconds. I got rejected the first two times, and then, the third let me in. When you start selling, it catches on. I became the top salesperson during those holidays.

It taught me a lot of things. For example, instead of walking up, I started on the top floor and walked down. I also memorized the elevator pitch and understood how to catch people's interest.

Sharon:

What was your mindset then? How do you condition yourself to even do it?

Joanne:

Well, I had no money, so it was staying at home and doing nothing or that, so I might as well do the latter. It was also a lot of fun because I got a couple of friends to join me. We had a great school holiday.

That's how my mom taught me. It made me feel that having money is always up to you and your creativity and hard work.

Sharon:

Your mother is progressive and ran her own marketing agency back in those days. What are some lessons you have learnt from her? Also, she advertised feet!

Joanne:

People always thought I would take over her agency, but the market was changing back then. Then I met this man who became our client who told me, 'Joanne, I think you are cut out for PR.'

I didn't know what PR was. He explained it to me and taught me how to do it. I will never forget my first client, jet peddlers. Then, he left for New York, and I had to host every journalist on my own. I never studied PR, I studied accountancy. But I did everything myself and built the firm.

My mother taught me that as long as you worked hard and had grit and integrity, good people will always follow you no matter what you do.

Sharon:

So, you really started from the ground up, right? Since you were ten, you were already making sales calls. How do you take rejection? That's also an interesting life lesson.

Joanne:

As an entrepreneur, we never take rejection to heart, right? I just went to sleep and told myself that if it wasn't because of the three selling points I did wrong, I would get over it the next morning.

Sharon:

You could put your failures in context, which is a great way to get over your supposed failures. Entrepreneurialism is a completely different ballgame, and it's not always about the pursuit of money.

Joanne:

It's actually about doing the right business with the right people. Then, money will follow. Put your mind at the right place and ensure that your team is aligned. I believe that it's 1 percent vision, and 99 per cent alignment. If you and your team are on the same page, magic will happen.

Sharon:

How do you decide on the finances in your household between you and your husband?

Joanne:

It's a joint decision. My husband manages the day-to-day stuff, and I am in charge of growing the pot, which means growing the team. When my team is good, they can give the best service so that the growth multiplies. I have other businesses and I empower my partners. One lesson I learned through the years is to put the best person at the best spot and they will shine. When everyone shines, then you have magic.

Sharon:

What are some of the money habits that you impart to your children?

Joanne:

We'll spend within our means. For example, if we go for a holiday, we always plan where to stay and what to eat. But we don't overplan it.

We love beautiful food and experiences, and we believe in living in the moment. But for the young children, I always remind them to be thrifty and save for the rainy day. They have to learn how to plan. I believe children will look at you and then become you, both for the small and big things. The way you treat other people, your parents, and even your helper will be how the children will treat you.

Sharon:

There is so much we can and need to impart to our children on saving and investing, but nothing beats making them work for their money!

Joanne:

My daughter started working at my agency when she was fourteen. In the initial years, I knew it was tough on her. I would be difficult on her to the point that my husband said that I should go easy because he thinks she didn't like it. But she learned a lot and was great at her work. She also came back nearly every year, and I could see my colleagues enjoyed working with her.

Even though the office knew that she was my daughter, they saw me telling her off. So, there was no favouritism. She even told me it's good that she went because she learned what to do and what not to do from a young age, and to work hard. It's definitely a gift because once, her boss called me to say that she's the one intern to make the biggest difference in such a short time.

I was thrilled for her when I got the call. But it's the start of a journey and I'm not sure where it will lead. However, having that real-life experience and ability to perform under pressure is not something every young person can handle.

Sharon:

What kind of legacy or business do you want to leave to your children?

Joanne:

I will definitely not leave my agency business to my children. I told my team that my legacy will be talented people. It's a people business, right? When I build relationships, I empower my team, which then benefits my clients. I can't be here forever. I'm already fifty, although I feel young and still want to work because working keeps me young and focused. But I want to do less. I hope to work less and play a bit more.

So, I'm building a team that can take over both monetarily and responsibly. Then I can pass the firm to this creative and amazing group of people. I have thought about succession planning and getting a second bench in the management team.

Sharon:

What is money to you?

Joanne:

Money isn't just about physical ownership but sharing. When I create new businesses, you can create something amazing if you can find superb partners. Even if you're just a small part of it, you're a small part of something amazing.

If I can think of an analogy, money is like a small seed you plant. The more seeds you plant, the more growth you'll have, and soon you'll have a full garden. I've never chased money. If your heart is at the right place and you are doing things to help people, whether clients or friends, the money will come. That's how I view life. If I can help, I will, even if it's just a phone call for a connection or an email. You don't have to give me anything. When you do that, then down the road, it'll pay off, like a seesaw.

Through the years, I have never advertised my business. It's purely been through word-of-mouth referrals. Karma is give and take, and I believe in building good karma.

Sharon:

The PR industry is incredibly competitive. I wanted to ask how you balance the perception of pricing yourself competitively with helping people? How do you reconcile this?

Joanne:

It's really just about doing your best because when people pay you a certain amount, you just have to deliver that value. But when you over-deliver, the person will be happy and spread to another person. Delivering significant results is critical in the industry and for my reputation. Like, for this book, for example, so many women came to help you because they believed in you. When you asked me, I immediately said yes.

Sharon:

I'm so grateful for that. We wanted to have this book as a platform for women to come out and share their stories, successes, and failures because all of us are from different industries. So, sometimes, we need to hear from others to help us look at life from different perspectives. How do you think about investing? Are you a risk taker?

Joanne:

I'm quite risk averse. I leave a lot of my investing to my private banker. We have bonds, and for investments, I like to buy property. I know it's old school. I keep 10 to 15 per cent for exciting investments. Occasionally, I've been an angel investor in some companies. My limit is just $50,000 though and I don't do a lot. I had one that did well during Covid-19. They were selling a lot of food items and have branched out to more than just food, so that's quite interesting. I'm not really involved in the business and have a few amazing partners running it.

Sharon:

Do you invest in areas that you are less familiar with, like technology?

Joanne:

Lesser, and I think it's because I have fewer opportunities. I might get more after talking to you, but I don't have a lot of debt coming my way. It's interesting to invest in companies because sometimes you find the good ones that fly, and you make new friends along the way.

Sharon:

How do you think about your own investment portfolio?

Joanne:

So, the allocation from safer to riskier assets is big. I must think about it properly and go at the right time. Most of what I have, however, I invest into my business because it's still the most important part of my life. I spend 90 per cent of my time and energy in my business and I believe it's typical for enterprises to reinvest a lot of their earnings into their businesses to get the biggest payoff. It is your baby.

Sharon:

You mentioned before that you are a saver. So, what do you spend your money on?

Joanne:

Family holidays are such precious experiences especially when the kids are growing up. As entrepreneurs, we are incredibly busy every day, so holidays are the only time you can spend with your children. Children of entrepreneurs know weekends can be very busy, which is why I will always spend on travel experiences.

I believe that money is also about feeling content because there will always be people who are richer than you. I always feel like I'm lucky. Even when I was a student with only $50 in the bank, I felt fine. I understood that life is a process, and you had to be content at every stage.

We live in a world now where we always compare because of social media. If you look at what you own and what you buy, how do you have this mindset that you will be content with what you have? My measure is caring about how happy I am every day.

Love yourself. That's incredibly important. We only live once. Being content and happy is important because we never know if something happens tomorrow that changes your life. So being happy is just a gift that we should treasure.

Sharon:

Yeah, I think that's a unique take on life or being content with what you have. Life is so volatile and none of us know what's going to happen.

Joanne:

Yeah. And I think we just worry too much about different things and lose sight of what is really important today. Sometimes, I will be in a difficult situation and lose myself in it, but after a few days, I pull myself out of that. I talk to positive friends and remind myself that if I still have my health and my family, nothing can be worse than that. Then I climb up the hill again.

Sharon:

If a billion dollars land in your bank account tomorrow, what would you do with that money?

Joanne:

I wouldn't change my lifestyle because if I make big changes, it will make me unhappy if I lose the money in the future and I want more and more. I would rather use the money to help other people, such as within my team and my family. After I settle them, then I'll reach out to other people. I find it more real if I donate to charity and I can see the tangible help that is being given out. You can see how you're affecting them. I'll invest the rest.

Sharon:

What is the kindest money-related act someone has done for you?

Joanne:

If I think back on my life, it would be that man who taught me PR. He didn't give me any monetary benefits, but he got me my first job and taught me how to do it. He believed in my potential. There were several other people who gave me big jobs and projects that helped to get people to notice me. I've met a lot of good people along the way who helped to make that difference. Without them, I don't think I could have made it to who I am today.

I'm also grateful to my team, many of whom have worked with me for several years. We have a great relationship. While I might be the boss, we are partners in this because we help each other grow the firm to what it is today.

Everyone has helped me in many little ways, and I think gratefulness is something that I always want to keep because I think it's important to always be grateful to everyone around you who has helped you become a better person.

Sharon:

Yes, that's true. This book is about women and money and the fact that women don't talk enough about money.

Joanne:

It's not wrong to talk about money. We need money to survive. It's just your view towards it. It must be with the right values and mindset. If the money you take with you is honourable, then it's yours. If the money is dishonourable, like snatching someone's client, that money will not last. I've seen it happen. Somehow, one day, you have to return the money.

I talk about money to my close friends and what we should do with it. Everyone's view is different and talking to many people will help you refine your view on it. But people get unhappy if you are too obsessed with it. There's a fine line.

Sharon:

We have heard so much from your experiences in PR and entrepreneurship and your refreshing philosophy on money. Thank you, Joanne!

20

Dr Jade Kua

Mental and emotional health is priceless.

Dr Jade Kua mans the frontlines of critical care in public hospitals and runs wellness-focused businesses. Her approach to wellness is rooted in practical mindfulness. She understands that true wealth encompasses not only financial prosperity but also the well-being of our mind and body. She also extends the reach of mindful practices into our everyday lives through various channels, including children's books and skincare lines. In this conversation, Dr Kua discusses the importance of balancing your mental and emotional well-being with the pursuit of prosperity.

KEY INSIGHTS

Mental and emotional health is the new wealth.

No amount of money can replace emotional and mental well-being. People are becoming more open to discussing mental health, recognizing that it's an issue that affects many. Prioritizing mental health and well-being can lead to a richer, more meaningful life. It's a reminder that health truly is the most valuable form of wealth, and it's something worth talking about openly and honestly.

Spending is not a bad thing.

Money often comes with complex emotions, and sometimes you might feel guilty about spending, even when you can afford it. However, it's crucial to realize that spending itself isn't inherently bad. What truly matters is how you choose to allocate your resources and what aligns with your values. Decisions related to money, especially investing, often come with emotions. It's beneficial to expose yourself to these experiences and not be afraid to make mistakes.

Know your value and push for your worth.

Negotiating for fair compensation can often feel uncomfortable, but there's a better way to approach it. It's crucial to be less emotional about these discussions. One valuable mindset shift is to embrace the idea of a willing seller and a willing buyer. If someone isn't keen on what you offer at your price, that's okay. It doesn't mean you've failed; it's just a part of life. If you're comfortable with your value and someone else prefers to allocate their resources differently, it's fine to let them walk away too.

THE CONVERSATION

Sharon:

How about a quick introduction?

Jade:

I work mainly around life and wellness. I cut my teeth in medicine as a senior consultant and paediatric emergency medicine, and work in public healthcare and it's been overwhelming. Somewhere in between, I spent a few years building several small businesses. One is a skincare company that takes heritage secrets and infuses it with modern technology. I also have a company focused on art, including a children's book, *Good Night Marion*, that is dedicated to parents and caregivers who struggle to put their children to bed. The book is in bookstores. And finally, the business that I spend most of my time on is Jade Like and Wellness. It's a coaching company focusing on health, life, and high-performance coaching for teens. It has been quite the journey. I've never been so nerdy in my life! I spent several years studying and clearing exams and getting fully accredited and qualified to coach, so I'm thrilled to be where I am today.

Sharon:

Wow, that's a powerful introduction! As a mother of six children, how do you balance it all?

Jade:

They rebalance themselves, to be honest. I have three young children that I do confinement for, and I have three older stepchildren that I didn't do confinement for. They're about to enter the workforce, so they help a lot at home with the younger children. The latter adore them and want to be like them. Everyone is independent with their own chores. The older children are thinking about careers and the future because they hear the older generation talk about it so much. So, in that respect, I feel like the conversations we have at home are so important in shaping young people's lives.

Sharon:

What are some conversations you have with the children about money?

Jade:

Well, a question that comes up after the Chinese New Year is, 'Mom, what happened to my money?' I think it's a wonderful question. So, we have a conversation about how much to spend and how much to put in the bank for savings. Then we discuss what we take out to put into investments for them. I've explored several investment platforms and allocated separate ones for each child before talking to them about it. It's interesting because I talk to them about investing in Netflix, for example, it's something they understand and perhaps use too much. But we talk to them about something else that might be a great idea, but they don't understand, we'll read the company profile and to get a better picture. Sometimes, it's still unclear what they do. But at least they learn more, and it feels real. While we're dealing with small amounts of money, it's still real for the children.

Sharon:

How do you talk to your children about savings and investments?

Jade:

Well, it's all about what we want to do with our resources. Spending is not necessarily a bad thing. You want to spend on education, classes, or a holiday. What do you consider an expense versus an investment? Saving is a way to grow our money slowly. Investing is more about growing your money meaningfully.

Beyond money, I also talk to them about time. These are disposable resources, so what do you want to do with it? Time is yours to use.

We also talk to them about various cycles. For example, when you make a decision that doesn't pan out, that's all right. Then we take a bit of money out to buy ice cream.

Then they have to decide. Do you stick it out and wait for another cycle? Or you decide that it's too scary and feel uncomfortable? These are the emotions that come with investing and it's great to expose them to these. It's also important to think about the process of investing and the outcomes. I think it's okay for children to lose a bit of money so that they understand the consequences and realize it's okay to make mistakes.

Sharon:

Since you're incredibly proactive about managing money, I'm curious to know what it was like for you growing up. Did your family talk a lot about money and business to you? What was your first interaction with money?

Jade:

It's hard to remember the first interaction. I had a rich childhood with lots of opportunities to travel, take wonderful lessons in music, art, and dance, and attend concerts. It was wonderful.

But I was also aware of the cost of things and what it would take to get there. My father was a doctor who taught us that if you work harder, you get more money and if you take time off, then it would be harder with less money.

They would also talk to us about insurance, investments, and savings. I appreciated that. It was one of the biggest lessons to learn that money is a great thing and can help you get far. I don't think I've ever told my parents that. I'm grateful that they talked about money as a part of life. You had to work hard, but they were also comfortable talking about investing and saving.

Sharon:

It's amazing how you talk to your children about money. They see the values and you working hard. Therefore, you do so many things, right? Is it something that will help you get more out of life?

Jade:

I guess I focus on the areas that interest me, which is health and wellness. Other than emergency medicine, which is a lot about physical health and the extremes, I'm also very interested in emotional and mental wellness. Right now, I think we're in a phase where people are more open to talking about the problem because it could be endemic. Many people experience isolation and depression, yet it was almost a stigma. People didn't want to feel like they had to talk about it.

If you had to discuss mental illness, there must be something wrong with you. And people don't want to have that feeling of weakness and exposure. I thought that was something worth bringing up. With every business venture I do, I go back to my core values: looking at things important to me.

When I started writing my book about mindful conversations with children, I felt this was important because I want to shield children. We want to build enough assets for them. We want them to head to a good university, have a wonderful career, and find an excellent partner. Then we can die happy. But that's not how life goes, unfortunately. It's more important to be prepared. I work in emergency medicine, so I know I can die at any point. I want my children to make excellent decisions independently.

What better way than in practice, right? It's helpful for them to be comfortable with their emotions and make better decisions for the future. All the things I do are focused on that concept of health and wellness, what it's like for me, and what I want for the kids so that they can live well without me.

Sharon:

How do you view money versus wealth?

Jade:

I think of it in the same terms as knowledge and wisdom. Money is one aspect that helps to create wealth, and being wealthy is a powerful and wonderful thing. But wealth is more than just the numbers. If you don't have peace of mind, it means nothing. It's more important to have financial freedom, which you can achieve with a lot less money but have the freedom to do the things you've always wanted to do. If you build your life around just gaining more money, it's difficult to live.

I think that's what my clients appreciate about coaching. I don't position myself as a money or health expert. But people come to me for coaching because I give them a different perspective, let them learn a bit more about themselves and the situation, and guide them to move forward to achieve their health and life goals.

Sharon:

What does money mean to you?

Jade:

I think my views about money accurately portray the different milestones of my life. At one point I focused on creating wealth. If you use wealth as an understanding for money, then in this instance, it was about growing it to a point where I didn't have to think about it all the time and just let it grow on its own. So, I had to make good investment decisions.

But now I feel like I'm at a point in my life where I'm happy to spend it in order to get happiness in other aspects of my life. For example, I'm happy to spend it to travel, to get a better experience, and to save time. Right now, I feel like the resource that's most depleted is time. I can do a lot of projects on my own, but if I can spend money to hire staff to do it more efficiently or implement technology, I would do it because time is the most precious resource now.

Sharon:

There are many emotions tied to money and specifically spending money. What are some of your emotions around money?

Jade:

I think this relates to how we've built our portfolios to a point where you feel you can buy a nice painting or a piece of jewellery and tell yourself it's an investment. It definitely makes you feel good, which isn't a bad thing too. But what about after? Do I feel that sense of regret? I've had that before. We have to move on from our emotions and a huge part of this is mapping everything out. That is part of our portfolio of emotions.

Sharon:

So how do you look at your own portfolio of investments and risk?

Jade:

My mortality plays a big part now. I've become more prudent in my investments, but it's also because I've been through so many cycles like this and know that there will be many more cycles to come. It's allowed me to be comfortable with technology and come to terms with things. That's why I have these conversations with my kids so that they have time to process their reactions.

You can take more risks when you are younger. At my age, I'm definitely a lot more prudent with income-generating assets. Investing is an emotional journey, and that's how we grow as a person.

Sharon:

The wellness aspects also tie everything together, right? You're now fairly comfortable and achieved a lot in your life. How do you plan for the future and for your children?

Jade:

My younger children try to listen in on our conversations. Sometimes, I get them to draw their feelings out so we can process it, but I've been driving them around and having them around as much as I can so that they can make more decisions on their own in the future. This is a bit of a gamble and they're not investing with immense sums but it's still real money. I've spent less time on financial conversations with them now because I've been busy with my businesses.

Sharon:

What are some of the money lessons you've learned over the years?

Jade:

As a business owner, I have learned to take calculated risks with available information. Every dollar counts when you're running your own business. But you also have to be more holistic when you look at finance and business growth.

It's always helpful to go back to your values when you're trying to make a big life decision. Those values can contribute that bit of strength because those will really help to guide the compass. So, if your strength is something big like strategy, you might think you can do it, but eventually overextend yourself.

You try to manage that. Play to your strengths when you look at your finances, then you can make big decisions and minimize the chances of making missteps. You'll also be able to process emotions better.

Sharon:

Are there specific mistakes that you would like to point out?

Jade:

It's probably when we invest in things that we know nothing about, But we have the fear of missing out and let envious emotions override reason. You might not get it, but you want to go along for the ride and the timing didn't work out. That can be tough to rationalize. But if you had more knowledge, you'd be more comfortable with your decision.

Sharon:

Do you talk about money with other women?

Jade:

We would discuss costs or certain decisions. But I feel like we don't really talk about money with other people. This is quite rampant in my professional community. We don't discuss salaries and other similar topics.

In fact, you'd be considered quite a money-minded, materialistic person if you want to talk too much about money, if at all. You're supposed to just put your head down and work, and not to think about issues like working for free or overtime or doing too many things where you might overextend yourself.

That was the situation I grew up in, so I never really talked about money with friends. That's why I'm glad we're having this conversation because there is a gap there where we don't talk about money with our friends and peers.

Sharon:

Let's talk about that. How do you place a dollar value on your work as a coach?

Jade:

That is one of the hottest topics that I have for myself. I felt uncomfortable when setting my rates. I looked around to figure out how other people did it, and I realized they were almost clinical about it.

I had to adopt the mentality of willing seller, willing buyer. If you're not keen, I can spend my time doing something else. Previously, I thought I couldn't do that because I would feel like a failure if someone walked away. But now I know that is part of life.

If you're comfortable with what you feel and other people would rather spend their resources elsewhere, then let them walk away and everyone's happy. It's not meant to be personal either and I have learned to be comfortable with that. And if it gets to a point that everyone wants a piece of the pie and has lowered their rates, then do something else.

Sharon:

That perception of value is interesting. What is the reason coaching is seen as such?

Jade:

So, some of that might be simply community education. I think many people are reluctant to pay for something related to mental wellness. They feel like it should be free or something like $30 an hour and seem offended that you have to pay for mental illness. But this person might dine in restaurants and buy designer bags. You get a sense of how their mind approaches these issues.

Some of that might be to do with education and understanding people who are advocates for wellness professionals in this area, many of them train and invest to be where they are now. If you respect that and the help that they render, then what's the fuss?

Spending on wellness really saves you the money that you might have to spend in the future when you get ill and have to be treated.

Sharon:

Do you think men and women have different perspectives on money?

Jade:

Yes, I do. And I think I can learn from a man's perspective. Why is it so easy for them to say a price and walk away, and then go for a beer and play golf? They're so relaxed about it. That was a lesson. I needed to learn how to process that emotional guilt I feel about calling out the right price and perceiving my value. I don't want to allocate gender to that, but I definitely see a lot more of this in men who understand what they are worth.

I think they're just more well versed in asking for higher fees. They are unemotional when talking about the price of a car or a house while ladies attach emotions to money.

We need to remove that emotion and the feeling that having these conversations makes us seem materialistic. We all work hard for our money and have built up our feminism.

Sharon:

How comfortable are you with talking about money?

Jade:

I don't know how to bring out questions around money. It's quite obvious from this chat. When we talk about broad concepts, such as health and wellness or my children, I feel like my energy is higher. I can speak more confidently about it. But when I'm recalling my own experiences about how I value myself, I feel like I'm sinking into my soul. My voice comes down and I can't look you in the eye. It's about building up that habit of talking about money.

Sharon:

You're right. We have done several interviews and there is always that resistance that we get from our interviewees, many of whom are embarrassed about some questions. One of them is this question. What would you do with a billion dollars?

Jade:

This is pretty funny. But when we were kids and we would watch a Miss Universe contest, and all the contestants would say, 'world peace', I thought it was such a silly thing to say. I thought it was more important to work towards something a bit more substantial than world peace.

Now, world peace looks like a great wish, especially when the traditional political superpowers are destabilized, and no one is really sure what is happening. Peace is not too bad, and a billion dollars could secure that. But I feel like that would mean having global conversations. So, a tech-enabled system involving the global community and human connection where people can have frank conversations in a brave space could go a long way.

There's also vast inequality. So, if there was a way to bridge that gap and have real meaningful work on a global scale in equality using that money, that would be great. But it won't be easy.

Sharon:

That's a brilliant answer. But I'm also curious. What would you do for your children and family? I guess I'm trying to get a sense of something more realistic.

Jade:

That's a good point. I guess it's because a billion dollars seems so much that you want to solve a big problem. But, if I had to start with myself, I guess I would buy back the beautiful properties that we sold in the past, such as some family shophouses. It would be so nice to have them back.

Then, I would give back to the community. That's a non-negotiable to me. When we consider all the experiences and mentors in our lives, it's only natural that we have to give back, whether it's in service or money.

So, I sit on a couple of boards, one of which is the Mental Health Film Festival. We seek to increase conversations on mental health through film because films are extremely powerful. That billion could go towards this community and understanding that we're part of a bigger wider system.

Sharon:

What is the kindest money-related thing someone has done for you?

Jade:

Every Chinese New Year, we have this vegetarian breakfast ceremony. It's an annual event and the kids get packets of money and I feel like that money is wrapped in kindness because it comes with blessings from the older generation to the younger ones who are the beacons of hope for the future.

This money is given to you by a family member who gives you good wishes, and while some of these wishes might be stereotypical, the meaning behind them is so powerful. That's genuine kindness, and it's a tradition I hope to continue. It's not just about the dollars and cents, and it's a different way of looking at kindness.

Sharon:

If I can ask you a more reflective question, what money advice would you give to your twenty-year-old self?

Jade:

I feel like I wouldn't change things because I know I made certain decisions based on where I was in my life. It wasn't just the numbers in my bank account but the emotions I felt.

What was meaningful were my interests. Sometimes, my money went to scuba diving or water sports, which I fell in love with. So, the money went towards a great time and not saving or investing. But that's okay. As I grew older, I spent little on buying stuff. I was saving as much as I could. Looking back, I could have probably afforded to spend more to give myself a break. But I felt like I couldn't until I got to a certain amount and felt more comfortable after that.

I know why I did certain things back then. Some turn out to be significant decisions, others could be better, but at least I did everything right. So, I'd go back to tell myself that it's all going to work out. Just trust your instincts and values and spend a bit more enjoying life and be comfortable with these decisions because sometimes I would spend a long time pondering my decisions. Then things didn't work out and I would spend a bit of time in that rut wondering what I should have done instead. To a certain extent, that retrospective thinking is good, but only to a certain point. So, I would tell myself to move on and don't spend even more time in that unhealthy space.

Sharon:

I really enjoyed our conversation, Jade.

21

Catherine Loh

When you believe you are going to have money,
it will come your way.

Catherine Loh has held leadership roles in prominent financial institutions such as Nomura, Lehman Brothers, and Goldman Sachs. Her journey began at the Government of Singapore Investment Corporation, but her true calling emerged when she joined the Community Foundation of Singapore (CFS). Since 2012, Catherine has steered CFS towards strategic growth, expanding donor funds, increasing donations, and amplifying social impact through effective grant-making. In this section, we explore how Catherine's dedication to philanthropy has left an indelible mark on the landscape.

KEY INSIGHTS

When you believe that you are going to have money, it will come your way.

Women underestimate the power they have to shape their financial realities. Having a strong desire to be financially successful can be a catalyst for abundance. Consider the example of saving for a significant financial goal, such as buying a home. If you believe strongly that you will achieve this goal, you're more likely to take consistent, disciplined actions to make it happen.

Saving and investing go hand in hand.

Since you were little, your folks probably talked about saving for a rainy day. But saving is just one side of the story. In the long run, it's not only about how much you save, but also how you put that money to work. Savings means your money sits in the bank, while investing means your money works for you. Make your money work for you.

With great (or small) wealth comes great responsibility.

Wealth can be a powerful tool for positive change, whether it's uplifting those in need or actively taking part in efforts to save our planet. This perspective underscores the profound opportunity wealth presents—to not only enhance your life but leave a lasting legacy that reflects your values and contributes to a better world.

THE CONVERSATION

Sharon:

You've spent a lot of time in the financial world with Goldman Sachs and Lehman Brothers before joining the Community Foundation of Singapore to help with strategic philanthropy. What's your earliest memory of money?

Catherine:

My earliest memory of money was receiving ang baos during Chinese New Year. And I have always been taught to save up the money from them. I grew up with my grandparents, who lived during World War II and shared how life was tough back then. They inculcated the value of saving for a rainy day in me. I feel blessed, however, to not have to face any real financial hardship. I knew money wasn't easy to earn. My father worked hard in the construction industry, so we learned to be careful with money.

But I also know that money is a tool and should be used when there is a need to. Saving enough helps me to use it when the right opportunity arises. And I feel that having money is security.

Sharon:

Saving is your first impression of money. How do you talk about money at home with your spouse and children?

Catherine:

We talk about money openly at home, especially when we make big financial decisions such as major purchases and investments. Now that the children are older, we also talk about investments. It's especially important now with online shopping. We have to teach them about instant gratification and to be careful not to get carried away by the impulse to buy. How do we help them realize that money should be saved instead of spending frivolously? It can be destructive.

Sharon:

How did your children get the understanding of how to invest?

Catherine:

It is amazing because children can learn so much from multiple channels. A lot of the information we used to get were from books. We didn't even have documentaries, let alone YouTube interviews. Now, everything is online and available for free. You can do research for any of your interests.

My son is interested in gaming and told me about the potential demand for computer chips. My daughter is more interested in healthcare, and she's shared several companies out there that produce innovative medical products. It's something I'm interested in as well because I believe that healthcare will grow in the future, especially in an ageing society.

Sharon:

It's great that you're learning from your children. They're giving you a different perspective on investing. It's probably because of the conversations you've had with them in the past about what's interesting out there. What are the values you hold regarding money that you want to pass to your children?

Catherine:

Saving is definitely part of it. The other angle is investing. I'd definitely want to teach them eventually about risk. There's always that trade-off between risk and return, and the risks grow whenever there are promises of high returns. We're in different stages of life now. I'm in early retirement while they are just about to start their lives, so we would have different risk profiles.

I explain to them that everyone has different approaches and risk appetites. They have to find a level that they are comfortable in and not get too carried away by social media or whatever is trendy at the moment.

Sharon:

So, what is your investment portfolio like? You've mentioned that you've changed over the years.

Catherine:

When I first started, I was a lot more aggressive. I would take on more risk and leverage myself more because I know I have a longer runway, working for the next twenty to thirty years. We both started in the financial sector, so you hear a lot of trade chatter and investment advice in the dealing room. So, I always knew I needed to invest during this opportune timing. Now that I'm older, I think about how much is enough. If I have a sum of money that is enough, then I'd put that sum aside and reduce the risk in my debt portfolio because I want to make sure I don't lose too much.

At the same time, I need to generate a certain return not eroded by time, so I would look into new ideas and technological advancements. For example, I was sharing about medical care and how it would be vastly different in the future compared to today.

Sharon:

You've mentioned savings several times and we're talking about risk now. What does money mean to you from an emotional perspective?

Catherine:

It's important to understand that money is only a medium of exchange and not the be-all and end-all. I think I have a positive attitude towards money because if you believe you are going to have money, it will come your way. That's true. And I believe that if you are doing your job well, no matter what you are doing, you will be rewarded monetarily or otherwise.

So, a healthy work ethic is important. Money has to be earned. It doesn't fall from the sky. Invest it prudently, but also spend on necessary things, like providing for the family. If you have enough to spare, too, then help people in your community.

Sharon:

On that point, how have you talked about that with potential donors from the Community Foundation of Singapore to broach the idea of money, wealth, and giving?

Catherine:

I come with this idea that with great power comes great responsibility. And for those who are blessed with wealth, I ask if the money could be put to better use than just on your own consumption? Could it be used to invest in the future of not just your children but the entire community? Or could the money uplift those who need a helping hand? Perhaps even create a better world? Now, with all this talk about sustainability, how can we save the planet?

So, potential donors have the option to spend on themselves, their families, or the larger community. For those with wealth, it can be really appealing to do something meaningful that speaks to them and their core values.

Sharon:

So, what is your view of money and wealth?

Catherine:

Well, as I shared earlier, money is a medium of exchange. Wealth, however, is the emotions you get when you spend it. Money doesn't equate to wealth. Being wealthy is having that sense of contentment and gratitude with what you have. That's the source of happiness, right? Even if you have a lot of money and spend it, you'll still feel envious, jealous, or inadequate when you see someone else doing better if you don't feel content. That is a source of wealth.

Sharon:

Are you in that contented state of mind, though?

Catherine:

I would like to think so *[laughs]*.

Sharon:

If you have a billion dollars sitting in your account, what would you do with it?

Catherine:

I'd take a portfolio approach. I'll set aside some for the family to make sure that they are going to be comfortable for life. The million-dollar question then is, what is comfortable? How much do I want to leave behind? Everyone has a different number. For me, it's probably providing the second and third generations with as much education as they want to go for and perhaps give them a leg up with their first property or a bit of support should they want to start a family.

In the long run, we have to make sure that this pot grows. So, I'll probably want to invest in something steady such as a fixed-income portfolio. The rest of the money could better myself, the family, and the world. I'll look at investments in the sustainability sector, or in medical technology, or even in STEM education. These are areas that can uplift many people.

Of course, I'd set aside money for people who need our support right now too.

It's a sensible portfolio allocation approach. Leaving the right legacy not just for the children, but the community, is important.

Sharon:

Education seems close to your heart. And helping women feel more confident about money and investing. What is your advice to women who may want to invest? How should they think about it?

Catherine:

First, start with a positive mindset, a belief that you can do it. Get rid of the fear that you might have, perhaps because of a traumatic financial crisis. Most of us have been through the Asian crisis and the global financial crisis. Many people would have vivid memories similar to those. A subject like the financial crises might also be something few will like, but it's important not to be afraid of it.

Nowadays, there is so much advice and support out there for people who are just starting out. I'd suggest speaking to somebody, like a mentor or someone who has been there and done that, and ask them for advice. It could even be your insurance agent.

Get different views and make up your own mind. In the past, like we talked earlier, there was no Internet, so we had to find information through books. Now, there are so many tools to help us.

So, it's really about taking that first step and overcoming the trauma of fear.

Finally, one last hurdle most people have is thinking that investments are difficult. Or believing that you need a lot of time to think about it because you have so many other things to do, such as your work, your children, or even your household chores. It's actually prudent to set aside time regularly to clean up your finances. It doesn't have to be every week or even every month, but at least set aside some time to discuss with your experts and your loved ones so that you can plan the journey together.

Sharon:

What is the best and worst advice you've gotten?

Catherine:

Well, the best advice I've received is also a bit of a funny story. My grandparents love to save. So, for every $5,000 they had, they would go to the bank and open a fixed deposit account. Back in the old days, you would receive a piece of paper that tells you the maturity date of your account and when it comes, you return to the bank and pass it to the teller, who would give you the principal with interest.

Those frequent trips to the bank made me think that it's a good idea to work in the bank. This was in the seventies. The bank was air-conditioned, and you could go to work wearing a beautiful uniform. And voila, I started my career in a bank. The frequent trips also proved to be great learning experiences because it showed me that money needed to be earned and having an excellent education provided me the pathway to work in a bank.

Bad advice? I remember when Sentosa was being built. It was an enormous construction site, and I was talking to an expert in real estate. I casually mentioned that this looked like a wonderful idea, to have a property facing the beach. He told me, 'Why would anybody want to live on this tiny island that's surrounded by construction for the next ten years? It's probably not a good time to go in right now.' And the rest is history.

Sharon:

What about the kindest advice you've received?

Catherine:

I started as a fund manager and after a while, I realized that fund management was just not for me. It's not that I don't understand the product, but I didn't have the right risk appetite that would make me a great fund manager. I was still young, and I would get emotional or fearful, which is not good. It also made me doubly nervous to invest other people's money.

So, I spoke to my then boss who suggested that I could head to the sell side from the buy side. That was actually brilliant advice. I felt more confident and calmer while still being in the market. I'm comfortable with statistics, so I could still talk to the client. Since I dealt with institutional clients, my job is to provide the best advice and customer service.

The role actually suited my personality a lot more, and I really enjoyed my job thereafter because of that.

Sharon:

Your personality also plays a big role in how you feel comfortable around money. If I could ask you a more personal question, were there times in your life when you felt financially vulnerable?

Catherine:

Yes, there was one genuine shock. I remember vividly the bankruptcy of Lehman Brothers during the Great Financial Crisis. My entire extended family came to my house the weekend when the bankruptcy was announced. Even though they wanted to comfort me, they didn't know what to say. At that point in time, nobody knew how bad it was going to be. They just knew that the company that I worked for went bankrupt. I'm sure they had questions, but I think they just came over as a physical expression of saying that they will be there if I needed help.

I got through that entire episode quite unscathed. Well, I mean, we lost our entire stock options. I try not to think about it and just consider it like buying a car and crashing it. The most important thing I learned is maintaining your integrity and ensuring that people can continue to trust you, no matter what.

I'm actually delighted to see that many of our colleagues have found jobs in the financial sector. The collapse of Lehman didn't stop us from continuing our careers and our friendships, in fact, it taught me we should always invest in our personal network and friendships. This is a lot more important than just the relentless pursuit of money.

It made me realize that chasing after money and promotions can be all for naught and disappear overnight. Even the biggest financial institution can go kaput.

Sharon:

Did you invest in anything recently that made you excited? I'm really thinking about your beautiful jewellery.

Catherine:

[laughs] Yes, I love jewellery and I think it can be an investment. But I don't envision any monetary returns. It's for memories and something I bought for myself. It's just something for future generations to remember me by. We've worked hard for our money, so we should spend it, and I think spending it on something that would make you happy is important.

To reiterate, it's about contentment. Don't spend the money because someone else has it or because you want to keep up with the Joneses. Instead, get something you really like and that speaks to you.

Sharon:

Indeed, we all need that wisdom and humility in our lives. Your work in the philanthropy space is a real inspiration. Thank you for your time, Catherine.

22

Serena Wong

*What's the point of having money if you don't have
people to enjoy it with?*

Serena Wong advocates for wealth management, family offices, and women in business. She spent over two decades building a career in finance serving in sovereign wealth funds, investment banking, and private banking. She held senior positions as Head of Indonesia at JPMorgan Private Bank, and helped grow Kamet Capital, a pre-eminent multi-family office for Asia's most innovative entrepreneurs. Her mission to empower and provide a voice for women arose from her work as a founding member of JPMorgan's Women Interactive Network and co-founder of Women in Family Offices in Singapore. Her work to help families manage their wealth and plan for the long term continues in her capacity as Managing Director at Julius Baer. In this interview, she reflects on the role that people and connections have played in her life, and how growing our relationships is the ultimate wealth creation.

KEY INSIGHTS

Invest in people and yourself.

In investing, you can only learn by doing and by trial and error. Invest in fund managers whom you respect and admire, and founders and business owners whom you believe in and want to support. But above all, you are your own best investment.

Transform money into wealth.

Use your means to bring joy, delight, and connection with people. In doing so, you'll touch more lives and have more impact on a larger population. That is transforming money into wealth. Money is not just about what you have. Some have less and some have more. It's how you behave, act, and direct what you have to enrich lives, including your own.

Use money as fuel.

We are the car, money is fuel, and the point of a car is not to have more fuel but to get somewhere. Just like a car needs fuel to take you places, we need money to reach our goals and destinations. But the goal isn't to accumulate fuel; it's about the journey and people you bring along. That is true wealth.

THE CONVERSATION

Sharon:

Family is very important to you. Let's understand how you grew up and what your early money memories were.

Serena:

We were a traditional Asian family that didn't talk about money, except for bills and payments. I grew up in a HDB household. My parents worked, so I would go to my aunt's house after school. She brought me up. My brother went to a nanny's house. Then, we came home on the weekends to my parent's.

I remember distinctly around the age of seven, I must have begged my parents to have my birthday celebration at McDonald's at Liat Towers. That was my first glimpse that money can buy you a party! It was my first money memory.

Subsequent money memories were probably around eight or nine years old. With school, you're exposed to more friends and more families. I remember taking public transport to school because we did not have a car. My friends did, however. It was a visual means of comparison and I remember we didn't have that. On the outside, I was a confident child. But inside, I had a growing insecurity and inferiority regarding money.

At twelve years old, we took the national (PSLE) exam. After that, we had a break, so I invited one of my friends to come and play at my house. After a while, we got bored because I didn't have a lot of toys. And she said, 'Hey, why don't you come to my house?' I said okay.

I was floored because she had a chauffeur who brought us to her massive white house. She opened her closet, and it was full of Esprit t-shirts. So, money became associated with the finer and beautiful things in life.

I never felt lacking in love at home. But there were a lot of material triggers outside of the home.

Sharon:

Thanks for sharing that story. When we were growing up, Singapore was developing at a quick pace, so the social gap widened and became obvious. How has that coloured your career and how you invest?

Serena:

My parents were laissez-faire with me for school and education. I could pursue my interests and I graduated with a degree in psychology. I started work in a sovereign wealth fund and investment banking. My decisions were driven by people rather than money.

I love being surrounded by really good and smart people. And because I didn't grow up with any financial vocabulary, my investing journey only started much later, in the past decade.

In investing, you can only learn by trial and error. I found my formula after many mistakes. My philosophy now is that I invest in people. So, I invest in fund managers whom I respect and admire, and founders and business owners whom I want to believe in and support. And above all, I invest in myself.

Sharon:

Does your background in psychology help you invest in the right people?

Serena:

There is no magic formula. Investing in the right people means spending time. You can do as much analysis as you want but you have to decide. That gut feel is important. This is my personal approach because if I make the choice, I also live with the consequences. So, I make no investment that I cannot lose.

I invest in public markets, private investments, ventures, and in new themes, whether it was crypto a few years back or in Web3, and now in climate and women or gender-related themes. To learn, I put some money in because you need skin in the game. I'm easy on myself about this because you win some, you may lose some. Hopefully you win more than you lose.

Sharon:

How have you invested in yourself?

Serena:

I believe the life journey is about understanding yourself, or at least coming to some radical acceptance of yourself.

In my twenties, it was hubris. Anything is possible, and you put yourself out there. But it wasn't a very examined life. In my thirties, I had a good job and good pay. On the exterior, it looked great. But I was conforming to some vision of what others expected of me or what they wanted me to be like. Now, with age and hopefully some wisdom, life and money decisions become a lot more intentional.

I do a couple of things to invest in myself. I invest in myself via self-care. I'm not afraid to say that I don't know everything. And the past few years, I've been open to speaking with coaches to help me frame how I want to be very intentional in the present and also in the future.

All my friends know I spend money on blow-outs for my hair. I go to the hair salon two to three times a week. That's my mane of confidence. I definitely spend on investing. I cannot save. So, because I know myself, I have to put my money away or transform it, so I don't touch it. So, part of it is invested for the longer term.

Sharon:

What is the deeper meaning that money brings to you?

Serena:

Money can bring a lot of anxiety because you see the good it can do, but the danger and fear that comes along with it. For example, when my brother graduated from polytechnic, he signed on for the Army. He did this to get the bonus to buy a motorcycle so he could have mobility and independence that every twenty-year-old craved. That was the beginning of problems for my parents and me because by midnight, if he was not home, my mum would be worried. Sometimes, there were close calls and minor skirmishes but there were a couple of serious accidents.

I saw that money can be used for selfish reasons. The consequence of that was creating fear and anxiety for the individual and family.

Money means meeting basic needs. Then transcending to financial freedom, which is the freedom from worry. The next step is to create impact. The impact I want to see money and wealth translate into is related to women—giving voice to and empowering them. I also want to use money to bring joy to others.

For me, money is external validation or value that people put on you or you put on something. Wealth is an internal value that I create or place on myself. That is the distinction for me.

At some point I hope money can translate into wealth. That process happens when we bring joy and delight through connecting with people. In that way, we can touch more lives and have more impact on a larger population.

Sharon:

How much money and wealth do you need? What is enough?

Serena:

It would be disingenuous to say that I don't like money. I love money and spend a lot of time thinking about it *[laughs]* and working with it. My personal and professional relationship with money is in a good place.

I work with many families and individuals, and advise, plan, and invest for them. I don't want to be a prescriptive adviser who tells you what to buy or sell. Instead, I want to be the adviser who journeys with you.

Previously, I used to tell clients to put money in private equity. I hadn't done it myself. Now I can put that small cheque, which can become a bigger cheque, with founders and companies. There is a thought process to investing and how it affects individuals and their objectives.

I don't have a number on what is enough. But I have a short answer to that. What's the point of having money if you don't have people around you to spend it or to enjoy it with?

'Enough' is personal and subjective. Rather than focus on that number, I'd focus on the process of nurturing the relationships and the people I surround myself with.

I have a great example for this. Last year, I went on a family holiday with eight aunties and uncles and eleven cousins. I made the slight gesture of paying for the hotels, but the impact and memories the trip created, and the ties that were formed and reforged has taken on more and more meaning for me.

For me, enough is what I have today. Today is enough. The number might be bigger tomorrow and that's enough. And the day after it may be a smaller number. The way for me to show up every day is: Whatever I have that day is enough.

Sharon:

That's a really healthy way of looking at it. I'm intrigued because how you think of wealth relates to people. You have always brought people together and cared for people around you.

Serena:

Yeah, I hope so. I've heard money being described as fuel. Cars need fuel. But the point of having a car is not to have more fuel. It's getting somewhere.

So, the analogy is money is fuel, we are the car, and life is the journey. Wealth is going deeper, going along with more people on the journey. That is what wealth is to me.

Sharon:

If money is no longer an issue, how do you want to use that money or wealth?

Serena:

It's a tough question because I'm lacking in imagination to know what to do. But I know instinctively that a lot of money means more responsibility, and that means we need to dare to dream about solving bigger problems, right? Try to do something at scale that has great impact.

I have to come back to what I stand for and what is within my realm to affect. I'm going to have to pick something around women and lifting women and bringing delight and joy to humanity.

So how do we do that? I hope that a conversation like this is one drop in the ocean. The more drops we collect, the more we can fill up the ocean with good ideas and good intentions.

Sharon:

What is your attitude towards risk, and do you think that has changed over time?

Serena:

My personality and upbringing is such that I will always err on the side of taking too little risk. I have to be conscious about getting out of my comfort zone, challenging myself, and taking risks. So, I have much more capacity for risk. It's good to be self-aware.

I think risk tolerance and risk appetite changes over time and over life events. So, it's not one formula or one set of portfolio allocation and risk profile the whole time.

Sharon:

Finally, what is the kindest thing anyone has done for you?

Serena:

I have to bring it back to my mother. When I was ten, I said, 'I want to learn French,' and parents love their children, so they make things happen. We would take the bus to Alliance Française in town and there was young Serena learning French. Later in my twenties I did work in France, and I used my French. You can only connect the dots looking back!

After my 'A' Level examinations, I wanted to travel like my friends. Again, my mother made it happen. She gave me the resources to buy a ticket. I went skiing with friends and saw snow for the first time.

Looking back, travel opened my worldview. It made the world accessible. I now work with people from all over the world, across cultures, and we connect as equals. Whether you're a billionaire or someone from a humbler background, to me we are the same. That's the beauty of humanity. I really want to thank my mother for her belief that opened up the world for me.

Sharon:

We have been friends for many years, but this conversation made me feel I know you even better. Thank you for opening up, Serena. You shared beautifully how the softness in relationships can be in harmony with the hardness of money.

23

Sharon Sim

Money means the freedom to craft your own future.

Sharon Sim has a purpose: to make meaningful change in the world through venture capital, family offices, and her organization, Women in Family Offices. As a financial industry veteran with over two decades of experience and the co-founder at Purpose Venture Capital, she's on a mission to build and invest in tech ventures that make a positive impact. Sharon is no stranger to capital markets and wealth management, having worked with major players like Goldman Sachs, Lehman Brothers, JPMorgan, and UBS. Sharon helms a Singapore-based family office, which she founded in 2019, and is a strategic adviser in the food and beverage industry. In this conversation, she explains her passion for getting women to talk about money.

KEY INSIGHTS

Money means freedom to craft your own future.

Money grants you an optionality to shape how you spend your time. It's about the freedom to pursue your passions, on your terms, whenever you desire, and for as long as you choose. It's a tool that enables you to live life on your own terms and make choices that align with your values and aspirations.

Don't wait, start investing.

The key is to begin small and stay committed to your investment goals. Embrace the magic of compounding. Let the power of time grow each dollar you invest, whether in the stock market, fixed income, or any fund that aligns with your strategy. Take the first step, educate yourself, and gradually build your investment portfolio.

Borrowing money is not necessarily a bad thing.

Taking calculated risks and strategic leverage can be your allies. Debt usually gets a bad rap, but it's not all black and white. Think of leverage like a double-edged sword—it can magnify both gains and losses. The key is to weigh your financial goals carefully and let leverage work in your favour.

THE CONVERSATION

Serena:

Take me back to your childhood. Were there any conversations around money in your household growing up?

Sharon:

We talked too much about money in my family. My mother is a stockbroker, and my father is an accountant by training. My family has been doing business for some time in various industries in Singapore and Hong Kong. So, it's normal in my household to have discussions about the stock markets and business during dinners or gatherings. I was comfortable with the concepts of how the stock market works, and failure, too, as businesses didn't work sometimes.

One memory that I draw on a lot was the huge stock market crash in the 1980s. My mother was severely affected because she had taken on a lot of credit risk for her clients, and they lost money and she couldn't get it back from the clients. She bears the loss for the firm. So, it was a stressful time for her, and she projected that to us.

Hence, I always had this notion that the stock market is a risky thing and people are affected. It's not just about losing money, but jobs and businesses. Money has many connotations for me. At the same time, it's also something I want to achieve with business while monitoring it closely because there is also a significant risk.

Serena:

Tell me more about those memories around money. How did that make you feel?

Sharon:

Money is always emotional, and I associate it with different tough periods in my life. Because of the stock market crash in the late eighties, my mom suffered losses and lost her job. My family's businesses failed because of mounting debts.

One of the most acute memories I had was when we had to sell our family home and rent a small flat. We had to adjust our lifestyle. As a ten-year-old, I didn't fully appreciate what the downturn meant but I remember feeling sad and unsettled as I had to leave my home, move into a smaller flat, and share a room with my two siblings. So, I told myself to stop buying frivolous things and save my pocket money. I loved to buy stationery like those Sanrio erasers from Isetan. I asked myself, 'Do I really need this? Do I need to buy this extra eraser or this cute pencil?'

That was when I realized we had to tighten our belts and save money. That helped my journey of mindfulness and frugality. I am not enamoured with brands or a lot of jewellery.

I'm a simple person and that experience made me realize that money was fluid. You can have it one day and lose it the next. As a parent now, I don't want my kids to go through that experience.

Serena:

Are you a spender or saver?

Sharon:

I'd say I have a good balance. I like to have beautiful things and love to travel. So, I spend on things that are important and make me happy.

But I'm also a disciplined saver. It's ingrained in me because of my childhood. I love to collect money and count the notes in the bank. It makes me feel secure. This has followed me throughout my career. I've always been careful with money. But I also understand that I have to invest to make the money grow, and compounding is one of the most powerful forces on this planet. There's a massive difference between every dollar you save and every dollar you invest that compounds in the long run. So, I do both, saving and also investing.

Serena:

So, you see spending and saving two sides of the same coin, which is aligned with your personality. You have a quiet side and an outgoing one.

Sharon:

Life is about balance. I have the same philosophy with money. Don't be obsessed with chasing the next dollar. However, having that dollar in your bank account means a lot. When you let it sit and it compounds, and you're consistent about it, your returns could really help the family years down the road.

Serena:

What's been your best investment?

Sharon:

The best investments for many of us are our properties. The house that you own, which is usually the public apartment that you stay in, has probably appreciated. Given where we are in the economic cycle, Singapore is well positioned.

Just like how I have an outgoing and quiet side, my investing philosophy has two sides as well. I can be a risk taker. I understand you cannot get high returns without taking an appropriate amount of risk. So, for me, the best investments have been property. I started investing in property fairly early in my late twenties, and I never looked back. Once you get the hang of it, you feel comfortable making property transactions.

I look at interest rates. For me, property has fewer variables than investing in stock markets or even venture capital, which some might argue sits at the extreme end of the risk profile. It's really about finding your niche and what you're comfortable in.

Serena:

Are you more analytical or instinctive in your investing?

Sharon:

Sometimes, I ask myself if I'm smart or just lucky. I think it's a combination of both. As they say, it's better to be lucky than smart. Luck in the sense that you are at the right place at the right time with the economic cycle in your favour. When I invested in property in my twenties, I was fortunate enough to have the capital to make that investment. But I'm also lucky because the cycle was turning in the early 2000s. Singapore's property market was down to flat for a long time and I caught that pivot when things were improving. So, timing is important in life.

I also like to think through the bigger cycle and the economic conditions and analyse the property's location. You can plan and research as much as you want, but sometimes it's also instinct and emotional. For example, you might want a property because it's close to your mother's house. So, it can be a combination of both. You have to understand what's driving the position.

Serena:

We spend a lot of time talking about money and thinking about it. What are some meanings you ascribe to money?

Sharon:

Money means different things to different people. There are so many studies and gurus who preach to you about how to make money. But what is not talked about is the emotions that go into money, which affects the way we think about investing. For me, money gives me optionality, which is the freedom to do the things I like at the time for as long as I like.

People work most of their lives to provide optionality to their family. They can send their children to good universities, which can help with their future career. They can have the right insurance policy to provide security. But ultimately, they're buying the little spark of happiness to do things they like. So, money is practical. The more you save, the more you invest, the more you feel confident that if anything goes wrong, you have the option to pull back and take some time out. That creates happiness for me. I've never exercised the option, but I know I have that security blanket.

There's also a sense of freedom and liberation. You might not quit your job tomorrow, but you have six months of savings in your account, so you feel optimistic about the future. That's what money brings to me.

Wealth is a different dimension. It's optimizing your current assets. I think about growing that wealth. It acts as information about how you want to do things in the future.

Serena:

So, wealth is freedom and the possibility of changing your current situation. I know you are a quantitative person, so how much do you think is enough? And what is your interpretation of enough?

Sharon:

I think 'enough' is a dangerous word. For most people, enough is never enough. And I think that's the danger of chasing that quantitative number.

When I was younger, I wanted to all be a millionaire because it was a huge number and you felt rich. Fast forward to today with inflation, a million doesn't buy much these days. So, if you're chasing the absolute number, it's never going to be enough because the goalpost always moves and the environment changes. What was enough for you a decade ago might not be enough now. So, I don't have a number in mind.

Serena:

So, what is your mental state that you are aiming towards?

Sharon:

I want to be in a state where I can wake up in the morning naturally without an alarm clock, plan my day as I wish, head out for lunch with a girlfriend, then either go to a seminar for work or talk to start-up founders that I potentially want to invest in. It's the freedom to choose how I want to spend my day. That's enough for me.

It's having that control over your day, your career, and your time. Time is finite for all of us and something that money cannot buy.

Serena:

Yeah, I love that. You invest with purpose and impact. Along those lines, how do you make money work for you? What kind of impact do you want to create with your money?

Sharon:

That's a question a lot of venture capitalists have to answer. When you invest in new ideas and technology, you're taking on a fair bit of risk. We all know the statistics of companies failing, especially early-stage ones. It's extremely high.

Hence, I think the impact that we're making is giving these new companies and founders that little extra boost to close that gap. We can be thoughtful around it and purposeful about how we want to deploy our capital.

When I invest, I want to know how we can amplify our dollar deployment. I always say this, 'Not every dollar is equal.' Giving a dollar to you versus another start-up founder can be different depending on the amplification.

So, thinking about the deployment of your capital is important and I'm fortunate to be at a stage where I can be careful about how to deploy my money. But there are also important areas that we need to step into, such as climate change. Supporting women founders is also critical, especially for the next two decades because we know females find it harder to talk about money. Fundraising is also challenging for female founders. So, I believe we need to give it to people who need that extra boost. Spending my money that way has a bigger chance of effecting massive change.

Serena:

If you woke up tomorrow and found a billion in your bank account, what would you do and what kind of impact would you make?

Sharon:

My answer remains the same. I want to use it to make change. I can bridge the financing gap for certain industries and purposes. It could be as simple as helping rural communities grow through micro-financing. Once you have a lot of money, the basics such as your kids and your well-being are taken care of. Then it's really about how you want to help and enable change. Having that capacity to invest in early-stage companies still makes sense because that's where the change you're creating pays forward.

Of course, things might fail, or the company might not make it. But you are betting on that 1 or 2 per cent that makes it and the creative massive value.

Serena:

What are some of these themes that you're invested in that you're excited about?

Sharon:

Everyone knows about climate change. One of the major consequences of this is biodiversity loss. We are destroying a lot more than we create. We have seen forests being destroyed and coral reefs degenerating. A lot of this damage in the ocean can thankfully be reversed. I've invested in a company that helps to regenerate corals. It's created a special ceramic tile to be placed at the bottom of the ocean that helps corals regrow. There's a lot we can really think about to help reverse the degeneration of natural resources in ecosystems.

Everybody's focused on decarbonization, and Singapore is probably at the forefront of net zero drive. But I think there are a few fundamental rights that we can really address such as marine communities. We can make a difference by investing in the right companies and technologies.

Serena:

Yes, everyone has to pick the battles that they feel best equipped to address. Coming back to you, like you shared earlier, money can make you feel insecure, small, and vulnerable. Are there instances in your past that made you feel small and inadequate?

Sharon:

Yes, all the time. We must be humble all the time because investing is a long journey and even the best plans, portfolio construction, and asset allocation can be badly affected by major unseen events such as Covid-19. No one can predict how crises happen. We've been through a few major financial ones during our lifetimes. Back to your point of vulnerability, we have to be vulnerable when we invest because that makes us very humble. I wouldn't know everything. I don't know about Warren Buffett, but I think the track record for most money managers or fund managers is probably about 50 per cent accuracy.

Serena:

That's a pretty good statistic. Fifty-one per cent actually means that you are probably one of the above-average managers.

Sharon:

Yes. So, my point is to be vulnerable because no one can predict the future and therefore no one can guarantee you financial returns either. And as you said, even the best of us are only 50 per cent right in the long run. That's the same chance as flipping a coin. So, there's no need to feel vulnerable because everybody is in that position.

But, for a personal story, it's definitely the 2008 Lehman Brothers crisis that nobody can forget because it left an impact on everybody. For me, the memory was so sharp because I was in the Singapore office of Lehman Brothers. That's when you feel totally exposed because I was not just professionally impacted, but also because I was just starting a family during that time. You feel very vulnerable because the entire world has changed.

Serena:

For younger readers, could you take us through that crisis? The collapse of Lehman Brothers was a key trigger point for the collapse of the entire financial system.

Sharon:

There was panic on the streets because no one knew which the next bank to go under would be. There was a lot of pain on Wall Street and Main Street. My experience is personal because I took a financial hit on both sides, meaning I could have lost my job and all my stock options. So, that created a sense for me that nothing is permanent even in the best financial institution. You can't predict that this will happen and if you return to that time, I don't think many predicted that Lehman would go under.

There was a lot of debate about how the bank was too big to fail and someone was going to step in. That was a big moral hazard at that point in time. However, the decision came about, having such a big institution go down and one that I believed in, joined, worked for, and knew the people made me feel that anything could happen in life. The best plans in life always fall prey to a black swan event.

Serena:

Have you been the benefactor of good advice?

Sharon:

We're in the business of giving advice, so we know it pertains to the circumstances and the nature of the client or person you're talking to. It's not about giving stock tips. No one can predict outcomes.

So, the best advice given to me is, first, don't be afraid of taking risks, and second, leverage is your friend. In Asia, we have this perception that we shouldn't take more loans and don't borrow money because we want to be conservative. Of course, there is the downside of taking too much leverage. But leverage cuts both ways. With leverage you can really optimize your personal balance sheet. Even for a company, having no debt is not a great thing at different stages of growth. So, the best advice is to take risks and to leverage.

In my earlier days in banking, my mentor and boss at the time supported me by saying that I should buy property at this stage. That gave me the confidence as a young person to borrow a lot of money from the bank. It was a thirty-year mortgage, and you weren't sure if you could pay it back. But she told me, 'Don't be afraid of leverage.'

Serena:

I've heard you mentioned that if you start earlier, you can recover.

Sharon:

As you move on with your career and have a family, you should adjust your leverage. I don't want to take on excessive debt at a time if I don't have that much time horizon or runway to recover losses. But it's all calculated risk. Don't fear things like debt or taking a bit of risk because I truly believe no one has a crystal ball. No investment guru can honestly say to you that this is going to be the best or the worst investment.

Serena:

Could you share something surprising about yourself that is money-related?

Sharon:

Most people know me for being in finance and investing. Something that is not so well known is that I also invest in a lot of alternative investments. For example, cryptocurrency. I don't look at it as a speculative investment. I started fairly early and invested in Bitcoin, maybe not as early as I would have liked to, but definitely from 2016 to 2017 onwards. When you have your own dollar invested, you have skin in the game. So, I think that's where I am more risk averse in the sense that I don't mind putting money into inane ideas because I want to learn something, or I want to see how that plays out.

And having ownership interest is always the best motivator. Coming back to your earlier question about the best advice someone else has given me, when I started my career in equity sales, my boss told me I have to invest in equities.

I asked, 'Why? I don't know enough about the companies, and I have only a little money since I just started working.' My mentor's answer was, 'So you know how it feels to lose money.' That was fantastic advice because it changed my entire investment mentality. We advise clients and institutions all the time, and you can't give the proper advice until you understand how the pain feels. It's different for fund managers or institutions because losing money is not a personal but a performance issue. It is other people's money and statistics.

But when it's your own money or advice, losing that money is different. The personal hit is emotional. I appreciated the advice because it made me realize that if I want to give advice, I better make sure I understand how it feels to be right or wrong.

Serena:

Coming back to the emotion of money, do you have any mantras around money that you used to share with your children?

Sharon:

Well, they are teenagers now, so I am not sure if they even listen to me at all. But we set some ground rules when they were young. We always gave them a monthly allowance, and we chose monthly because we want them to think through their spending for the month and make those decisions on their own. And so maybe that has given them a bit more confidence around looking at their own finances, and how they want to plan their allowances.

So, they would have to ask how much it is when they buy something. Sometimes most young kids would want something but never ask about cost.

But once they have that number, then they can process if it's worth buying. My daughter is wonderful that way, as she's cognizant about why some brands are more expensive than others. In their minds, they have the basic concepts of money and we used to nag at them all the time and share how a carton of milk that used to cost $2 is now $2.50, and how that's a big percentage change. We just want to keep impressing on them that there's value for money and there's always a compromise when you buy this.

Serena:

How do you divide the financial responsibilities at home?

Sharon:

When we got married as well, we agreed to have a joint family household account. We had our own accounts that we keep separate from the family plot. But I think what is interesting is that we want to be equals in the entire household, especially in buying things for the kids, the mortgage, and everything.

We naturally came to this agreement. We both contribute equally into the joint account. It's different from other couples who might have one person put more or less depending on how much they earn. But we went with the equality route.

That's the way we've constructed the household finances. But that also means I have control over my personal accounts and that we have an understanding when we have different approaches to investing.

We have different investment profiles. My husband is more meticulous than I am. He accounts for every expenditure and is incredibly mathematical. I'm less so, but because of that, I feel that I'm able to take on more risk. I can close one eye and say, 'Oh, I'm not sure, but maybe there's a chance that this would be an excellent investment.' I'm willing to live with that uncertainty and I can live with the potential losses.

That liberates me. I can choose my way. So, we have a shared investment portfolio and also individual ones. We can make our own independent decisions. For example, we may discuss the bigger themes like cryptocurrencies and that I bought some Bitcoin, but I don't need his approval to do it. It's important that I consider how he thinks and feels, but I don't need his agreement.

Serena:

Wow, do you think that translates to women and how we invest? I know you have some well thought out opinions on this.

Sharon:

We don't talk enough about money. There is this aversion to bringing up the topic about money or investing and it is almost taboo in social settings. Even in private, it is incredibly difficult to have heart-to-heart conversations around money. I find it hard to draw it out from females. It becomes almost awkward because I am open to sharing and passionate about investing. You may feel less confident when you are starting your investment journey and think that you don't know enough or you think you're asking a stupid question, but the truth is no one really knows what they're doing all the time.

The simplest way to get started is to start small but consistently. It is this concept of compounding. Every dollar you put into the stock market, a fixed income product or any kind of fund works. It's just a matter of sticking it through that time period and longer because the cycles come and go. Staying invested for the long run is the only way to get performance.

Serena:

If we want to get started, what do you encourage us to do? What do you encourage women to do if they don't have that full portfolio or a decade of experience?

Sharon:

This is the right place and the right time. We have technology tools and a spectrum of wealth-tech companies out there where we can learn from. You can put in smaller investment amounts, and they help you understand what the funds are about. What are you investing in on the basic level? The lack of access to information is no longer the barrier to getting started, especially to women, because most don't know who to ask or how to find that information.

With various robot-advisers out there, there is really no excuse not to do it. Then is it a question of fear or complacency? So, you push it back. My advice is really to just start and do something about it.

It could be as simple as reading an article and that triggers your thinking, or opening an online trading account or even talking to a friend to invest together. There are many ways to get past this inertia. I think a lot of women kind of avoid thinking about those topics and become complacent after a while. It boils down to getting over that initial vulnerability that you're not sure what you're doing. In terms of access to information, access to funds or investment opportunities is as democratic as it ever has been.

Serena:

We covered a lot of ground, Sharon. You are definitely one of my top choices when I want to talk about women and money.

Afterword

At the tail end of this book, I find myself reflecting on the incredibly emotional ride we've taken together. This book started with my curiosity about how women are thinking and feeling about money. As someone who spent more than half her life in finance, I still find it awkward to speak openly about my financial fears and goals, especially with women. This made me even more determined to dig deeper and unravel the emotional entanglement we have with money.

Little did I know it would develop into a journey of shared experiences from phenomenal women from all walks of life. Their stories, spanning from early childhood memories about money to crippling self-doubt and overcoming financial struggles and achieving financial freedom, have shed so much light on my understanding of women's complex relationship with money. We are not alone, and we can change our inner financial dialogue.

I am humbled and energized by these stories. Writing this book has pushed me to reassess my financial blind spots, to confront my discomfort about asking for more, and to embrace discussing money openly. More importantly, I am buoyed by the life lessons that were shared in these real, unfiltered, and candid conversations. My three biggest takeaways on money, women, and life:

1. **On Money:** Be aware of your inner money narrative. What I have heard from the twenty-four women is that we all have our blind spots when it comes to managing our finances. Take time to pinpoint specific fears or anxieties related to money. Having candid discussions about money can have a transformative impact on our financial mindset and decision-making.
2. **On Women:** There is power when women join together to rewrite their money journeys. The stories shared by women in the book

underscore the strength that comes from breaking the silence surrounding money. When women unite, share their experiences, and support one another, we amplify and lift each other

3. **On Life:** Wealth is not just about money. As Oprah Winfrey wisely puts it, 'There's a wealth that has nothing to do with dollars, that comes from the perspective and wisdom of paying attention to your life.' Money is a great enabler but what brings the most joy is finding wealth in health, purposeful living, and pursuing passions.

Last, this book isn't just a collection of stories, it's a catalyst for change. It's a call for women to own their financial narratives and break free from the silence. As I move forward, I carry with me the resilience, wisdom, and strength of the incredible women who have contributed to this project.

Thank you for being part of this journey. May our stories continue to inspire and pave the way for generations to come.

—Sharon Sim
Founder and General Partner
at Purpose Venture Capital,
Co-Founder of Women in Family Offices

II

A confession. My catalyst for writing this book was not altruistic. After four decades of living by the expectations of others, and two decades of running the career rat race, I had lost my voice. The voice that sings to my tune and my own words—what makes me, me—had gone silent. A book project seemed like a head-on rescue strategy. The urgency of a deadline would surely be the most direct route to the lost and found department.

How naïve, but how brave I was!

In corralling this incredible group of twenty-four women, I was pulled into a web of old friends, new friends, and near strangers with whom I instantly connected. The common thread—we were all apprehensive about talking so openly about money and dragging our families into the stories. But we had no other choice because we knew deep down that ease with money should be as important a skill as reading a map (if you were born before 1980s), coding (born after 2000s), and learning to disagree agreeably (for all).

We dug deep, clarified, and sharpened our money narratives. What did I learn?

On Women

- We must lift each other higher through action. And find other men and women allies to do the same.
- We live mostly in our own thoughts. A gentle nudge from a friend could be all it takes for us to pop out of our heads and see different possibilities.

On Money

- We have a choice. We can choose to keep or change our money narratives. Because our parents didn't talk about money, doesn't mean that we can't.
- Investing is empowering. Making our own money, and making our money grow, is intoxicating.
- Start investing with whatever little we can put aside as early as possible.
- Compounding is the key ingredient to growing money.
- Saving and investing must go hand in hand. Saving itself cannot help us reach financial freedom; we need to invest as well.

On Why Women Must Talk Money

- We are worthy. Know our worth and say it confidently. Practise this.
- Action leads to manifestation. By talking about money in the open, we clear the neural pathways to thought, action, and outcome. It is a skill and habit we can build. It breaks the taboo and becomes the norm.

We wrote at the start that nothing bad happens when more money is in the hands of women. The World Economic Forum's Global Gender Gap Report 2022 reminds us 'gender pay gaps, unequal career progression trajectories, gender gaps in financial literacy, and life events that disrupt women's work participation'[9] are factors we need to address to bridge the gender wealth gap. These words stir in me a powerful emotion and conviction.

We must do better. That must be a worthy use of my voice. Of all our voices.

—Serena Wong
Managing Director at Julius Baer,
Co-Founder of Women in Family Offices

---

[9] World Economic Forum. 'Global Gender Gap Report 2022,' July 13, 2022. https://www.weforum.org/publications/global-gender-gap-report-2022/.

Acknowledgements

Some words of appreciation to the wonderful and generous folks who made *Why Women Don't Talk Money* possible. In no particular order:

Nora Nazerene Abu Bakar, who took a chance on us.
Cheng Limin, who challenges us to dream big.
Benny Loy, your attention to detail is calming for us.
Farhan Shah, whose guidance is invaluable.
Anna Shatilova, who helps without hesitation.

And to the brave and amazing women who believe in and inspire us, Anthonia Hui, Quah Ting Wen, Cecilia Tan, Angela Loh, Choo Oi-Yee, Christine Amour-Levar, Dr Jade Kua, Catherine Loh, Harmin Kaur, Joanne Ho, Joy Tan, Mint Lim, Ning Chong, Petrina Kow, Sunita Gill, Veronica Phua, Hui Ting Koh, Ong Bee Yan, Madeline Liu and Zheng Yizhou, Felicia Heng, and Lily Choh.

Thank you.